T0332710

# LONDON MATHEMATICAL SOCIETY STUDENT TEXTS

Managing Editor: Ian J. Leary,
Mathematical Sciences, University of Southampton, UK

London Mathematical Society Student Texts 107

# Inverse Problems and Data Assimilation

DANIEL SANZ-ALONSO
*University of Chicago*

ANDREW STUART
*California Institute of Technology*

ARMEEN TAEB
*University of Washington*

# CAMBRIDGE
## UNIVERSITY PRESS

Shaftesbury Road, Cambridge CB2 8EA, United Kingdom

One Liberty Plaza, 20th Floor, New York, NY 10006, USA

477 Williamstown Road, Port Melbourne, VIC 3207, Australia

314–321, 3rd Floor, Plot 3, Splendor Forum, Jasola District Centre,
New Delhi – 110025, India

103 Penang Road, #05–06/07, Visioncrest Commercial, Singapore 238467

Cambridge University Press is part of Cambridge University Press & Assessment,
a department of the University of Cambridge.

We share the University's mission to contribute to society through the pursuit of
education, learning and research at the highest international levels of excellence.

www.cambridge.org
Information on this title: www.cambridge.org/9781009414326

DOI: 10.1017/9781009414319

First published 2023

*A catalogue record for this publication is available from the British Library*

*A Cataloging-in-Publication data record for this book is available from the
Library of Congress*

ISBN 978-1-009-41432-6 Hardback
ISBN 978-1-009-41429-6 Paperback

To my wife, parents and brother
DS-A

To the much-loved Crazy 8
AMS

To my parents and my brother and sister
AT

# Contents

# Preface

These notes developed as a result of courses taught at Caltech and at the University of Chicago, and aim at providing a clear and concise introduction to the subjects of inverse problems and data assimilation. To cater to students with diverse backgrounds and interests, we complement the material covered in our courses with hands-on assignments; these notes contain several exercises that we have used for this purpose. Additionally, we have found it pedagogically beneficial to ask students to complete an independent project, implementing the methods studied in class to solve an applied problem of their choice. Students can use the bibliographic comments included at the end of each chapter to help them choose and formulate their own projects. The notes are intended to be self-contained, and thus to be useful not only as a teaching resource, but also for independent self-guided learning.

## Acknowledgements

A first draft of these notes was created in LaTeX by the students in the Caltech course ACM159 (now ACM/IDS 154), based on lectures presented by the instructor Andrew Stuart, and on input from the course teaching assistant Armeen Taeb. The authors are very grateful to these students, without whom these notes would not exist. The individuals responsible for typesetting the notes, listed in alphabetical order, are: Blancquart, Paul; Cai, Karena; Chen, Jiajie; Cheng, Richard; Cheng, Rui; Feldstein, Jonathan; Huang, De; Idíni, Benjamin; Kovachki, Nikola; Lee, Marcus; Levy, Gabriel; Li, Liuchi; Muir, Jack; Ren, Cindy; Seylabi, Elnaz; Schäfer, Florian; Singhal, Vipul; Stephenson, Oliver; Song, Yichuan; Su, Yu; Teke, Oguzhan; Williams, Ethan; Wray, Parker; Xiao, Fangzhou; Zhan, Eric; Zhang, Shumao. Furthermore, the following students added content to the notes, beyond the materials presented by the instructors: Parker Wray – created an early draft of the Overview; Jiajie Chen – found an alternative proof of early presentations of under-determined inverse problems and smoothing in Gaussian data assimilation; Fangzhou Xiao – providing numerical illustrations of prior, likelihood, and posterior; Elnaz Seylabi and Fangzhou Xiao – catching many typographical errors in an early draft of these notes; Cindy Ren – numerical simulations to enhance understanding of importance sampling; Cindy Ren and De Huang – improving the constants in initial presentations of the approximation error of importance sampling; Richard Cheng and Florian Schäfer – illustrations to enhance understanding of the coupling argument used to study convergence of MCMC algorithms by presenting the finite state-space case; and Ethan Williams and Jack Muir – numerical simulations and illustrations of ensemble Kalman filter and extended Kalman filter that appeared in an early version of these notes. The authors are also grateful to Tapio Helin (LUT University) who used the notes in his own course and provided very helpful feedback on an early draft. The authors are also thankful to Yuming Chen, Andrew Dennehy, Ruoxi Jiang, Phillip Lo, and Walter Zhang (University of Chicago) and Eitan Levin (Caltech) for their generous feedback; they are also grateful to Hwanwoo Kim (University of Chicago) for making substantial improvements to the figures initially provided by the individuals listed above. Finally, the authors are thankful to David Tranah (CUP) whose advice helped to shape this book.

The work of Daniel Sanz-Alonso has been funded by DOE, NGIA, and NSF (USA), and by FBBVA (Spain). The work of Andrew Stuart has been funded by AFOSR, ARL, DoD, NIH, NSF, and ONR (USA), by EPSRC (UK), and by ERC (EU). The work of Armeen Taeb has been funded by the Resnick Fellowship (USA) and by the ETH Foundations of Data Science (Switzerland). All of this funded research has helped to shape the presentation of the material in these notes and is gratefully acknowledged.

# Introduction

## Aim and Overview of the Notes

The aim of these notes is to provide a clear and concise mathematical introduction to the subjects of Inverse Problems and Data Assimilation, and their interrelations, together with bibliographic pointers to literature in this area that goes into greater depth. The target audiences are advanced undergraduates and beginning graduate students in the mathematical sciences, together with researchers in the sciences and engineering who are interested in the systematic underpinnings of methodologies widely used in their disciplines.

In its most basic form, inverse problem theory is the study of how to estimate model parameters from data. Often the data provide indirect information about these parameters, corrupted by noise. The theory of inverse problems, however, is much richer than just parameter estimation. For example, the underlying theory can be used to determine the effects of noisy data on the accuracy of the solution; it can be used to determine what kind of observations are needed to accurately determine a parameter; and it can be used to study the uncertainty in a parameter estimate and, relatedly, is useful, for example, in the design of strategies for control or optimization under uncertainty, and for risk analysis. The theory thus has applications in many fields of science and engineering.

To apply the ideas in these notes, the starting point is a mathematical model mapping the unknown parameters to the observations: termed the "forward" or "direct" problem, and often a subject of research in its own right. A good forward model will not only identify how the data is dependent on parameters, but also what sources of noise or model uncertainty are present in the postulated relationship between unknown parameters and data. For example, if the desired forward problem cannot be solved analytically, then the forward model may be approximated by a numerical simulation; in this case, discretization may be considered as a source of error. Once a relationship between model parameters, sources of error, and data is clearly defined, the inverse problem of estimating parameters from data can be addressed. The theory of inverse problems can be separated into two cases: (1) the ideal case where data is not corrupted by noise and is derived from a known perfect model; and (2) the practical case where data is incomplete and imprecise. The first case is useful for classifying inverse problems and determining if a given set of observations can, in principle, allow to fully reconstruct the model parameters; this provides insight into conditions needed for existence, uniqueness, and stability of a solution to the inverse problem. The second case is useful for the formulation of practical algorithms to learn about parameters, and uncertainties in their estimates, and will be the focus of these notes.

A model for which a solution exists, is unique, and changes continuously with input (stability) is termed "well-posed." Conversely, a model lacking any of these properties is termed "ill-posed." Ill-posedness is present in many inverse problems, and mitigating it is an extensive part of the subject. Out of the different approaches to formulating an inverse problem, our notes emphasize the Bayesian framework. Nonetheless, practical algorithms in this area include a variety of related optimization approaches, and these are also discussed in detail.

The goal of the Bayesian framework is to find a probability measure that assigns a probability to each possible solution for a parameter $u$, given the data $y$. Bayes' formula states that

$$\mathbb{P}(u \mid y) = \frac{1}{\mathbb{P}(y)} \, \mathbb{P}(y \mid u) \, \mathbb{P}(u).$$

This formula enables calculation of the posterior probability on $u \mid y$, $\mathbb{P}(u \mid y)$, in terms of the product of the data likelihood $\mathbb{P}(y \mid u)$ and the prior information on the parameter encoded in $\mathbb{P}(u)$. The likelihood describes the probability of the observed data $y$ if the input parameter were set to be $u$; it is determined by the forward model, and the structure of the noise. The normalization constant $\mathbb{P}(y)$ ensures that $\mathbb{P}(u \mid y)$ is a probability measure. There are four primary benefits to this framework: (1) it provides a clear theoretical setting in which the forward model choice, the description of how noise enters the data and the forward model, and *a priori* information on the unknown parameter are all explicit; (2) it provides information about the entire solution space for possible input parameter choices; (3) it naturally leads to quantification of uncertainty and risk in parameter estimates; (4) it is generalizable to a wide class of inverse problems, in finite and infinite dimension, and comes with a well-posedness theory mitigating the ill-posedness of a naive deterministic approach.

The first part of the notes is dedicated to studying the Bayesian framework for inverse problems. Techniques such as importance sampling and Markov Chain

| Topic | Inverse Problems | Data Assimilation |
| --- | --- | --- |
| Bayesian Formulation | Chapter 1 | Chapter 7 |
| Linear Setting | Chapter 2 | Chapter 8 |
| Optimization Perspective | Chapter 3 | Chapter 9 |
| Gaussian Approximation | Chapter 4 | Chapter 10 |
| Sampling | Chapters 5 and 6 | Chapters 11 and 12 |
| Kalman Inversion | Chapter 13 | |

Table 1 *Structure of the notes: the organization of the material emphasizes the unity between the subjects of inverse problems and data assimilation.*

Monte Carlo (MCMC) methods are introduced; these methods have the desirable property that in the limit of an infinite number of samples they reproduce the full posterior distribution. Since it is often computationally intensive to implement these methods, especially in high-dimensional problems, techniques to approximate the posterior by a Dirac or a Gaussian distribution are also discussed, along with related optimization algorithms to determine the best approximation.

The second part of the notes covers data assimilation. This refers to a particular class of inverse problems in which the unknown parameter is the initial condition of a dynamical system or, in the case of stochastic dynamics, the entire sequence of subsequent states of the system, and the data comprises partial and noisy observations of the (possibly stochastic) dynamical system. A primary use of data assimilation is in forecasting, where the purpose is to provide better future estimates than can be obtained using either the data or the model alone. All the methods from the first part of the course may be applied directly, but there are other new methods which exploit the Markovian structure to update the state of the system sequentially, rather than to learn about the initial condition. (But, of course, knowledge of the initial condition may be used to inform the state of the system at later times.)

The third and final part of the notes describes methods for generic inverse problems that build on data assimilation ideas, thus bringing together the material in the first two parts. The structure of the notes, as well as the presentation, emphasizes the inter-relations between inverse problems and data assimilation.

As summarized in Table 1, each chapter in the first part (inverse problems) has its counterpart in the second part (data assimilation).

## Notation

Throughout the notes we use $\mathbb{N}$ to denote the positive integers $\{1, 2, 3, \ldots\}$, and $\mathbb{Z}^+$ to denote the non-negative integers $\mathbb{N} \cup \{0\} = \{0, 1, 2, 3, \ldots\}$. The symbol $I_d$ denotes the identity matrix on $\mathbb{R}^d$, and $Id$ denotes the identity mapping. We use $|\cdot|$ to denote the Euclidean norm corresponding to the inner-product $\langle a, b \rangle = a^\top b$; we also use the notation $|\cdot|$ to denote the induced norm on matrices.

A symmetric matrix $A$ is positive definite (resp. positive semi-definite) if $\langle u, Au \rangle$ is positive (resp. non-negative) for all $u \neq 0$. This will sometimes be denoted by $A > 0$ (resp. $A \geq 0$). For $A > 0$, we denote by $|\cdot|_A$ the weighted norm defined by $|v|_A^2 = v^\top A^{-1} v$. The corresponding weighted Euclidean inner-product is given by $\langle \cdot, \cdot \rangle_A := \langle \cdot, A^{-1} \cdot \rangle$. We use $\otimes$ to denote the outer product between two vectors: $(a \otimes b)c = \langle b, c \rangle a$. We let $B(u, \delta)$ denote the open ball of radius $\delta$ at $u$, in the Euclidean norm. We also use det and Tr to denote the determinant and trace functions on matrices.

Throughout, we denote by $\mathbb{P}(\cdot), \mathbb{P}(\cdot \mid \cdot)$ the probability density function (pdf) of a random variable and its conditional pdf, respectively. We write

$$\rho(f) = \mathbb{E}^\rho[f] = \int_{\mathbb{R}^d} f(u)\rho(u)du$$

to denote expectation of $f \colon \mathbb{R}^d \mapsto \mathbb{R}$ with respect to pdf $\rho$ on $\mathbb{R}^d$. The distribution of the random variables in these notes will often have density with respect to Lebesgue measure, but occasional use of Dirac masses will be required; we will use the notational convention that Dirac mass at point $v$ has "density" $\delta(\cdot - v)$, also denoted by $\delta_v(\cdot)$. When a random variable $u$ has pdf $\rho$ we will write $u \sim \rho$. We use $\Rightarrow$ to denote weak convergence of probability measures; that is, $\rho_n \Rightarrow \rho$ if $\rho_n(f) \to \rho(f)$ for all bounded and continuous $f \colon \mathbb{R}^d \mapsto \mathbb{R}$.

# PART I

INVERSE PROBLEMS

# 1

# Bayesian Inverse Problems and Well-Posedness

In this chapter we introduce the Bayesian approach to inverse problems in which the unknown parameter and the observed data are viewed as random variables. In this probabilistic formulation, the solution of the inverse problem is the posterior distribution on the parameter given the data. We will show that the Bayesian formulation leads to a form of well-posedness: small perturbations of the forward model or the observed data translate into small perturbations of the posterior distribution. Well-posedness requires a notion of distance between probability measures. We introduce the total variation and Hellinger distances, giving characterizations of them, and bounds relating them, that will be used throughout these notes. We prove well-posedness in the Hellinger distance.

The chapter is organized as follows. Section 1.1 introduces the formulation of Bayesian inverse problems. In Section 1.2 we derive a formula for the posterior pdf and explain how several estimators for the unknown parameter can be obtained using the posterior. Section 1.3 describes the well-posedness of the Bayesian formulation together with the necessary background on distances between probability measures. The chapter closes with bibliographical remarks in Section 1.4.

## 1.1 Formulation of Bayesian Inverse Problems

We consider the following setting. We let $G : \mathbb{R}^d \to \mathbb{R}^k$ define the forward model and aim to recover an unknown parameter $u \in \mathbb{R}^d$ from data $y \in \mathbb{R}^k$ given by

$$y = G(u) + \eta, \qquad (1.1)$$

where $\eta \in \mathbb{R}^k$ represents observation noise. We view $(u, y) \in \mathbb{R}^d \times \mathbb{R}^k$ as a random variable, whose distribution is specified by means of the following

3

assumption on the distribution of $(u, \eta) \in \mathbb{R}^d \times \mathbb{R}^k$ and the relationship between $u$, $y$ and $\eta$ postulated in equation (1.1).

**Assumption 1.1** *The distribution of the random variable $(u, \eta) \in \mathbb{R}^d \times \mathbb{R}^k$ is defined by:*

- $u \sim \rho(u), u \in \mathbb{R}^d$.
- $\eta \sim \nu(\eta), \eta \in \mathbb{R}^k$.
- *$u$ and $\eta$ are independent, written $u \perp \eta$.*

Here $\rho$ and $\nu$ describe the pdfs of the random variables $u$ and $\eta$, respectively. Then $\rho(u)$ is called the *prior* pdf and, for each fixed $u \in \mathbb{R}^d$, $y \mid u \sim \nu(y - G(u))$ determines the *likelihood* function. In this probabilistic perspective, the solution to the inverse problem is the conditional distribution of $u$ given $y$, which is called the *posterior* distribution, and will be denoted by $u \mid y \sim \pi^y(u)$. The posterior pdf determines, for any candidate parameter value in $\mathbb{R}^d$, how probable that parameter is, based on prior assumptions and the link between parameter and data, all expressed probabilistically. In particular, the posterior contains information about the level of uncertainty in the parameter recovery: for instance, large posterior covariance typically indicates that the data contains insufficient information to accurately recover the input parameter.

## 1.2 Formula for Posterior pdf: Bayes' Theorem

Bayes' theorem is a bridge connecting the prior, the likelihood, and the posterior.

**Theorem 1.2** (Bayes' Theorem)   *Let Assumption 1.1 hold, and assume that*

$$Z = Z(y) := \int_{\mathbb{R}^d} \nu(y - G(u))\rho(u)du > 0.$$

*Then $u \mid y \sim \pi^y(u)$, where*

$$\pi^y(u) = \frac{1}{Z}\nu(y - G(u))\rho(u). \tag{1.2}$$

*Proof*   Denote by $\mathbb{P}(\cdot)$ the pdf of a random variable and by $\mathbb{P}(\cdot \mid \cdot)$ its conditional pdf. We have

$$\mathbb{P}(u, y) = \mathbb{P}(u \mid y)\,\mathbb{P}(y), \text{ if } \mathbb{P}(y) > 0,$$
$$\mathbb{P}(u, y) = \mathbb{P}(y \mid u)\,\mathbb{P}(u), \text{ if } \mathbb{P}(u) > 0.$$

Note that the marginal pdf on $y$ is given by

$$\mathbb{P}(y) = \int_{\mathbb{R}^d} \mathbb{P}(u, y)\,du$$
$$= \int_{\mathbb{R}^d} \mathbb{P}(y \mid u)\,\mathbb{P}(u)\,du = Z > 0.$$

Then

$$\mathbb{P}(u \mid y) = \frac{1}{\mathbb{P}(y)}\,\mathbb{P}(y \mid u)\,\mathbb{P}(u) = \frac{1}{\mathbb{P}(y)} v\big(y - G(u)\big)\rho(u) \qquad (1.3)$$

for both $\mathbb{P}(u) = \rho(u) > 0$ and $\mathbb{P}(u) = \rho(u) = 0$. $\qquad\square$

We will often denote the likelihood function by $l(u) := v\big(y - G(u)\big)$. We then write

$$\pi^y(u) = \frac{1}{Z} l(u)\rho(u),$$

omitting the data $y$ in the likelihood function; when no confusion arises we will also simply write $\pi(u)$ for the posterior pdf, rather than $\pi^y(u)$.

**Remark 1.3** The proof of Theorem 1.2 shows that in order to apply Bayes' formula (1.2) one needs to guarantee that the normalizing constant $\mathbb{P}(y) = Z$ is positive; in other words, the marginal density of the observed data $y$ needs to be positive. This is simply the natural assumption that the observed data could indeed have been observed, given the probabilistic conditions in Assumption 1.1. From now on it will be assumed without further notice that $\mathbb{P}(y) = Z > 0$. Finally, we remark that throughout these notes we will denote normalizing constants generically by $Z$, and depending on the context the normalizing constant may sometimes be interpreted as the marginal density of an underlying data set. $\quad\diamond$

The posterior distribution $\pi^y(u)$ contains all the knowledge on the parameter $u$ available in the prior and the data. In applications it is often useful, however, to summarize the posterior distribution through a few numerical values. Summarizing the posterior is particularly important if the parameter is high-dimensional, since then visualizing the posterior or detecting regions of high posterior probability is nontrivial. Two natural numerical summaries are the posterior mean and the posterior mode.

**Definition 1.4** The *posterior mean estimator* of $u$ given data $y$ is the mean of the posterior distribution:

$$u_{\mathrm{PM}} = \int_{\mathbb{R}^d} u\pi^y(u)\,du.$$

The *maximum a posteriori (MAP) estimator* of $u$ given data $y$ is the mode of the posterior distribution $\pi^y(u)$, defined as

$$u_{\text{MAP}} = \arg\max_{u \in \mathbb{R}^d} \pi^y(u).$$

This maximum may not be uniquely defined, in which case we talk about $a$, rather than *the*, MAP estimator. $\diamond$

The importance of the MAP and the posterior mean already suggest the need to compute maxima (for the MAP estimator) and integrals (for the posterior mean) in order to extract actionable information from the Bayesian formulation of inverse problems and data assimilation. For this reason, optimization (to compute maxima) and sampling (to compute integrals) will play an important role in these notes. In practice it is often useful to quantify the uncertainty in the parameter reconstruction, and numerical summaries such as the posterior mean and the MAP estimators can be complemented by credible intervals; that is, parameter regions of prescribed posterior probability. In order to make tractable the computation of estimators and credible intervals, the posterior can be approximated by a simple distribution, such as a Gaussian or a Gaussian mixture; optimization can be used to determine such approximations. In a similar spirit, sampling may be viewed as approximating the posterior by a combination of Dirac masses to enable computation of integrals. An optimization perspective for inverse problems and data assimilation will be studied in Chapters 3 and 9, respectively, and Gaussian approximations will be discussed in Chapters 4 and 10, respectively; Dirac approximations constructed via sampling will be studied in Chapters 5 and 6 (inverse problems) and in Chapters 11 and 12 (data assimilation).

We next consider two simple examples of a direct application of Bayes' theorem.

**Example 1.5** (MAP and Posterior Mean Estimators)   Let $d = k = 1$, $\eta \sim \nu = \mathcal{N}(0, \gamma^2)$, and let

$$\rho(u) = \begin{cases} \frac{1}{2}, & u \in (-1, 1), \\ 0, & u \in (-1, 1)^c. \end{cases}$$

Suppose that the observation is generated by $y = u + \eta$. Using Bayes' Theorem 1.2, we derive the posterior pdf

$$\pi^y(u) = \begin{cases} \frac{1}{2Z} \exp(-\frac{1}{2\gamma^2}|y - u|^2), & u \in (-1, 1), \\ 0, & u \in (-1, 1)^c, \end{cases}$$

where $Z$ is a normalizing constant ensuring that $\int_{\mathbb{R}} \pi^y(u)\,du = 1$. Now we find the MAP estimator. From the explicit formula for $\pi^y$, we have

$$u_{\mathrm{MAP}} = \arg\max_{u \in \mathbb{R}} \pi^y(u) = \begin{cases} y & \text{if } y \in (-1, 1), \\ -1 & \text{if } y \leq -1, \\ 1 & \text{if } y \geq 1. \end{cases}$$

In this example, the prior on $u$ is supported on $(-1, 1)$ and the posterior on $u \mid y$ is supported on $(-1, 1)$. If the data lies in $(-1, 1)$ then the MAP estimator is the data itself; otherwise it is the extremal point of the prior support which matches the sign of the data. The posterior mean is

$$u_{\mathrm{PM}} = \frac{1}{2Z} \int_{-1}^{1} u \exp\left(-\frac{1}{2\gamma^2}|y - u|^2\right) du,$$

which may be approximated using, for instance, the sampling methods described in Chapters 5 and 6. ◇

The following example illustrates once again the application of Bayes' theorem, and shows that the posterior may concentrate near a low-dimensional manifold in the input parameter space $\mathbb{R}^d$. In such a case it is important to understand the geometry of the support of the posterior density, which cannot be captured by point estimation or Gaussian approximations.

**Example 1.6** (Concentration of Posterior on a Manifold)   Let $d = 2$, $k = 1$, $\rho \in C(\mathbb{R}^2, \mathbb{R})$, and suppose that there is $\rho_{\max} > 0$ such that, for all $u \in \mathbb{R}^2$, we have $0 < \rho(u) \leq \rho_{\max} < \infty$. Suppose that the observation is generated by

$$y = G(u) + \eta,$$
$$G(u) = u_1^2 + u_2^2,$$
$$\eta \sim \nu = \mathcal{N}(0, \gamma^2), \quad 0 < \gamma \ll 1,$$

and assume that $y > 0$. Using Bayes' theorem we obtain the posterior pdf

$$\pi^y(u) = \frac{1}{Z} \exp\left(-\frac{1}{2\gamma^2}|u_1^2 + u_2^2 - y|^2\right)\rho(u).$$

We now show that the posterior concentrates near the manifold defined by the circumference $\{u \in \mathbb{R}^2 : u_1^2 + u_2^2 = y\}$. Denote $A^{\pm} := \{u \in \mathbb{R}^2 : |u_1^2 + u_2^2 - y|^2 \leq \gamma^{2\pm\delta}\}$, for some fixed $\delta \in (0, 2)$. The set $A^-$ is defined so that it captures most of the posterior probability, and $A^+$ so that it captures little of the posterior probability. They are defined this way because the observational noise has variance $\gamma^2$; considering a neighborhood of the circumference which scales as $\gamma$ raised to a power slightly smaller than 2 captures most of the posterior probability; considering a neighborhood of the circumference in which the exponent is slightly larger than this captures little of the posterior probability. Define $B$ to be the closed ball of radius $2\sqrt{y}$ centered at the origin. Let $u^+ \in A^+ \subset B, u^- \in (A^-)^c$ and let $\rho_{\min} = \inf_{u \in B} \rho(u)$. Since $\rho(u)$ is positive and continuous and $B$ is compact, $\rho_{\min} > 0$. Taking the small noise limit yields

$$\frac{\pi^y(u^+)}{\pi^y(u^-)} \geq \exp\left(-\frac{1}{2}\gamma^\delta + \frac{1}{2}\gamma^{-\delta}\right)\frac{\rho_{\min}}{\rho_{\max}} \to \infty, \text{ as } \gamma \to 0^+.$$

Therefore, noting that $y > 0$, the posterior $\pi^y$ concentrates, as $\gamma \to 0^+$, on the circumference with radius $\sqrt{y}$.          $\diamond$

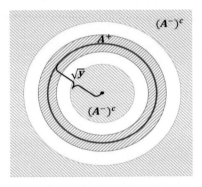

Figure 1.1 The posterior measure concentrates on a circumference with radius $\sqrt{y}$. Here, the blue shadow area is $A^+$ and the green shadow area is $(A^-)^c$.

## 1.3 Well-Posedness of Bayesian Inverse Problems

In this section we show that the Bayesian formulation of inverse problems leads to a form of well-posedness. More precisely, we study the sensitivity of the posterior pdf to perturbations of the forward model $G$. In many inverse problems the ideal forward model $G$ is not accessible but can be approximated by some computable $G_\delta$; consequently $\pi^y$ is replaced by $\pi^y_\delta$. An example that is often found in applications, to which the theory contained herein may be generalized, is when $G$ is an operator acting on an infinite-dimensional space which is approximated, for the purposes of computation, by some finite-dimensional operator $G_\delta$. We seek to prove that, under certain assumptions, the small difference between $G$ and $G_\delta$ (forward error) leads to a similarly small difference between $\pi^y$ and $\pi^y_\delta$ (inverse error):

**Meta Theorem** (Well-Posedness)

$$|G - G_\delta| = O(\delta) \implies d(\pi^y, \pi_\delta^y) = O(\delta)$$

*for small enough $\delta > 0$ and some metric $d(\cdot, \cdot)$ on probability densities.*

This result will be formalized in Theorem 1.15 below, which shows that the $O(\delta)$-convergence of $\pi_\delta^y$ with respect to some distance $d(\cdot, \cdot)$ can be guaranteed under certain assumptions on the likelihood. We will conclude the chapter by showing an example where these assumptions hold true. In order to discuss these issues we will need to introduce metrics on probability densities.

### 1.3.1 Metrics on Probability Densities

Here we introduce the total variation and the Hellinger distance, both of which have been used to show well-posedness results. In this chapter we will use the Hellinger distance to establish well-posedness of Bayesian inverse problems, and in Chapter 7 we employ the total variation distance to establish well-posedness of Bayesian formulations of filtering and smoothing in data assimilation.

**Definition 1.7** The *total variation distance* between two pdfs $\pi$ and $\pi'$ is defined by

$$d_{\mathrm{TV}}(\pi, \pi') := \frac{1}{2} \int |\pi(u) - \pi'(u)| du = \frac{1}{2} \|\pi - \pi'\|_{L^1}.$$

The *Hellinger distance* between two pdfs $\pi$ and $\pi'$ is defined by

$$d_{\mathrm{H}}(\pi, \pi') := \left( \frac{1}{2} \int |\sqrt{\pi(u)} - \sqrt{\pi'(u)}|^2 du \right)^{1/2} = \frac{1}{\sqrt{2}} \|\sqrt{\pi} - \sqrt{\pi'}\|_{L^2}.$$

$\diamond$

In the rest of this subsection we will establish bounds between the Hellinger and total variation distance, and show how both distances can be used to bound the difference of expected values computed with two different densities; these results will be used in subsequent chapters. Before doing so, the next lemma motivates our choice of normalization constant $1/2$ for total variation distance and $1/\sqrt{2}$ for Hellinger distance: they are chosen so that the maximum possible distance between two densities is one. The proof also shows that $\pi$ and $\pi'$ have total variation and Hellinger distance equal to one if and only if they have disjoint supports; that is, if $\int \pi(u)\pi'(u)du = 0$.

**Lemma 1.8** *For any pdfs $\pi$ and $\pi'$,*

$$0 \le d_{\mathrm{TV}}(\pi, \pi') \le 1, \quad 0 \le d_{\mathrm{H}}(\pi, \pi') \le 1.$$

*Proof* The lower bounds follow immediately from the definitions, so we only need to prove the upper bounds. For total variation distance,

$$d_{\text{TV}}(\pi, \pi') = \frac{1}{2} \int |\pi(u) - \pi'(u)| du \leq \frac{1}{2} \int \pi(u) du + \frac{1}{2} \int \pi'(u) du = 1,$$

and for Hellinger distance,

$$d_{\text{H}}(\pi, \pi') = \left( \frac{1}{2} \int \left| \sqrt{\pi(u)} - \sqrt{\pi'(u)} \right|^2 du \right)^{1/2}$$

$$= \left( \frac{1}{2} \int \left( \pi(u) + \pi'(u) - 2\sqrt{\pi(u)\pi'(u)} \right) du \right)^{1/2}$$

$$\leq \left( \frac{1}{2} \int \left( \pi(u) + \pi'(u) \right) du \right)^{1/2}$$

$$= 1.$$

$\square$

The following result gives bounds between total variation and Hellinger distance.

**Lemma 1.9** *For any pdfs $\pi$ and $\pi'$,*

$$\frac{1}{\sqrt{2}} d_{\text{TV}}(\pi, \pi') \leq d_{\text{H}}(\pi, \pi') \leq \sqrt{d_{\text{TV}}(\pi, \pi')}.$$

*Proof* From the Cauchy–Schwarz inequality it follows that

$$d_{\text{TV}}(\pi, \pi') = \frac{1}{2} \int \left| \sqrt{\pi(u)} - \sqrt{\pi'(u)} \right| \left| \sqrt{\pi(u)} + \sqrt{\pi'(u)} \right| du$$

$$\leq \left( \frac{1}{2} \int \left| \sqrt{\pi(u)} - \sqrt{\pi'(u)} \right|^2 du \right)^{1/2} \left( \frac{1}{2} \int \left| \sqrt{\pi(u)} + \sqrt{\pi'(u)} \right|^2 du \right)^{1/2}$$

$$\leq d_{\text{H}}(\pi, \pi') \left( \frac{1}{2} \int \left( 2\pi(u) + 2\pi'(u) \right) du \right)^{1/2}$$

$$= \sqrt{2} d_{\text{H}}(\pi, \pi').$$

Notice that $|\sqrt{\pi(u)} - \sqrt{\pi'(u)}| \leq |\sqrt{\pi(u)} + \sqrt{\pi'(u)}|$ since $\sqrt{\pi(u)}, \sqrt{\pi'(u)} \geq 0$.

Thus we have

$$
\begin{aligned}
d_{\mathrm{H}}(\pi, \pi') &= \left( \frac{1}{2} \int \left| \sqrt{\pi(u)} - \sqrt{\pi'(u)} \right|^2 du \right)^{1/2} \\
&\leq \left( \frac{1}{2} \int \left| \sqrt{\pi(u)} - \sqrt{\pi'(u)} \right| \left| \sqrt{\pi(u)} + \sqrt{\pi'(u)} \right| du \right)^{1/2} \\
&\leq \left( \frac{1}{2} \int \left| \pi(u) - \pi'(u) \right| du \right)^{1/2} \\
&= \sqrt{d_{\mathrm{TV}}(\pi, \pi')}.
\end{aligned}
$$

$\square$

The following two lemmas show that if two densities are close in total variation or in Hellinger distance, expectations computed with respect to both densities are also close. In addition, the following lemma also provides a useful characterization of the total variation distance that will be used repeatedly throughout these notes.

**Lemma 1.10** *Let $f$ be a function such that $|f|_\infty := \sup_{u \in \mathbb{R}^d} |f(u)| < \infty$. It holds that*

$$
\left| \mathbb{E}^\pi[f] - \mathbb{E}^{\pi'}[f] \right| \leq 2|f|_\infty d_{\mathrm{TV}}(\pi, \pi').
$$

*Moreover, the following variational characterization of the total variation distance holds:*

$$
d_{\mathrm{TV}}(\pi, \pi') = \frac{1}{2} \sup_{|f|_\infty \leq 1} \left| \mathbb{E}^\pi[f] - \mathbb{E}^{\pi'}[f] \right|. \tag{1.4}
$$

*Proof* For the first part of the lemma, note that

$$
\begin{aligned}
\left| \mathbb{E}^\pi[f] - \mathbb{E}^{\pi'}[f] \right| &= \left| \int_{\mathbb{R}^d} f(u) \big( \pi(u) - \pi'(u) \big) du \right| \\
&\leq 2|f|_\infty \cdot \frac{1}{2} \int_{\mathbb{R}^d} |\pi(u) - \pi'(u)| du \\
&= 2|f|_\infty d_{\mathrm{TV}}(\pi, \pi').
\end{aligned}
$$

This in particular shows that, for any $f$ with $|f|_\infty = 1$,

$$
d_{\mathrm{TV}}(\pi, \pi') \geq \frac{1}{2} \left| \mathbb{E}^\pi[f] - \mathbb{E}^{\pi'}[f] \right|.
$$

Our goal now is to show a choice of $f$ with $|f|_\infty = 1$ that achieves equality. Define $f(u) := \mathrm{sign}\big( \pi(u) - \pi'(u) \big)$, so that $f(u)\big( \pi(u) - \pi'(u) \big) = |\pi(u) - \pi'(u)|$. Then it holds that $|f|_\infty = 1$, and

$$
\begin{aligned}
d_{\mathrm{TV}}(\pi, \pi') &= \frac{1}{2} \int_{\mathbb{R}^d} |\pi(u) - \pi'(u)| \, du \\
&= \frac{1}{2} \int_{\mathbb{R}^d} f(u) \big(\pi(u) - \pi'(u)\big) \, du \\
&= \frac{1}{2} \Big| \mathbb{E}^\pi[f] - \mathbb{E}^{\pi'}[f] \Big|.
\end{aligned}
$$

This completes the proof of the variational characterization.     □

**Lemma 1.11**   *Let $f$ be a function such that $f_2 := \big(\mathbb{E}^\pi[|f|^2] + \mathbb{E}^{\pi'}[|f|^2]\big)^{\frac{1}{2}} < \infty$. Then*

$$
\big| \mathbb{E}^\pi[f] - \mathbb{E}^{\pi'}[f] \big| \le 2 f_2 d_{\mathrm{H}}(\pi, \pi').
$$

*Proof*   Using the Cauchy–Schwarz inequality gives

$$
\begin{aligned}
\big| \mathbb{E}^\pi[f] - \mathbb{E}^{\pi'}[f] \big| &= \left| \int_{\mathbb{R}^d} f(u) \big(\sqrt{\pi(u)} - \sqrt{\pi'(u)}\big)\big(\sqrt{\pi(u)} + \sqrt{\pi'(u)}\big) \, du \right| \\
&\le \left( \frac{1}{2} \int \big|\sqrt{\pi(u)} - \sqrt{\pi'(u)}\big|^2 \, du \right)^{1/2} \\
&\quad \times \left( 2 \int |f(u)|^2 \big|\sqrt{\pi(u)} + \sqrt{\pi'(u)}\big|^2 \, du \right)^{1/2} \\
&\le d_{\mathrm{H}}(\pi, \pi') \left( 4 \int |f(u)|^2 \big(\pi(u) + \pi'(u)\big) du \right)^{1/2} \\
&= 2 f_2 \, d_{\mathrm{H}}(\pi, \pi').
\end{aligned}
$$

□

***Remark* 1.12**   Note that the result for Hellinger only assumes that $f$ is square integrable with respect to $\pi$ and $\pi'$. In contrast, the result for total variation distance assumes that $f$ is bounded, which is a stronger condition. Lemma 1.9 also demonstrates that smallness in the Hellinger metric is a more stringent condition than smallness in total variation. Our aim in the following section is to show well-posedness in some metric on probability densities. The preceding observations suggest that establishing such a result in the Hellinger metric makes a stronger statement than doing so in total variation.     ◇

### 1.3.2 Approximation Theorem

We denote by

$$
\mathsf{I}(u) = \nu\big(y - G(u)\big) \quad \text{and} \quad \mathsf{I}_\delta(u) = \nu\big(y - G_\delta(u)\big)
$$

the likelihoods associated with $G(u)$ and $G_\delta(u)$, so that

$$\pi^y(u) = \frac{1}{Z}\mathsf{l}(u)\rho(u) \quad \text{and} \quad \pi^y_\delta(u) = \frac{1}{Z_\delta}\mathsf{l}_\delta(u)\rho(u),$$

where $Z, Z_\delta > 0$ are the corresponding normalizing constants. Before we proceed to our main result, we make some assumptions.

**Assumption 1.13** *There exist $\delta^+ > 0$ and $K_1, K_2 < \infty$ such that, for all $\delta \in (0, \delta^+)$,*

(i) $|\sqrt{\mathsf{l}(u)} - \sqrt{\mathsf{l}_\delta(u)}| \leq \varphi(u)\delta$ *for some $\varphi(u)$ such that $\mathbb{E}^\rho[\varphi^2(u)] \leq K_1^2$;*

(ii) $\sup_{u \in \mathbb{R}^d}(|\sqrt{\mathsf{l}(u)}| + |\sqrt{\mathsf{l}_\delta(u)}|) \leq K_2$.

***Remark* 1.14** Assumption 1.13 only involves conditions on the likelihood $\mathsf{l}$ and the approximate likelihood $\mathsf{l}_\delta$. Our presentation in this chapter emphasizes the situation in which this approximation is necessitated in order to approximate the forward model $G$. However, another important scenario which is covered by the theory is approximation due to perturbations of the data $y$. As an example, we will establish in Chapter 7 a well-posedness result that guarantees stability of Bayesian smoothing under perturbations of the data. More generally, the theoretical framework introduced here is very flexible, and it may be employed to study the stability of many Bayesian formulations of inverse problems and data assimilation under a wide range of perturbations. ◇

Now we state the main result of this section:

**Theorem 1.15** (Well-Posedness of Posterior) *Under Assumption 1.13 we have*

$$d_{\mathrm{H}}(\pi^y, \pi^y_\delta) \leq c\delta, \quad \delta \in (0, \Delta),$$

*for some $\Delta > 0$ and some $c \in (0, +\infty)$ independent of $\delta$.*

Notice that this theorem, together with Lemma 1.11, guarantees that expectations computed with respect to $\pi^y$ and $\pi^y_\delta$ are order $\delta$ apart. To prove Theorem 1.15, we first show a lemma which characterizes the normalization factor $Z_\delta$ in the small $\delta$ limit.

**Lemma 1.16** *Under Assumption 1.13 there exist $\Delta > 0$, $c_1, c_2 \in (0, +\infty)$ such that*

$$|Z - Z_\delta| \leq c_1\delta \quad \text{and} \quad Z, Z_\delta > c_2, \quad \text{for } \delta \in (0, \Delta).$$

*Proof* Since $Z = \int \mathsf{l}(u)\rho(u)du$ and $Z_\delta = \int \mathsf{l}_\delta(u)\rho(u)du$, we have

$$|Z - Z_\delta| = \left| \int \big(\mathsf{l}(u) - \mathsf{l}_\delta(u)\big)\rho(u)du \right|$$

$$\leq \left( \int \left|\sqrt{\mathsf{l}(u)} - \sqrt{\mathsf{l}_\delta(u)}\right|^2 \rho(u)du \right)^{1/2} \left( \int \left|\sqrt{\mathsf{l}(u)} + \sqrt{\mathsf{l}_\delta(u)}\right|^2 \rho(u)du \right)^{1/2}$$

$$\leq \left( \int \delta^2 \varphi(u)^2 \rho(u)du \right)^{1/2} \left( \int K_2^2 \rho(u)du \right)^{1/2}$$

$$\leq K_1 K_2 \delta, \quad \delta \in (0, \delta^+).$$

Therefore, for $\delta \leq \Delta := \min\{\frac{Z}{2K_1 K_2}, \delta^+\}$, we have

$$Z_\delta \geq Z - |Z - Z_\delta| \geq \frac{1}{2}Z.$$

The lemma follows by taking $c_1 = K_1 K_2$ and $c_2 = \frac{1}{2}Z$. $\qquad\square$

*Proof of Theorem 1.15* We break the total error into two contributions, one reflecting the difference between $Z$ and $Z_\delta$, and the other the difference between $\mathsf{l}$ and $\mathsf{l}_\delta$:

$$d_{\mathrm{H}}(\pi^y, \pi_\delta^y) = \frac{1}{\sqrt{2}} \left\| \sqrt{\pi^y} - \sqrt{\pi_\delta^y} \right\|_{L^2}$$

$$= \frac{1}{\sqrt{2}} \left\| \sqrt{\frac{\mathsf{l}\rho}{Z}} - \sqrt{\frac{\mathsf{l}\rho}{Z_\delta}} + \sqrt{\frac{\mathsf{l}\rho}{Z_\delta}} - \sqrt{\frac{\mathsf{l}_\delta\rho}{Z_\delta}} \right\|_{L^2}$$

$$\leq \frac{1}{\sqrt{2}} \left\| \sqrt{\frac{\mathsf{l}\rho}{Z}} - \sqrt{\frac{\mathsf{l}\rho}{Z_\delta}} \right\|_{L^2} + \frac{1}{\sqrt{2}} \left\| \sqrt{\frac{\mathsf{l}\rho}{Z_\delta}} - \sqrt{\frac{\mathsf{l}_\delta\rho}{Z_\delta}} \right\|_{L^2}.$$

Using Lemma 1.16 we have, for $\delta \in (0, \Delta)$,

$$\left\| \sqrt{\frac{\mathsf{l}\rho}{Z}} - \sqrt{\frac{\mathsf{l}\rho}{Z_\delta}} \right\|_{L^2} = \left| \frac{1}{\sqrt{Z}} - \frac{1}{\sqrt{Z_\delta}} \right| \left( \int \mathsf{l}(u)\rho(u)du \right)^{1/2}$$

$$= \frac{|Z - Z_\delta|}{(\sqrt{Z} + \sqrt{Z_\delta})\sqrt{Z_\delta}}$$

$$\leq \frac{c_1}{2c_2}\delta,$$

and

$$\left\| \sqrt{\frac{\mathsf{l}\rho}{Z_\delta}} - \sqrt{\frac{\mathsf{l}_\delta\rho}{Z_\delta}} \right\|_{L^2} = \frac{1}{\sqrt{Z_\delta}} \left( \int \left| \sqrt{\mathsf{l}(u)} - \sqrt{\mathsf{l}_\delta(u)} \right|^2 \rho(u)du \right)^{1/2} \leq \sqrt{\frac{K_1^2}{c_2}}\delta.$$

Therefore

$$d_{\mathrm{H}}(\pi^y, \pi_\delta^y) \leq \frac{1}{\sqrt{2}}\frac{c_1}{2c_2}\delta + \frac{1}{\sqrt{2}}\sqrt{\frac{K_1^2}{c_2}}\delta = c\delta,$$

with $c = \frac{1}{\sqrt{2}} \frac{c_1}{2c_2} + \frac{K_1}{\sqrt{2c_2}}$, which is independent of $\delta$.          □

### 1.3.3 Example: Well-Posedness for Parameter Estimation in an ODE

Many inverse problems arise from differential equations with unknown input parameters. Here we consider a simple but typical example where $G(u)$ comes from the solution of an ordinary differential equation (ODE), which needs to be solved numerically. Let $x(t)$ be the solution to the initial value problem

$$\frac{dx}{dt} = F(x; u), \quad x(0) = 0, \tag{1.5}$$

where $F; \mathbb{R}^k \times \mathbb{R}^d \longrightarrow \mathbb{R}^k$ is a function such that $F(x; u)$ and the partial Jacobian $D_x F(x; u)$ are uniformly bounded with respect to $(x, u)$, i.e.

$$|F(x; u)|, |D_x F(x; u)| < F_{\max}, \quad \text{for all } (x, u) \in \mathbb{R}^k \times \mathbb{R}^d,$$

for some constant $F_{\max}$, and thus $F(x; u)$ is Lipschitz in $x$ in that, for all $u \in \mathbb{R}^d$,

$$|F(x; u) - F(x'; u)| \le F_{\max}|x - x'|, \quad \text{for all } x, x' \in \mathbb{R}^k.$$

Note that $u \in \mathbb{R}^d$ defines parametric dependence of the vector field defining the differential equation.

Now consider the inverse problem setting

$$y = G(u) + \eta,$$

where

$$G(u) := x(1) = x(t)|_{t=1},$$

and $\eta \sim \mathcal{N}(0, \gamma^2 I_k)$. We assume that the exact mapping $G(u)$ is replaced by some numerical approximation $G_\delta(u)$. In particular, $G_\delta(u)$ is given by using the forward Euler method to solve the ODE (1.5). Define $X_0 = 0$ and

$$X_{\ell+1} = X_\ell + \delta F(X_\ell; u), \quad \ell \ge 0,$$

where $\delta = \frac{1}{L}$ for some large integer $L$. Finally define $G_\delta(u) := X_L$.

In what follows, we will prove that $G_\delta(u)$ is uniformly bounded and close to $G(u)$ when $\delta$ is small, and that $G$ and $G_\delta$ both satisfy the same global bound. Then we will use these results to show that Assumption 1.13 is satisfied. Therefore, we can apply Theorem 1.15 to this example to establish that the approximate posterior $\pi_\delta^y$, defined by approximate forward model $G_\delta$, is close to the true posterior $\pi^y$ with exact forward model $G$.

In showing that Assumption 1.13 is satisfied, we use Lemmas 1.17 and 1.18 below. Recall that $\eta \sim \mathcal{N}(0, \gamma^2 I_k)$, and thus

$$\sqrt{l(u)} = \sqrt{\nu(y - G(u))} = \frac{1}{(2\pi)^{k/4}\gamma^{k/2}} \exp\left(-\frac{1}{4\gamma^2}|y - G(u)|^2\right),$$

$$\sqrt{l_\delta(u)} = \sqrt{\nu(y - G_\delta(u))} = \frac{1}{(2\pi)^{k/4}\gamma^{k/2}} \exp\left(-\frac{1}{4\gamma^2}|y - G_\delta(u)|^2\right).$$

- For Assumption 1.13(i) notice that the function $e^{-w}$ is Lipschitz for $w > 0$, with Lipschitz constant 1. Therefore we have

$$\left|\sqrt{l(u)} - \sqrt{l_\delta(u)}\right| \leq \frac{1}{(2\pi)^{k/4}\gamma^{k/2}} \cdot \frac{1}{4\gamma^2} \cdot \left||y - G(u)|^2 - |y - G_\delta(u)|^2\right|$$

$$= \frac{1}{(2\pi)^{k/4}\gamma^{k/2}} \cdot \frac{1}{4\gamma^2} \cdot |2y - G(u) - G_\delta(u)||G(u) - G_\delta(u)|$$

$$\leq \frac{1}{(2\pi)^{k/4}\gamma^{k/2}} \cdot \frac{1}{4\gamma^2} \cdot (2|y| + 2F_{\max})c\delta$$

$$= \tilde{c}\delta.$$

That is, Assumption 1.13(i) is satisfied with $\varphi(u) = \tilde{c}$ and $\int_{\mathbb{R}^d} \varphi^2(u)\rho(u)\,du = \tilde{c}^2 < \infty$.

- Assumption 1.13(ii) is satisfied, since

$$\sqrt{l(u)} = \frac{1}{(2\pi)^{k/4}\gamma^{k/2}} \exp\left(-\frac{1}{4\gamma^2}|y - G(u)|^2\right) \leq \frac{1}{(2\pi)^{k/4}\gamma^{k/2}},$$

$$\sqrt{l_\delta(u)} = \frac{1}{(2\pi)^{k/4}\gamma^{k/2}} \exp\left(-\frac{1}{4\gamma^2}|y - G_\delta(u)|^2\right) \leq \frac{1}{(2\pi)^{k/4}\gamma^{k/2}}.$$

The preceding verification of Assumption 1.13 used the following two lemmas, and the first of these uses the Gronwall inequality which follows them. Define $t_\ell = \ell\delta, x_\ell = x(t_\ell)$. The following lemma gives an estimate on the error generated from using the forward Euler method.

**Lemma 1.17**    *Let $E_\ell := x_\ell - X_\ell$. Then there is $c < \infty$ independent of $\delta$ such that*

$$|E_\ell| \leq c\delta, \quad 0 \leq \ell \leq L.$$

*In particular,*

$$|G(u) - G_\delta(u)| = |E_L| \leq c\delta.$$

*Proof*    For simplicity of exposition, we consider the case $k = 1$; the case $k > 1$ is almost identical, simply requiring the integral form for the remainder term in the Taylor expansion. Using Taylor expansion in the case $k = 1$, there is $\xi_\ell \in [t_\ell, t_{\ell+1}]$ such that

$$x_{\ell+1} = x_\ell + \delta \frac{dx}{dt}(t_\ell) + \frac{\delta^2}{2} \frac{d^2 x}{dt^2}(\xi_\ell)$$

$$= x_\ell + \delta F(x_\ell; u) + \frac{\delta^2}{2} D_x F(x(\xi_\ell); u) F(x(\xi_\ell); u).$$

Thus we have

$$|E_{\ell+1}| = |x_{\ell+1} - X_{\ell+1}|$$

$$= \left| x_\ell - X_\ell + \delta \Big( F(x_\ell; u) - F(X_\ell; u) \Big) + \frac{\delta^2}{2} D_x F(x(\xi_\ell); u) F(x(\xi_\ell); u) \right|$$

$$\leq |x_\ell - X_\ell| + \delta \big| F(x_\ell; u) - F(X_\ell; u) \big| + \frac{\delta^2}{2} \big| D_x F(x(\xi_\ell); u) \big| \big| F(x(\xi_\ell); u) \big|$$

$$\leq |E_\ell| + \delta F_{\max} |E_\ell| + \frac{\delta^2}{2} F_{\max}^2.$$

Noticing that $|E_0| = 0$, the discrete Gronwall inequality (Theorem 1.19) gives

$$|E_\ell| \leq (1 + \delta F_{\max})^\ell |E_0| + \frac{(1 + \delta F_{\max})^\ell - 1}{\delta F_{\max}} \cdot \frac{\delta^2}{2} F_{\max}^2$$

$$\leq \left( \Big( 1 + \frac{F_{\max}}{L} \Big)^L - 1 \right) \cdot \frac{F_{\max} \delta}{2}$$

$$\leq \frac{(e^{F_{\max}} - 1) F_{\max}}{2} \delta.$$

The lemma follows by taking $c = \frac{(e^{F_{\max}} - 1) F_{\max}}{2}$. $\qquad\square$

**Lemma 1.18** *For any $u \in \mathbb{R}^d$,*

$$|G(u)|, |G_\delta(u)| \leq F_{\max}.$$

*Proof*  For $G(u)$ we use that $F(x; u)$ is uniformly bounded, so that

$$|G(u)| = |x(1)| = \left| \int_0^1 F(x(t); u) dt \right| \leq \int_0^1 |F(x(t); u)| dt \leq F_{\max}.$$

As for $G_\delta(u)$, we first notice that

$$|X_{\ell+1}| = |X_\ell + \delta F(X_\ell; u)| \leq |X_\ell| + \delta |F(X_\ell; u)| \leq |X_\ell| + \delta F_{\max},$$

and by induction

$$|X_\ell| \leq |X_0| + \ell \delta F_{\max} = \ell \delta F_{\max}.$$

In particular,

$$|G_\delta(u)| = |X_L| \leq L \delta F_{\max} = F_{\max}.$$

□

The following discrete Gronwall inequality is used several times in these notes, and is stated and proved here for completeness.

**Theorem 1.19** (Discrete Gronwall Inequality)   *Let a positive sequence $\{Z_\ell\}_{\ell=0}^{L}$ satisfy*

$$Z_{\ell+1} \leq CZ_\ell + D, \qquad \text{for all } \ell = 0, \ldots, L-1$$

*for some constants $C, D$ with $C > 0$. Then*

$$Z_\ell \leq \frac{D}{1-C}(1 - C^\ell) + Z_0 C^\ell \qquad \text{for all } \ell = 0, \ldots, L, \quad C \neq 1$$

*and*

$$Z_\ell \leq \ell D + Z_0 \qquad \text{for all } \ell = 0, \ldots, L, \quad C = 1.$$

*Proof*   The proof is by induction. We start with the case $C \neq 1$. The result holds for $\ell = 0$. Assume it is true for $\ell < L$. Then, using the defining inequality,

$$Z_{\ell+1} \leq \frac{CD}{1-C}(1 - C^\ell) + Z_0 C^{\ell+1} + D.$$

Rearranging yields

$$Z_{\ell+1} \leq \frac{D}{1-C}(1 - C^{\ell+1}) + Z_0 C^{\ell+1}$$

and the result follows by induction.

When $C = 0$ we again note that the result holds for $\ell = 0$. Assume it is true for $\ell < L$. Then, using the defining inequality with $C = 1$,

$$Z_{\ell+1} \leq \ell D + Z_0 + D = (\ell + 1)D + Z_0$$

and the result follows by induction.                                    □

## 1.4  Discussion and Bibliography

Kaipio and Somersalo (2006) provides an introduction to the Bayesian approach to inverse problems, especially in the context of differential equations, and Calvetti and Somersalo (2007) gives an introduction to Bayesian scientific computing. An overview of the subject of Bayesian inverse problems in differential equations, with a perspective informed by the geophysical sciences, is given in Tarantola (2015a) (see, especially, Chapter 5). For non-statistical approaches to inverse problems, we refer to the books Tikhonov and Arsenin (1977), Engl et al.

(1996), Vogel (2002), and the lecture notes Bal (2012) and Miller and Karl (2003).

The subject of Bayesian inverse problems may be developed beyond the specific setting of equation (1.1) to study problems of the form

$$y = G(u, \eta).$$

Our emphasis on additive noise $\eta$, often assumed to be Gaussian, simplifies some algorithms and enables us to be explicit about some formulae, but is not fundamental in any way. We refer to Dunlop (2019) for well-posedness theory and a study of MAP estimation with multiplicative noise. In addition, the setting of equation (1.1) presupposes that the forward model $G$ is given to us, but in some cases the forward model itself may need to be learned from data.

In Stuart (2010) the Bayesian approach to regularization is reviewed, developing a function space viewpoint on the subject; a similar development of this approach is described in Lasanen (2012a,b). A well-posedness theory and some algorithmic approaches which are used when adopting the Bayesian approach to inverse problems are introduced. The function space viewpoint on the subject is developed in more detail in the lecture notes of Dashti and Stuart (2017). An early application of this function space methodology to a large-scale applied inverse problem, taken from the geophysical sciences, may be found in Martin et al. (2012). Lieberman et al. (2010) demonstrates the potential for the use of dimension reduction techniques from control theory within statistical inverse problems.

We refer to Gibbs and Su (2002) for further study on the subject of metrics, and other distance-like functions, on probability measures. The first published paper to discuss stability and well-posedness of the Bayesian inverse problem was Marzouk and Xiu (2009), in which the Kullback–Leibler divergence (see Chapter 4) is employed. Related results on stability and well-posedness, but using other distances and divergences, may be found in Latz (2020). The articles Stuart (2010) and Dashti and Stuart (2017) study well-posedness of Bayesian inverse problems in the Hellinger metric, with respect to perturbations in the data; Cotter et al. (2010) and Harlim et al. (2020) consider stability of the posterior distribution with respect to numerical approximation of partial differential equations appearing in the forward model. Hosseini and Nigam (2017); Hosseini (2017) discuss generalizations of the well-posedness theory to various classes of specific non-Gaussian priors. On the other hand, Iglesias et al. (2014b) contains an interesting set of examples where the Meta Theorem stated in this chapter fails in the sense that, whilst well-posedness holds, the posterior is Hölder with exponent less than 1, rather than Lipschitz, with respect to perturbations.

The Bayesian approach to inverse problems builds on, and benefits from, the vast literature on Bayesian statistics. Fienberg (2006) provides a historical overview of the development and popularization of Bayesian statistics, starting with the introduction of Bayes' formula (Bayes, 1763) and emphasizing the leading role of Savage (1972) in axiomatizing and popularizing the subjective view of probability pioneered by De Finetti (2017). We refer to Gelman et al. (2013) for a recent and comprehensive textbook on Bayesian methodology. See Nickl (2022) for an overview of Bayesian inversion and, in particular, statistical consistency results in this context.

A topic of debate in Bayesian statistics, and specifically in the Bayesian approach to inverse problems, is how to construct prior probability measures from available prior information, which is typically not described probabilistically. Owhadi et al. (2015a,b) demonstrate that this is an important question: different priors, both consistent with available prior information, can lead to wildly different Bayesian inference when computing posterior expectations: what the authors term *Bayesian brittleness*. Arguably, this issue may be dealt with through application of the scientific method: a given prior and likelihood are postulated, and posterior predictions are made; data acquired after making posterior predictions may then be used to evaluate the Bayesian probabilistic model employed, and in particular the prior and likelihood and, if necessary, modify it.

The body of work on Bayesian brittleness builds on related analysis in the context of forward uncertainty quantification (Owhadi et al., 2013), a topic concerned with propagating uncertainty on parameters through a model into predictions. The subject of uncertainty quantification, both the forward and inverse varieties, is overviewed in Sullivan (2015) and Smith (2013).

# 2

# The Linear-Gaussian Setting

Recall the inverse problem of estimating an unknown parameter $u \in \mathbb{R}^d$ from data $y \in \mathbb{R}^k$ under the model assumption

$$y = G(u) + \eta. \tag{2.1}$$

In this chapter we study the linear-Gaussian setting, where the forward model $G(\cdot)$ is linear and both the prior on $u$ and the distribution of the observation noise $\eta$ are Gaussian. This setting is highly amenable to analysis and arises frequently in applications. Moreover, as we will see throughout these notes, many methods employed in nonlinear or non-Gaussian settings build on ideas from the linear-Gaussian case by performing linearization or invoking Gaussian approximations. After establishing a formula for the posterior pdf in Section 2.1, we investigate in Section 2.2 the effect that the choice of prior has on our solution by quantifying the spread of the posterior distribution in the small noise (approaching zero) limit. This investigation provides intuitive understanding concerning the impact of the prior for overdetermined, determined, and underdetermined regimes, corresponding to $d < k, d = k$, and $d > k$, respectively. Extensions of the theory and references to the literature are discussed in Section 2.3.

The following will be assumed throughout this chapter.

**Assumption 2.1** *The relationship between unknown $u \in \mathbb{R}^d$, data $y \in \mathbb{R}^k$, and noise $\eta \in \mathbb{R}^k$ defined by equation (2.1) holds. Moreover,*

- *Linearity of the forward model: $G(u) = Au$, for some $A \in \mathbb{R}^{k \times d}$.*
- *Gaussian prior: $u \sim \rho(u) = \mathcal{N}(\widehat{m}, \widehat{C})$, where $\widehat{C}$ is positive definite.*
- *Gaussian noise: $\eta \sim \nu(\eta) = \mathcal{N}(0, \Gamma)$, where $\Gamma$ is positive definite.*
- *$u$ and $\eta$ are independent: $u \perp \eta$.*

## 2.1 Derivation of the Posterior Distribution

Under Assumption 2.1 the likelihood on $y$ given $u$ is Gaussian,

$$y|u \sim \mathcal{N}(Au, \Gamma). \tag{2.2}$$

Therefore, using Bayes' formula (1.2) we see that the posterior $\pi^y(u)$ is given by

$$
\begin{aligned}
\pi^y(u) &= \frac{1}{Z} \nu(y - Au)\rho(u) \\
&= \frac{1}{Z} \exp\left(-\frac{1}{2}|y - Au|_{\Gamma}^2\right) \exp\left(-\frac{1}{2}|u - \widehat{m}|_{\widehat{C}}^2\right) \\
&= \frac{1}{Z} \exp\left(-\frac{1}{2}|y - Au|_{\Gamma}^2 - \frac{1}{2}|u - \widehat{m}|_{\widehat{C}}^2\right) \\
&= \frac{1}{Z} \exp(-\mathsf{J}(u)),
\end{aligned}
$$

with

$$\mathsf{J}(u) = \frac{1}{2}|y - Au|_{\Gamma}^2 + \frac{1}{2}|u - \widehat{m}|_{\widehat{C}}^2. \tag{2.3}$$

Note that here

$$\log \mathsf{l}(u) = -\frac{1}{2}|y - Au|_{\Gamma}^2. \tag{2.4}$$

Since the posterior pdf can be written as the exponential of a quadratic in $u$ it follows that the posterior is Gaussian. Its mean and covariance are given in the following result.

**Theorem 2.2** (Posterior is Gaussian)   *Under Assumption 2.1 the posterior distribution is Gaussian,*

$$u|y \sim \pi^y(u) = \mathcal{N}(m, C). \tag{2.5}$$

*The posterior mean $m$ and $C$ are given by the following formulae:*

$$m = (A^{\top}\Gamma^{-1}A + \widehat{C}^{-1})^{-1}(A^{\top}\Gamma^{-1}y + \widehat{C}^{-1}\widehat{m}), \tag{2.6}$$

$$C = (A^{\top}\Gamma^{-1}A + \widehat{C}^{-1})^{-1}. \tag{2.7}$$

*Proof*   Since $\pi^y(u) = \frac{1}{Z}\exp(-\mathsf{J}(u))$ with $\mathsf{J}(u)$ given by (2.3), a quadratic function of $u$, it follows that the posterior is Gaussian. Denoting the mean and variance of $\pi^y(u)$ by $m$ and $C$, we can write $\mathsf{J}(u)$ in the following form

$$\mathsf{J}(u) = \frac{1}{2}|u - m|_C^2 + q, \tag{2.8}$$

where the term $q$ does not depend on $u$. Now matching the coefficients of the quadratic and linear terms in equations (2.3) and (2.8), we get

$$C^{-1} = A^\top \Gamma^{-1} A + \widehat{C}^{-1},$$
$$C^{-1}m = A^\top \Gamma^{-1} y + \widehat{C}^{-1}\widehat{m}.$$

Therefore equations (2.6) and (2.7) follow. □

We saw in the previous chapter that the posterior mean estimator and the MAP estimator are typically different. However, equation (2.8) shows that in the current linear-Gaussian setting the posterior mean $m$ minimizes $J(u)$ given in (2.3). Thus, the MAP estimator and the posterior mean coincide.

**Corollary 2.3** (Characterization of Bayes Estimators) *The posterior mean and MAP estimators under Assumptions 2.1 agree, and are given by $u_{\text{MAP}} = u_{\text{PM}} = m$ defined in equation* (2.6).

Furthermore, the formula (2.3) demonstrates that the posterior mean is found as a compromise between maximizing the likelihood (by making the *loss* term $\frac{1}{2}|y - Au|_\Gamma^2$ small) and minimizing deviations from the prior mean (by making the *regularization* term $\frac{1}{2}|u - \widehat{m}|_{\widehat{C}}^2$ small). The relative importance given to both objectives is determined by the relative size of the prior covariance $\widehat{C}$ and the noise covariance $\Gamma$. An important feature of the linear-Gaussian setting is that the posterior covariance $C$ does not depend on the data $y$; this is not true in general.

We conclude this subsection with an example.

**Example 2.4** Let $\Gamma = \gamma^2 I$, $\widehat{C} = \sigma^2 I$, $\widehat{m} = 0$, and set $\lambda = \frac{\gamma^2}{\sigma^2}$. Then

$$J_\lambda(u) := \gamma^2 J(u) = \frac{1}{2}|y - Au|^2 + \frac{\lambda}{2}|u|^2.$$

Since $m$ minimizes $J_\lambda(\cdot)$ it follows that

$$(A^\top A + \lambda I)m = A^\top y. \tag{2.9}$$

◇

Example 2.4 provides a link between Bayesian inversion and optimization approaches to inversion: $J_\lambda(u)$ can be seen as the objective function in a linear regression model with a regularizer $\frac{\lambda}{2}|u|^2$, as used in ridge regression. Equation (2.9) for $m$ is exactly the normal equation with regularizer in the least-squares problem. In fact, in the general linear-Gaussian setting of Assumption 2.1, equation (2.6) can also be viewed as a generalized normal equation. This perspective helps us understand the structure of Bayesian regularization by linking it to the deep understanding of optimization approaches to problems. A more extensive account of the optimization perspective and its interplay with Bayesian formulations will be given in the following chapter.

## 2.2 Small Noise Limit of the Posterior Distribution

In this section we study the small observation noise limit of the posterior in the linear-Gaussian setting. While most of the ideas and results can be extended beyond this setting, explicit calculations that are possible in the linear-Gaussian setting provide helpful intuition. Throughout this section we assume the following.

**Assumption 2.5** *In addition to Assumption 2.1 (the linear-Gaussian setting), we assume that $\eta := \gamma\eta_0$, where $\eta_0 \sim \mathcal{N}(0, \Gamma_0)$; thus $\Gamma = \gamma^2\Gamma_0$.*

Note that substituting $\Gamma = \gamma^2\Gamma_0$ into (2.6) and (2.7), we obtain that

$$m = (A^\top\Gamma_0^{-1}A + \gamma^2\widehat{C}^{-1})^{-1}(A^\top\Gamma_0^{-1}y + \gamma^2\widehat{C}^{-1}\widehat{m}), \qquad (2.10)$$

$$C = \gamma^2(A^\top\Gamma_0^{-1}A + \gamma^2\widehat{C}^{-1})^{-1}. \qquad (2.11)$$

In the next three subsections we study the behavior of the posterior mean $m$ and covariance $C$ as $\gamma \to 0^+$ – the small noise limit. We remark that $m$, $C$, and the posterior $\pi^y$ depend on the noise level $\gamma$, but we will not make explicit said dependence in our notation. We separately consider the overdetermined, determined, and underdetermined regimes. We recall that $\Rightarrow$ denotes weak convergence of probability measures. We will use repeatedly that weak convergence of Gaussian distributions is equivalent to the convergence of their means and covariances. In particular, the weak limit of a sequence of Gaussians with means converging to $m^+$ and covariance matrices converging to the zero matrix is a Dirac mass $\delta_{m^+}$.

### 2.2.1 Overdetermined Case

We start with the overdetermined case $d < k$.

**Theorem 2.6** (Small Noise Limit of Posterior Distribution – Overdetermined) *Suppose that Assumption 2.5 holds, that $\mathrm{Null}(A) = 0$, and that $d < k$. Then, in the limit $\gamma \to 0^+$,*

$$\pi^y \Rightarrow \delta_{m^+},$$

*where $m^+$ is the solution of the least-squares problem*

$$m^+ = \arg \min_{u \in \mathbb{R}^d} |\Gamma_0^{-1/2}(y - Au)|^2. \tag{2.12}$$

*Proof* Since Null($A$) = 0 and $\Gamma_0$ is invertible we deduce that there is $\alpha > 0$ such that, for all $u \in \mathbb{R}^d$,

$$\langle u, A^\top \Gamma_0^{-1} A u \rangle = |\Gamma_0^{-1/2} A u|^2 \geq \alpha |u|^2.$$

Thus $A^\top \Gamma_0^{-1} A$ is positive definite (and hence invertible). It follows that as $\gamma \to 0^+$, the posterior covariance converges to the zero matrix, $C \to 0$, and the posterior mean satisfies the limit

$$m \to m^* = (A^\top \Gamma_0^{-1} A)^{-1} A^\top \Gamma_0^{-1} y.$$

This proves the weak convergence of $\pi^y$ to $\delta_{m^*}$. It remains to characterize $m^*$. Since Null($A$) = 0, the minimizers of the scaled loss [1]

$$\mathsf{L}(u) := \frac{1}{2}|\Gamma_0^{-1/2}(y - Au)|^2$$

are unique and satisfy the normal equations $A^\top \Gamma_0^{-1} A u = A^\top \Gamma_0^{-1} y$. Hence $m^*$ solves the desired least-squares problem and coincides with $m^+$ given in (2.12). $\qquad \square$

We have shown that in the overdetermined case where $A^\top \Gamma_0^{-1} A$ is invertible, the small observational noise limit leads to a posterior which is a Dirac, centered at the solution of the least-squares problem (2.12). Therefore, in this limit the prior plays no role in the Bayesian inference.

**Theorem 2.7** (Posterior Consistency – Overdetermined) *Suppose that the assumptions of Theorem 2.6 hold and that the data satisfies*

$$y = Au^\dagger + \gamma \eta_0^\dagger, \qquad \text{for fixed } u^\dagger \in \mathbb{R}^d, \eta_0^\dagger \in \mathbb{R}^k.$$

*Then, for any sequence $M(\gamma) \to \infty$ as $\gamma \to 0^+$,*

$$\mathbb{P}^{\pi^y}\left(|u - u^\dagger|^2 > M(\gamma)\gamma^2\right) \to 0,$$

*where $\mathbb{P}^{\pi^y}$ denotes probability under the posterior distribution.*

**Remark 2.8** For any $\varepsilon > 0$, set $M(\gamma) = \frac{\varepsilon^2}{\gamma^2}$ in Theorem 2.10 to obtain

$$\mathbb{P}^{\pi^y}\left(|u - u^\dagger| > \varepsilon\right) \to 0.$$

This shows that the posterior probability concentrates around the truth in the small noise limit. ◇

[1] Note that this is a rescaling by $\gamma^2$ of the negative log-likelihood from equation (2.4).

*Proof of Theorem 2.7*    Throughout this proof we let $c$ be a constant independent of $\gamma$ that may change from line to line, and we denote by $\mathbb{E}$ expectation with respect to the posterior distribution, which is Gaussian with mean $m$ and covariance $C$ given by equations (2.10) and (2.11). Denote

$$m^* = (A^\top \Gamma_0^{-1} A)^{-1} A^\top \Gamma_0^{-1} y$$

as in the proof of the previous theorem. We have that

$$\mathbb{E}\big[|u - u^\dagger|^2\big] \leq c\Big(\mathbb{E}\big[|u - m|^2\big] + |m - m^*|^2 + |m^* - u^\dagger|^2\Big). \qquad (2.13)$$

We now bound each of the three terms in the right-hand side.

For the first one,

$$\begin{aligned}
\mathbb{E}\big[|u - m|^2\big] &= \mathbb{E}\big[(u - m)^\top (u - m)\big] = \mathbb{E}\big[\mathrm{Tr}[(u - m) \otimes (u - m)]\big] \\
&= \mathrm{Tr}\,\mathbb{E}\big[(u - m) \otimes (u - m)\big] \\
&= \mathrm{Tr}(C) \leq \gamma^2 \mathrm{Tr}\Big[(A^\top \Gamma_0^{-1} A)^{-1}\Big].
\end{aligned}$$

For the second term, note that

$$\begin{aligned}
(A^\top \Gamma_0^{-1} A) m^* &= A^\top \Gamma_0^{-1} y, \\
(A^\top \Gamma_0^{-1} A + \gamma^2 \widehat{C}^{-1}) m &= A^\top \Gamma_0^{-1} y + \gamma^2 \widehat{C}^{-1} \widehat{m}.
\end{aligned}$$

Therefore

$$m - m^* = \gamma^2 (A^\top \Gamma_0^{-1} A)^{-1} (\widehat{C}^{-1} \widehat{m} - \widehat{C}^{-1} m).$$

Since $m$ converges it is bounded, and so there is $c > 0$ such that

$$|m - m^*|^2 \leq c\gamma^4.$$

Finally, for the third term we write

$$\begin{aligned}
m^* &= (A^\top \Gamma_0^{-1} A)^{-1} A^\top \Gamma_0^{-1} A u^\dagger + \gamma (A^\top \Gamma_0^{-1} A)^{-1} A^\top \Gamma_0^{-1} \eta_0^\dagger \\
&= u^\dagger + \gamma (A^\top \Gamma_0^{-1} A)^{-1} A^\top \Gamma_0^{-1} \eta_0^\dagger,
\end{aligned}$$

which gives

$$|m^* - u^\dagger|^2 \leq c\gamma^2.$$

Using Markov inequality and the three bounds above,

$$\mathbb{P}^{\pi^y}\big(|u - u^\dagger|^2 > M(\gamma)\gamma^2\big) \leq \frac{\mathbb{E}[|u - u^\dagger|^2]}{M(\gamma)\gamma^2} \leq \frac{c}{M(\gamma)} \to 0, \text{ as } \gamma \to 0^+.$$

$\square$

## 2.2.2 Determined Case

As a byproduct of the proof of Theorem 2.6, we can determine the limiting behavior of $\pi^y$ in the boundary case $d = k$.

**Theorem 2.9** (Small Noise Limit of Posterior Distribution – Determined) *Suppose that Assumption 2.5 holds, Null$(A) = 0$, and $d = k$. Then, in the small noise limit $\gamma \to 0^+$,*

$$\pi^y \Rightarrow \delta_{A^{-1}y}.$$

*Proof*  In the proof of Theorem 2.6, the assumption $d < k$ is used only in that $A$ is not a square matrix and thus $A, A^\top$ are not invertible. Denote by $(m, C)$ the mean and variance of the posterior $u \mid y$. Using the same argument, we have $C \to 0$ and

$$m \to m^* = (A^\top \Gamma_0^{-1} A)^{-1} A^\top \Gamma_0^{-1} y.$$

Using that $A, A^\top$ are square invertible matrices, we obtain

$$m^* = (A^{-1} \Gamma_0 (A^\top)^{-1}) A^\top \Gamma_0^{-1} y = A^{-1} y.$$

Therefore, $\pi^y(u) \Rightarrow \delta_{m^*} = \delta_{A^{-1}y}$.  □

Note that here, as in the overdetermined case, the prior plays no role in the small noise limit. Moreover, it can be shown as above that posterior consistency holds. The proof is very similar to that in the overdetermined case, and therefore omitted.

**Theorem 2.10** (Posterior Consistency – Determined)  *Suppose that the assumptions of Theorem 2.9 hold, and that the data satisfies*

$$y = Au^\dagger + \gamma \eta_0^\dagger, \qquad \text{for fixed } u^\dagger, \eta_0^\dagger \in \mathbb{R}^d.$$

*Then, for any sequence $M(\gamma) \to \infty$ as $\gamma \to 0^+$,*

$$\mathbb{P}^{\pi^y}\left(|u - u^\dagger|^2 > M(\gamma)\gamma^2\right) \to 0.$$

## 2.2.3 Underdetermined Case

Finally we consider the underdetermined case $d > k$. We assume that $A \in \mathbb{R}^{k \times d}$ with Rank$(A) = k$ and write

$$A = (A_0 \ 0)Q^\top = (A_0 \ 0)(Q_1 \ Q_2)^\top = A_0 Q_1^\top, \qquad (2.14)$$

with $A_0 \in \mathbb{R}^{k \times k}$ an invertible matrix, $Q = (Q_1 \ Q_2) \in \mathbb{R}^{d \times d}$ an orthogonal matrix so that $Q^\top Q = I$, $Q_1 \in \mathbb{R}^{d \times k}$, $Q_2 \in \mathbb{R}^{d \times (d-k)}$. We have the following result:

**Theorem 2.11** (Small Noise Limit of Posterior Distribution – Underdetermined) *Suppose that Assumption 2.5 holds, that* $\text{Rank}(A) = k$, *and* $d > k$. *In the small noise limit* $\gamma \to 0^+$,

$$\pi^y \Rightarrow \mathcal{N}(m^+, C^+),$$

*where*

$$m^+ = \widehat{C}Q_1(Q_1^\top \widehat{C} Q_1)^{-1} A_0^{-1} y + Q_2(Q_2^\top \widehat{C}^{-1} Q_2)^{-1} Q_2^\top \widehat{C}^{-1} \widehat{m},$$
$$C^+ = Q_2(Q_2^\top \widehat{C}^{-1} Q_2)^{-1} Q_2^\top.$$

Since $\text{Rank}(C^+) = \text{Rank}(Q_2) = d - k < d$ this theorem demonstrates that, in the small observational noise limit, the posterior has no uncertainty in a subspace of dimension $k$, but retains uncertainty in a subspace of dimension $d - k$. As a consequence, there is no posterior consistency in the underdetermined case.

**Example 2.12** (Small Noise Limit – Underdetermined)    To help understand the result in Theorem 2.11, we consider a simple explicit example. Assume that $A = (A_0 \; 0) \in \mathbb{R}^{k \times d}, \Gamma = \gamma^2 \Gamma_0 = \gamma^2 I_k, \widehat{C} = I_d, \widehat{m} = 0$. Let $u = (u_1, u_2)^\top \sim \mathcal{N}(0, I_d)$, with $u_1 \in \mathbb{R}^k$, and $u_2 \in \mathbb{R}^{d-k}$. The data then satisfies

$$y = Au + \eta = A_0 u_1 + \eta, \quad \eta \sim \mathcal{N}(0, \gamma^2 I_k).$$

The posterior $u \mid y$ is $\pi^y(u) = \frac{1}{Z_\gamma} \exp(-\mathsf{J}_\gamma(u))$, where

$$\mathsf{J}_\gamma(u) = \frac{1}{2\gamma^2} |y - A_0 u_1|^2 + \frac{1}{2} |u|^2$$
$$= \left( \frac{1}{2\gamma^2} |y - A_0 u_1|^2 + \frac{1}{2} |u_1|^2 \right) + \frac{1}{2} |u_2|^2. \tag{2.15}$$

It is clear that

$$\pi^y(u_1) \Rightarrow \delta_{A_0^{-1} y}(u_1).$$

Once $u_1$ is fixed as $A_0^{-1} y$, the first term in (2.15) is a constant $\frac{1}{2} |A_0^{-1} y|^2$. Since $u_1$ and $u_2$ are independent we can derive, formally, the limiting posterior as follows:

$$\pi^y(u) \Rightarrow \delta_{A_0^{-1} y}(u_1) \otimes \frac{1}{Z} \exp\left( -\frac{1}{2} |u_2|^2 \right) = \delta_{A_0^{-1} y}(u_1) \otimes \mathcal{N}(0, I_{d-k}),$$

where $Z = \int_{\mathbb{R}^{d-k}} \exp(-\frac{1}{2} |u_2|^2) du_2$. In fact, this is exactly the limiting posterior measure given in Theorem 2.11. $\diamond$

To prove Theorem 2.11, we use the following decomposition of the identity $I_d$.

**Lemma 2.13** *Let $\widehat{C} \in \mathbb{R}^{d \times d}$ be invertible and $Q = [Q_1 \, Q_2]$ be an orthogonal matrix with $Q_1 \in \mathbb{R}^{d \times k}, Q_2 \in \mathbb{R}^{d \times (d-k)}$. We have the following decomposition of $I_d$:*

$$I_d = \widehat{C} Q_1 (Q_1^\top \widehat{C} Q_1)^{-1} Q_1^\top + Q_2 (Q_2^\top \widehat{C}^{-1} Q_2)^{-1} Q_2^\top \widehat{C}^{-1}. \qquad (2.16)$$

*Proof*    Denote by $R$ the right-hand side of (2.16). Since $Q$ is orthogonal, we have $Q_1^\top Q_2 = 0, Q_2^\top Q_1 = 0$ and thus

$$Q_1^\top (R - I) = 0, \quad Q_2^\top \widehat{C}^{-1} (R - I) = 0.$$

If $B := (Q_1 \, \widehat{C}^{-1} Q_2)$ is full rank, the above identities imply that $B^\top (R - I) = 0$ and thus $R = I$. Note that

$$Q^\top B = \left[ \begin{array}{c} Q_1^\top \\ Q_2^\top \end{array} \right] [Q_1 \, \widehat{C}^{-1} Q_2] = \left[ \begin{array}{cc} I_k & Q_1^\top \widehat{C}^{-1} Q_2 \\ 0 & Q_2^\top \widehat{C}^{-1} Q_2 \end{array} \right].$$

Since the last matrix is invertible, $B$ is invertible and the proof is complete.    □

*Proof of Theorem 2.11*    Using (2.16) we can decompose $u$ as follows

$$u = \underbrace{\widehat{C} Q_1 (Q_1^\top \widehat{C} Q_1)^{-1}}_{S} \underbrace{Q_1^\top u}_{u_1} + \underbrace{Q_2 (Q_2^\top \widehat{C}^{-1} Q_2)^{-1}}_{T} \underbrace{Q_2^\top \widehat{C}^{-1} u}_{u_2} = S u_1 + T u_2.$$

Here $u_1$ and $u_2$ are Gaussian with $u_2 \sim \mathcal{N}(Q_2^\top \widehat{C}^{-1} \widehat{m}, Q_2^\top \widehat{C}^{-1} Q_2)$. The identity

$$\mathrm{Cov}(u_1, u_2) = Q_1^\top \mathrm{Cov}(u, u) \widehat{C}^{-1} Q_2 = Q_1^\top Q_2 = 0$$

shows that $u_1$ and $u_2$ are independent, written $u_1 \perp u_2$. From (2.14), we have

$$y = Au + \eta = A_0 Q_1^\top u + \eta = A_0 u_1 + \eta. \qquad (2.17)$$

Since $u \perp \eta$ and $u_1 \perp u_2$, we have that $u_2 \perp y, u_1$. We apply conditional probability to yield

$$\pi^y(u_1, u_2) := \mathbb{P}(u_1, u_2 \mid y) = \mathbb{P}(u_2) \, \mathbb{P}(u_1 \mid y).$$

Equation (2.17) and Theorem 2.9 show that $\mathbb{P}(u_1 \mid y) \Rightarrow \delta_{A_0^{-1} y}(u_1)$ as the noise vanishes; that is, as $\gamma \to 0^+$. Note that $u_2 \perp u_1$ and $u_2 \perp y$. The limiting posterior measure $(u_1, u_2) \mid y$ is

$$\pi^y(u_1, u_2) \Rightarrow \mathbb{P}(u_2) \otimes \delta_{A_0^{-1} y}(u_1) \qquad (2.18)$$

as $\gamma \to 0^+$. Recall $u = S u_1 + T u_2$ and $u_2 \sim \mathcal{N}(Q_2^\top \widehat{C}^{-1} \widehat{m}, Q_2^\top \widehat{C}^{-1} Q_2)$. The mean and variance of the limiting posterior measure $u \mid y$ are

$$m^+ = \mathbb{E}[S u_1 + T u_2 \mid y] = S A_0^{-1} y + T \, \mathbb{E}[u_2] = S A_0^{-1} y + T Q_2^\top \widehat{C}^{-1} \widehat{m},$$

$$C^+ = \mathrm{Cov}\,(S u_1 + T u_2 \mid y) = \mathrm{Cov}\,(T u_2) = T Q_2^\top \widehat{C}^{-1} Q_2 T^\top = Q_2 (Q_2^\top \widehat{C}^{-1} Q_2)^{-1} Q_2^\top.$$

We have thus completed the proof.                                        □

Equation (2.18) shows that in the limit of zero observational noise, the uncertainty is only in the variable $u_2$. Since $\mathrm{Span}(T) = \mathrm{Span}(Q_2)$ and $u = SA_0^{-1}y + Tu_2$, the uncertainty we observed is in $\mathrm{Span}(Q_2)$. The prior plays a role in the posterior measure, in the limit of zero observational noise, but only in the variables $u_2$.


## 2.3 Discussion and Bibliography

The linear setting plays, for several reasons, a central role in the study of inverse problems. First, linear inverse problems are ubiquitous in applications, and are challenging to solve when the matrix defining the linear forward model is ill-conditioned, or when the system is severely underdetermined. Second, in the linear-Gaussian setting explicit solutions are available; these explicit solutions can be used to give insight into the solution of nonlinear inverse problems. Underlying the derivation of these formulae is the fact, shown in this chapter, that a Gaussian likelihood function supplemented with a Gaussian prior leads to a posterior that is again Gaussian. In statistical terms, this constitutes an example of a *conjugate prior* (Gelman et al., 2013), namely a choice of prior for a given likelihood such that the posterior belongs to the same family as the prior. A third reason for the central importance of linear inverse problems is that they arise naturally in sequential data assimilation, as we will see in the second part of these notes. Franklin (1970), which concerns the linear-Gaussian setting, was arguably the first to formulate Bayesian inversion in function space, for the specific problem of determining the initialization of the heat equation from the solution at later times. Lehtinen et al. (1989) studied the linear-Gaussian setting more generally. A computational framework for discretization of linear-Gaussian Bayesian inverse problems in function space was introduced in Bui-Thanh et al. (2013).

In this chapter we have studied several small noise limits, and established a basic form of posterior consistency. Intuitively, small observation noise would seem desirable in the reconstruction of the unknown parameter; however, and perhaps counterintuitively, it often makes the computational solution to the inverse problem more challenging. A concrete manifestation of this phenomenon is analyzed in the context of importance sampling in Agapiou et al. (2017a). For a treatment of posterior consistency in infinite dimensions we refer to Knapik et al. (2011), Agapiou et al. (2013), and Nickl (2020), and for the consistency problem in the classical statistical setting to the books of Gine and Nickl (2015) and der

Vaart (1998). In certain large data regimes, the Bernstein–von Mises theorem (Doob, 1949) guarantees that the Bayesian posterior solution is approximately Gaussian (Nickl, 2020; Nickl and Söhl, 2019; Giordano and Nickl, 2020) and that the prior distribution plays a negligible role in the posterior, thus providing theoretical support to the Bayesian approach. We emphasize, however, that in the underdetermined inverse problem setting one cannot expect the conclusions to hold, as demonstrated in this chapter. Furthermore, recent work (Nickl and Paternain, 2021) demonstrates specific phenomena, including potential obstacles to consistency theorems, that may result in the setting of infinite-dimensional Bayesian inversion. For non-statistical optimization-based approaches to inverse problems, and consistency in particular, see Engl et al. (1996) and the references therein.

# 3

# Optimization Perspective

In this chapter we explore the properties of Bayesian inversion from the perspective of an optimization problem which corresponds to maximizing the posterior probability; that is, to finding a maximum *a posteriori* (MAP) estimator, or mode of the posterior distribution. We demonstrate the properties of the point estimator resulting from this optimization problem, showing its positive and negative attributes, the latter motivating our work in the following three chapters. We also introduce, and study, basic gradient-based optimization algorithms.

The chapter is organized as follows. We first introduce the problem setting in Section 3.1. Two theoretical results are presented in Section 3.2. The first shows that the MAP estimator is attained under appropriate assumptions, while the second provides an interpretation of MAP estimation in terms of maximizing the probability of infinitesimally small balls. Section 3.3 contains several examples that illustrate some possible limitations of MAP estimation. Gradient descent and stochastic gradient descent algorithms are described in Section 3.4. Both of these algorithms are important examples of gradient-based optimization algorithms, which we interpret as arising from time-discretization of an underlying differential equation. The chapter closes in Section 3.5 with bibliographical remarks.

## 3.1 The Setting

Once again we work in the inverse problem setting of finding $u \in \mathbb{R}^d$ from $y \in \mathbb{R}^k$ given by

$$y = G(u) + \eta$$

with noise $\eta \sim \nu$ and prior $u \sim \rho$, as in Assumption 1.1. The posterior pdf $\pi^y(u)$ on $u \mid y$ is given by Theorem 1.2 and has the form

$$\pi^y(u) = \frac{1}{Z}\nu(y - G(u))\rho(u).$$

Generalizing the definition from the previous chapter, concerning only the Gaussian setting, we define a *loss function*

$$\mathsf{L}(u) = -\log \nu(y - G(u)),$$

and a *regularizer*

$$\mathsf{R}(u) = -\log \rho(u).$$

Note that the loss is equal to the negative log-likelihood: $\mathsf{L}(u) = -\log \mathsf{l}(u)$. When added together, these two functions of $u$ comprise an *objective function* of the form

$$\mathsf{J}(u) = \mathsf{L}(u) + \mathsf{R}(u).$$

Furthermore,

$$\pi^y(u) = \frac{1}{Z}\nu(y - G(u))\rho(u) \propto e^{-\mathsf{J}(u)}.$$

We see that minimizing the objective function $\mathsf{J}(\cdot)$ is equivalent to maximizing the posterior pdf $\pi^y(\cdot)$. Therefore, recalling Definition 1.4, the MAP estimator can be rewritten in terms of $\mathsf{J}$ as follows:

$$u_{\text{MAP}} = \arg\max_{u \in \mathbb{R}^d} \pi^y(u)$$
$$= \arg\min_{u \in \mathbb{R}^d} \mathsf{J}(u).$$

We will provide conditions under which the MAP estimator is attained in Theorem 3.5, and we will give an interpretation of MAP estimators in terms of maximizing the probability of infinitesimal balls in Theorem 3.8. This interpretation can be used to generalize the definition of MAP estimators to measures that do not possess a Lebesgue density.

**Example 3.1** (MAP Estimator – Linear-Gaussian Setting)   Consider the linear-Gaussian setting of Assumption 2.1. Then, since the posterior is Gaussian, its mode agrees with its mean, which is given by $m$ as defined in Theorem 2.2.   ◇

**Example 3.2** (Loss Function – Gaussian Observational Noise)   If $\eta = \mathcal{N}(0, \Gamma)$, then $\nu(y - G(u)) \propto \exp(-\frac{1}{2}|y - G(u)|_\Gamma^2)$. So the loss in this case is $\mathsf{L}(u) = \frac{1}{2}|y - G(u)|_\Gamma^2$, a $\Gamma$-weighted $\ell_2$ loss.   ◇

**Example 3.3** ($\ell_2$ Regularizer – Gaussian Prior)    If we have prior $\rho(u) = \mathcal{N}(0, \widehat{C})$, then ignoring $u$-independent normalization factors, which appear as constant shifts in $\mathsf{J}(\cdot)$, we may take the regularizer as $\mathsf{R}(u) = \frac{1}{2}|u|^2_{\widehat{C}}$. In particular, if $\widehat{C} = \lambda^{-1}I$, then $\mathsf{R}(u) = \frac{\lambda}{2}|u|^2$, an $\ell_2$ regularizer.    $\diamond$

If we combine Examples 3.2 and 3.3, we obtain a canonical objective function

$$\mathsf{J}(u) = \frac{1}{2}\left|y - G(u)\right|^2_\Gamma + \frac{\lambda}{2}\left|u\right|^2.$$

To connect with future discussions, here $\lambda$ corresponds to prior precision, and may be learned from data: an example of a *hierarchical* formulation of Bayesian inversion.

**Example 3.4** ($\ell_1$ Regularizer – Laplace Prior)    As an alternative to the $\ell_2$ regularizer, consider $u = (u_1, \ldots, u_d)$ with $u_i$ having prior distribution i.i.d. Laplace. Then $\rho(u) \propto \exp(-\lambda \sum_{i=1}^d |u_i|) = \exp(-\lambda|u|_1)$. In this case $\mathsf{R}(u) = \lambda|u|_1$, an $\ell_1$ regularizer. If we combine this prior with the weighted $\ell_2$ loss above, then we obtain the objective function

$$\mathsf{J}(u) = \frac{1}{2}|y - G(u)|^2_\Gamma + \lambda|u|_1.$$

Even though this objective function promotes sparse solutions, samples from the underlying posterior distribution are typically not sparse.    $\diamond$

## 3.2 Theory

For any optimization problem for an objective function with a finite infimum, it is of interest to determine whether the infimum is attained. We have the following result which shows that, under suitable conditions on $\mathsf{J}$, the infimum of $\mathsf{J}$ is attained and hence that the formulation of the MAP estimator through maximization of $\pi^y$ (equivalently minimization of $\mathsf{J}$) is well defined.

**Theorem 3.5** (Attainable MAP Estimator)    *Assume that $\mathsf{J}$ is non-negative, continuous and that $\mathsf{J}(u) \to \infty$ as $|u| \to \infty$. Then $\mathsf{J}$ attains its infimum. Therefore, the MAP estimator of $u$ based on the posterior $\pi^y(u) \propto \exp(-\mathsf{J}(u))$ is attained.*

*Proof*    By the assumed growth and non-negativity of $\mathsf{J}$, there is $R$ such that $\inf_{u \in \mathbb{R}^d} \mathsf{J}(u) = \inf_{u \in B(0,R)} \mathsf{J}(u)$, where (recall) $B(0, R)$ denotes the closed ball of radius $R$ around the origin. Since $\mathsf{J}$ is assumed to be continuous, its infimum over $B(0, R)$ is attained and the proof is complete.    $\square$

**Remark 3.6**   Suppose that:

(1) $G \in C(\mathbb{R}^d, \mathbb{R}^k)$, i.e. $G$ is a continuous function;
(2) the objective function $J(u)$ has $\ell_2$ loss as defined in Example 3.2 and $\ell_p$ regularizer $R(u) = \frac{\lambda}{p}|u|_p^p$, $p \in [1, \infty)$.

Then the assumptions on J in Theorem 3.5 are satisfied. This shows that if $G$ is continuous, the infimum of J defined with $\ell_2$ loss and $\ell_p$ regularizer is attained at the MAP estimator of the corresponding Bayesian problem with posterior pdf proportional to $\exp(-J(u))$.  ⬦

**Remark 3.7**   Notice that the assumption that $J(u) \to \infty$ is not restrictive. this condition needs to hold in order to be able to normalize $\pi^y(u) \propto \exp(-J(u))$ into a pdf, which is implicitly assumed in the second part of the theorem statement.  ⬦

Intuitively, the MAP estimator maximizes posterior probability. We make this precise in the following theorem, which links the objective function $J(\cdot)$ to small ball probabilities.

**Theorem 3.8** (Objective Function and Posterior Probability)   *Under the same assumptions as in Theorem 3.5, let*

$$\alpha(u, \delta) := \int_{v \in B(u, \delta)} \pi^y(v)dv = \mathbb{P}^{\pi^y}\big(B(u, \delta)\big)$$

*be the posterior probability of a ball with radius $\delta$ centered at u. Then, for all $u, u' \in \mathbb{R}^d$, we have*

$$\lim_{\delta \to 0} \frac{\alpha(u, \delta)}{\alpha(u', \delta)} = e^{J(u')-J(u)}.$$

*Proof*   Let $u, u' \in \mathbb{R}^d$ and let $\epsilon > 0$. By continuity of J we have that, for all $\delta$ sufficiently small,

$$e^{-J(u)-\epsilon} \le e^{-J(v)} \le e^{-J(u)+\epsilon} \quad \text{for all } v \in B(u, \delta),$$
$$e^{-J(u')-\epsilon} \le e^{-J(v)} \le e^{-J(u')+\epsilon} \quad \text{for all } v \in B(u', \delta).$$

Therefore, for all $\delta$ sufficiently small,

$$B_\delta e^{-J(u)-\epsilon} \le \int_{v \in B(u, \delta)} e^{-J(v)}dv \le B_\delta e^{-J(u)+\epsilon},$$
$$B_\delta e^{-J(u')-\epsilon} \le \int_{v \in B(u', \delta)} e^{-J(v)}dv \le B_\delta e^{-J(u')+\epsilon},$$

where $B_\delta$ is the Lebesgue measure of a ball with radius $\delta$. Taking the ratio of $\alpha$s and using the above bounds we obtain that, for all $\delta$ sufficiently small,

$$e^{J(u')-J(u)-2\epsilon} \leq \frac{\alpha(u,\delta)}{\alpha(u',\delta)} \leq e^{J(u')-J(u)+2\epsilon}.$$

Since $\epsilon > 0$ is arbitrary, the desired result follows.

□

***Remark 3.9***   This theorem shows that maximizing the probability of an infinitesimally small ball is the same as minimizing the objective function $J(\cdot)$. This is intuitive in finite dimensions, but the proof above generalizes beyond measures which possess a Lebesgue density, and may be used in infinite dimensions.   ◇

## 3.3 Examples

By means of examples, we now probe whether the MAP estimator captures useful information about the posterior distribution.

**Example 3.10** (Summarizing Single-Peaked Posterior)   If the posterior is single-peaked, such as a Gaussian or a Laplace distribution, as shown in Figure 3.1, the MAP estimator, i.e. minimizer of the objective function, reasonably summarizes the most likely value of the unknown parameter.   ◇

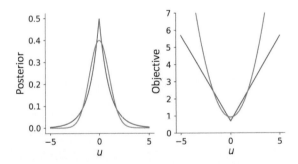

Figure 3.1 Posterior (left) and objective function (right) for $\mathcal{N}(0, 1)$ posterior (orange) and Laplace$(0, 1)$ posterior (blue).

We next consider several examples where a point estimator – or a $\delta$-radius ball with small $\delta$ – fails to adequately summarize the posterior distribution.

**Example 3.11** (Summarizing Multiple-Peaked Posterior)   If the posterior is rather unevenly distributed, such as a slab-and-spike distribution, as shown in

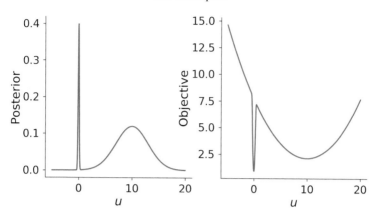

Figure 3.2 Posterior (left) and objective function (right) for a posterior that is a sum of two Gaussian distributions, $\mathcal{N}(0, 0.1^2)$ with probability 0.1 and $\mathcal{N}(10, 3^2)$ with probability 0.9.

Figure 3.2, then it is less clear that the MAP estimator usefully summarizes the posterior. For example, for the case in Figure 3.2 we may want the solution output of our Bayesian problem to be a weighted average of two Gaussian distributions, or two point estimators each with a separate mean located at one of the two minima of the objective functions, and weight describing the probability mass associated with each of those two points. ◇

**Example 3.12** (Summarizing Rough Posteriors) In addition to a multiple-peak posterior, there are cases where the objective function and the associated posterior pdf are simply very rough. In these cases, the small-scale roughness should be ignored, while the large-scale variation should be captured. For example, the objective function in Figure 3.3 is very rough and has a unique minimizer at a point far from 0. However, it also has a larger-scale pattern: it tends to be smaller around 0, while larger away from 0. The MAP estimator cannot capture this large scale pattern, as it is found by minimizing the objective function. It is arguably the case that $u = 0$ is a better point estimate. An alternative way to interpret this phenomenon is that there is a natural "temperature" to this problem, in the sense that variations lower than this temperature could be viewed as random noise that do not capture meaningful information. ◇

The preceding examples suggest that multi-peak distributions, or multi-minimum objective functions, can cause problems for MAP estimation. Next we illustrate that if the dimension $d$ of the parameter $u \in \mathbb{R}^d$ is high, then a single

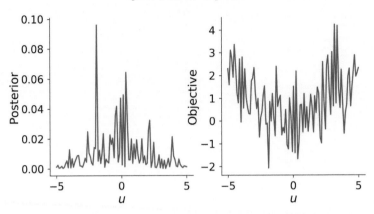

Figure 3.3 Posterior (left) and objective function (right) from an objective function that is very rough in the small scale, but contains a regular pattern on the larger scale. This specific example is generated by white noise summed with a quadratic function for the objective function, and the posterior is computed from the objective function.

point estimator, even if a MAP estimator, is typically not a good summary of the posterior.

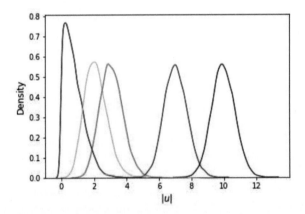

Figure 3.4 Empirical density of $\ell_2$ norm of $\mathcal{N}(0, I)$ random vectors for various dimension: $d = 1$ (blue), $d = 5$ (orange), $d = 10$ (green), $d = 50$ (red), and $d = 100$ (purple). The empirical density is obtained from 10 000 samples for each distribution.

**Example 3.13** (Summarizing High-Dimensional Posterior) We consider what is the "typical size" of a vector $u$ drawn from the standard Gaussian distribution

$\mathcal{N}(0, I)$, as the dimension increases. In Figure 3.4 we display the empirical density of the norm of such random vectors. We can see that at low dimensions, such as when $d = 1$, obtaining a value close to the mode $u = 0$ is highly likely. In higher dimensions, however, the probability for a vector from this distribution to have a small $\ell_2$-norm becomes increasingly small as $d$ grows. For example, let us consider the probability for the norm to be less than 5. Then $\mathbb{P}(|u| < 5)$ is 0.99999943 when $d = 1$, 0.99986 when $d = 5$, 0.99465 when $d = 10$, 0.001192 when $d = 50$, and $1.135 \times 10^{-15}$ when $d = 100$. So we see that, as the dimension increases, with probability close to 1 a sample from the posterior would have a norm far from 0. Indeed, for $d = 1000$, the 5th and 95th percentiles are respectively 30.3464 and 32.7823. This means when $d = 1000$, we most likely will find a vector with size around 31, not 0. Another way to see this is that, since the components $u_i$ of $u$ are i.i.d. standard unit Gaussians we have, by the strong law of large numbers, that

$$\frac{1}{d} \sum_{i=1}^{d} u_i^2 \to 1$$

as $d \to \infty$ almost surely. Thus, with high probability, the $\ell_2$-norm is of size $\sqrt{d}$. This example suggests that in high dimension, a point estimator may not capture enough information about the density. ◇

The preceding examples demonstrate that MAP estimators should be treated with caution, as they may not capture the desired posterior information in many cases. This motivates the study of alternative ways – beyond MAP estimators – to capture information from the posterior distribution. One such approach is to fit one or several Gaussian distributions to the posterior by minimizing an appropriate distance-like measure between distributions. This is the topic of the next chapter. However, in the remainder of this chapter we discuss gradient-based methods for minimization. These may be useful for MAP estimation, and also for fitting Gaussian approximations.

## 3.4 Gradient-Based Optimization Algorithms

In this section we discuss algorithms for the minimization of $J: \mathbb{R}^d \mapsto \mathbb{R}$. Algorithms for the optimization of functions of this type are numerous, and vary considerably in type. In order to focus our discussion, we devote our attention entirely to gradient-based algorithms. These are organized around a single important principle, and are also of interest due to their use in parameter estimation arising in machine learning (a form of inverse problem).

### 3.4.1 Gradient Flow

Our starting point is the differential equation

$$\frac{du}{dt} = -DJ(u), \quad u(0) = u_0. \tag{3.1}$$

A straightforward calculation shows that

$$\frac{d}{dt}\big(J(u)\big) = \left\langle DJ(u), \frac{du}{dt}\right\rangle = -|DJ(u)|^2.$$

This calculation is at the core of gradient-based optimization algorithms. Since the time-derivative of $u(t)$ gives the tangent to the trajectory, it demonstrates that evolving in the direction of the negative gradient of $J(u)$ will cause $J\big(u(t)\big)$ to be non-increasing as a function of time; indeed $J\big(u(t)\big)$ will actually decrease until $u$ is at a critical point of $J(\cdot)$: a point at which the gradient is zero, including local minima, local maxima, and saddle points.

For any $K \in \mathbb{R}^{d \times d}$, that we will assume positive definite in what follows, we may also consider the *preconditioned* gradient flow

$$\frac{du}{dt} = -KDJ(u), \quad u(0) = u_0. \tag{3.2}$$

### 3.4.2 Gradient Descent

In order to turn the gradient flow (3.2) into an optimization algorithm, we discretize it by the Euler method with variable time-step $\alpha_\ell > 0$.

---

**Algorithm 3.1** Gradient Descent Algorithm

---

1: **Input**: Objective function $J \colon \mathbb{R}^d \to \mathbb{R}$, positive definite matrix $K$, initialization $u_0 \in \mathbb{R}^d$, number of steps $L$, rule for choosing the step-sizes $\{\alpha_\ell\}_{\ell=0}^{L-1}$.

2: **Gradient Updates**: For $\ell = 0, 1, \ldots, L - 1$ do:

$$u_{\ell+1} = u_\ell - \alpha_\ell KDJ(u_\ell).$$

3: **Output**: Deterministic iterates $u_0, u_1, \ldots, u_L$.

---

It is natural to ask how $\alpha_\ell$ should be chosen. In order to get insight into this issue, we study in detail the case where $K = I$ and $J(u)$ is quadratic. The latter condition ensures that the iteration for $u_\ell$ is linear in the case of fixed $\alpha_\ell$; it is however nonlinear when $\alpha_\ell$ is adapted, as it is here, on the basis of $u_\ell$.

Let $A \in \mathbb{R}^{d \times d}$ be positive definite, let $b \in \mathbb{R}^d$, and define

$$J(u) = \frac{1}{2}|b - Au|_A^2. \tag{3.3}$$

This strictly convex function has minimum $u^\star$ which is the solution of the linear system

$$Au^\star = b. \tag{3.4}$$

The gradient flow (3.1) gives the linear differential equation

$$\frac{du}{dt} = b - Au$$

and has unique globally attracting fixed point at $u^\star$.

The resulting discrete time-step algorithm is

$$u_{\ell+1} = u_\ell + \alpha_\ell(b - Au_\ell).$$

The first question we ask is how $\alpha_\ell$ should be chosen to maximize the decrease in $J(\cdot)$ in one step of the algorithm. We address this in the next lemma and then, using this optimal time-step, we study the convergence properties of the algorithm. With this goal in mind, it is helpful to define the *residual function* $r \colon \mathbb{R}^d \to \mathbb{R}^d$ by $r(u) = b - Au$. Given the sequence $\{u_\ell\}$ we may then define the *residual vector* $r_\ell = r(u_\ell)$. Then $J(u) = \frac{1}{2}|r(u)|_A^2$, $J(u_\ell) = \frac{1}{2}|r_\ell|_A^2$ and

$$u_{\ell+1} = u_\ell + \alpha_\ell r_\ell.$$

**Lemma 3.14** *Choosing*

$$\alpha_\ell = \frac{|r_\ell|^2}{|r_\ell|_{A^{-1}}^2}$$

*leads to the maximal decrease in* $J(\cdot)$ *and to the algorithm*

$$u_{\ell+1} = u_\ell + \frac{|r_\ell|^2}{|r_\ell|_{A^{-1}}^2} r_\ell. \tag{3.5}$$

*Proof* We have

$$Au_{\ell+1} = Au_\ell + \alpha_\ell Ar_\ell,$$
$$b = b,$$

so that subtracting gives

$$r_{\ell+1} = r_\ell - \alpha_\ell Ar_\ell.$$

From this it follows that

$$J(u_{\ell+1}) = J(u_\ell) - \alpha_\ell|r_\ell|^2 + \frac{1}{2}\alpha_\ell^2|r_\ell|_{A^{-1}}^2. \tag{3.6}$$

The right-hand side is quadratic in $\alpha_\ell$ and minimized at the prescribed choice of $\alpha_\ell$. $\square$

**Theorem 3.15** (Conditioning of $A$ and Decrease of $J$)   *Let $A$ have maximal and minimal eigenvalues $\lambda_{\max} \geq \lambda_{\min} > 0$, respectively. Then*

$$J(u_{\ell+1}) \leq \left(1 - \frac{\lambda_{\min}}{\lambda_{\max}}\right)J(u_\ell). \qquad (3.7)$$

*Proof*   Substituting the optimal choice of $\alpha_\ell$ into equation (3.6) gives

$$J(u_{\ell+1}) = J(u_\ell) - \frac{1}{2}\frac{|r_\ell|^4}{|r_\ell|^2_{A^{-1}}}$$

$$= J(u_\ell) - \frac{|r_\ell|^4}{|r_\ell|^2_{A^{-1}}|r_\ell|^2_A}J(u_\ell).$$

Applying the result of Lemma 3.17 below gives the desired result. $\square$

***Remark* 3.16**   Inequality (3.7) suggests slow convergence of the algorithm for matrices $A$ which have a large condition number, i.e. for which $\lambda_{\max} \gg \lambda_{\min}$. In principle this can be ameliorated by preconditioning the algorithm by choosing $K = A^{-1}$ so that the preconditioned steepest descent iteration becomes

$$u_{\ell+1} = u_\ell + \alpha_\ell(A^{-1}b - u_\ell).$$

The optimal choice of $\alpha_\ell$ for this iteration becomes $\alpha_\ell = 1$, which gives $u_{\ell+1} = A^{-1}b$. Thus, the algorithm converges in one step, regardless of the initial condition. However, implementing the algorithm with $K = A^{-1}$ would require computation of $A^{-1}b$; the goal of the descent algorithm is, of course, to avoid computation of $A^{-1}$ in the first place. This discussion illustrates nonetheless the potential practical advantage of preconditioning using a positive definite matrix $K \approx A^{-1}$ whose action on vectors can nonetheless be computed much more cheaply than that of $A^{-1}$ itself. $\diamond$

**Lemma 3.17**   *For any $u \in \mathbb{R}^d$,*

$$\frac{|u|^4}{|u|^2_{A^{-1}}|u|^2_A} \geq \frac{\lambda_{\min}}{\lambda_{\max}}.$$

*Proof*   Since $A$ is assumed to be positive definite, the eigenvalue problem for $A$ has solutions with the form

$$A\varphi_i = \lambda_i\varphi_i, \quad i = 1, \ldots, d,$$
$$\langle \varphi_i, \varphi_j \rangle = \delta_{ij}, \quad i, j = 1, \ldots, d,$$

where we may assume the ordering

$$0 < \lambda_{\min} := \lambda_1 \leq \cdots \leq \lambda_d =: \lambda_{\max}.$$

Expanding $u \in \mathbb{R}^d$ in this eigenbasis, we have

$$u = \sum_{i=1}^d u_i \varphi_i$$

with $u_i = \langle u, \varphi_i \rangle$. Now, noting that

$$|u|^2 = \sum_{i=1}^d u_i^2, \quad |u|_{A^{-1}}^2 = \sum_{i-1}^d \lambda_i u_i^2, \quad |u|_A^2 = \sum_{i-1}^d \frac{u_i^2}{\lambda_i},$$

we get

$$|u|^2 = \sum_{i=1}^d u_i^2 \geq \lambda_{\min} |u|_A^2,$$

$$|u|_{A^{-1}}^2 = \sum_{i=1}^d \lambda_i u_i^2 \leq \lambda_{\max} |u|^2.$$

The desired result follows. $\qquad\qquad\qquad\qquad\qquad\qquad\qquad\qquad\square$

### 3.4.3 Stochastic Gradient Descent

Here we consider optimizing a stochastically defined objective function. This concerns the setting where

$$J(u) = \int_B F(u, z) \zeta(z) \, dz, \qquad (3.8)$$

$B \subseteq \mathbb{R}^{d_z}$, and $\zeta$ is the pdf of a random variable $z \in B$. The goal is optimization of $J(u)$.

Stochastic gradient descent is designed to numerically solve this optimization problem in cases where explicit evaluation of $J(u)$, and its gradient $DJ(u)$, is not possible because doing so involves an integration over $B$. It is assumed, however, that $D_u F(u, z)$ can be evaluated for any fixed $z \in B \subseteq \mathbb{R}^{d_z}$. The proposed algorithm is then the following:

---

**Algorithm 3.2** Stochastic Gradient Descent Algorithm

---

1: **Input**: Objective function J defined implicitly by (3.8), positive definite matrix $K$, initialization $u^{(0)} \in \mathbb{R}^d$, number of steps $L$, rule for choosing the step-sizes $\{\alpha_\ell\}_{\ell=0}^{L-1}$.

2: **Stochastic Gradient Updates**: For $\ell = 0, 1, \ldots, L-1$ do:
$u^{(\ell+1)} = u^{(\ell)} - \alpha_\ell K D_u F(u^{(\ell)}, z^{(\ell)})$  with $z^{(\ell)} \sim \zeta$ i.i.d.

3: **Output**: Random iterates $u^{(0)}, u^{(1)}, \ldots, u^{(L)}$.

---

The output of the algorithm defines an (in general) inhomogeneous Markov chain; it will be homogeneous if $\alpha_\ell$ is constant in $\ell$. Markov chains are discussed in more detail in Chapter 6. In what follows we will show the convergence of the algorithm in a simple setting, amenable to a concrete analysis. We will also motivate the importance of the algorithm in a machine learning context.

Our convergence analysis will rely on the following assumption.

**Assumption 3.18** *The objective function J in (3.8) satisfies:*

(i) *There exists $c_1$ such that, for all $u \in \mathbb{R}^d$, $\sup_{z \in B} |D_u F(u, z)|^2 \leq c_1$.*
(ii) *There exists $c_2 > 0$ such that, for all $u, v \in \mathbb{R}^d$,*

$$J(v) \geq J(u) + \langle DJ(u), v - u \rangle + \frac{c_2}{2}|u - v|^2. \tag{3.9}$$

Note that item (i) in Assumption 3.18 implies a Lipschitz condition on $F$ over its second argument, while the second item assumes strong convexity of J. In particular, this second condition implies that, if J is sufficiently smooth, its Hessian satisfies $D^2 J \geq c_2 I$, that is, for all $u \in \mathbb{R}^d$ the matrix $D^2 J(u) - c_2 I$ is positive definite.

**Theorem 3.19** (Convergence of Stochastic Gradient Descent)  *Suppose that Assumption 3.18 holds. Suppose further that the step-sizes are positive with $\alpha_\ell \to 0$ and $\sum_{\ell=0}^\infty \alpha_\ell = \infty$. Then the objective function J has a unique minimizer $u^\star$ and the output of Algorithm 3.2 satisfies $\mathbb{E}[|u^{(\ell)} - u^\star|^2] \to 0$ as $\ell \to \infty$.*

*Proof*  The existence and uniqueness of the minimizer $u^\star$ of J follows by the strong convexity in Assumption 3.18 item (ii). Write $e_\ell = \mathbb{E}[|u^{(\ell)} - u^\star|^2]$. Then, from the definition of the stochastic gradient descent updates, we have that

$$e_{\ell+1} = \mathbb{E}\left[|u^{(\ell)} - u^\star - \alpha_\ell D_u F(u^{(\ell)}, z^{(\ell)})|^2\right]$$

$$= e_\ell + \alpha_\ell^2 \mathbb{E}\left[|D_u F(u^{(\ell)}, z^{(\ell)})|^2\right] - 2\alpha_\ell \mathbb{E}\left[\langle u^{(\ell)} - u^\star, D_u F(u^{(\ell)}, z^{(\ell)})\rangle\right]. \tag{3.10}$$

By the law of total expectation and the definition of J in (3.8), we can rewrite the last expectation in the right-hand side as

$$
\mathbb{E}\left[\mathbb{E}\left[\langle u^{(\ell)} - u^\star, D_u F(u^{(\ell)}, z^{(\ell)})\rangle \mid u^{(1)}, \ldots, u^{(\ell)}, z^{(1)}, \ldots, z^{(\ell-1)}\right]\right] \tag{3.11}
$$
$$
= \mathbb{E}\left[\langle u^{(\ell)} - u^\star, DJ(u^{(\ell)})\rangle\right].
$$

Therefore, using Assumption 3.18 items (i) and (ii) to bound the second and third terms in the right-hand side of (3.10), we deduce that

$$
e_{\ell+1} \le (1 - \alpha_\ell c_2)e_\ell + \alpha_\ell^2 c_1.
$$

It follows that, for any $\epsilon > 0$,

$$
e_{\ell+1} - \epsilon \le (1 - \alpha_\ell c_2)(e_\ell - \epsilon) + \alpha_\ell(\alpha_\ell c_1 - \epsilon c_2).
$$

Note that, for all sufficiently large $\ell$, $\alpha_\ell(\alpha_\ell c_1 - \epsilon c_2) < 0$. Thus we obtain that, for all sufficiently large $\ell$,

$$
e_{\ell+1} - \epsilon \le (1 - \alpha_\ell c_2)(e_\ell - \epsilon).
$$

Iterating this inequality gives that, for some $\ell$ sufficiently large and all $m \in \mathbb{N}$,

$$
e_{\ell+m} - \epsilon \le \prod_{j=0}^{m-1}(1 - \alpha_{\ell+j}c_2)(e_\ell - \epsilon).
$$

Recall that for $x \in (0, 1)$ we have that $\log(1 - x) \le -x$ (a proof can be found in Chapter 4, Lemma 4.3). Now notice that, as $m \to \infty$,

$$
0 \le \prod_{j=0}^{m-1}(1 - \alpha_{\ell+j}c_2) \le \exp\left(\sum_{j=0}^{m-1} -\alpha_{\ell+j}c_2\right) \to 0 \tag{3.12}
$$

since by assumption $\sum_{\ell=0}^{\infty} \alpha_\ell = \infty$. Thus $e_{\ell+m} \le \epsilon$ for all $m$ large enough, and the desired result follows since $\epsilon$ is arbitrary. $\square$

**Example 3.20** (Stochastic Gradient Descent in Machine Learning)   Although the original motivation for the algorithm was settings in which $DJ(u)$ is not explicitly calculable, the methodology has gained importance in machine learning optimization tasks where the motivation is different. Consider an objective function defined by

$$
J(u) = \frac{1}{2}\sum_{i=1}^{d_z} |y^i - G^i(u)|^2,
$$

where each $y^i \in \mathbb{R}^k$ represents data arising from a forward model $G^i$. We may write this objective in the form of equation (3.8) as follows. Define

$$F(u, z) = \frac{d_z}{2} \sum_{i=1}^{d_z} z_i |y^i - G^i(u)|^2$$

with $z := (z_1, \ldots, z_{d_z}) \in \mathbb{R}^{d_z}$. Define $e^i := (0, \ldots, 1, \ldots, 0)^\top$, the $i$th unit vector and let

$$\zeta(z) = \frac{1}{d_z} \sum_{i=1}^{d_z} \delta(z - e^i).$$

Then

$$J(u) = \int_B F(u, z)\zeta(z)\, dz$$

with $B$ any bounded set containing all the unit vectors $\{e^i\}_{i=1}^{d_z}$. This is because if $z \sim \zeta$, then $\mathbb{E}[z] = d_z^{-1}(1, \ldots, 1)^\top \in \mathbb{R}^{d_z}$.

In this setting the stochastic gradient descent algorithm becomes

$$i(\ell) \sim \mathfrak{u}(\{1, \ldots, d_z\}) \text{ i.i.d.}$$
$$u^{(\ell+1)} = u^{(\ell)} + \alpha_\ell d_z DG^{i(\ell)}(u^{(\ell)})^\top \left(y^{i(\ell)} - G^{i(\ell)}(u^{(\ell)})\right), \quad (3.13)$$

where the notation signifies that $i(\ell)$ is chosen uniformly at random from the index set $\{1, \ldots, d_z\}$. In the context of machine learning this algorithm has several potential advantages over standard gradient descent: (i) if $d_z$ is massive (large data sets) then it is not necessary to hold the entirety of $DJ(u)$ in memory at any one time; (ii) if the data is received in a streaming fashion then the algorithm can be implemented in a non-random fashion where the indices $i(\ell)$ are traversed systematically as the components of the data are received; (iii) it is observed empirically that the randomness induced by sampling terms from the summand defining $DJ(u)$ promotes improved optimization for nonconvex $J(u)$, in comparison with standard gradient descent, because the randomness allows escape from local minima and allows for more rapid traversing of saddle-point neighborhoods.                                                                    ◇

We now consider the setting of Example 3.20 in which $G^i(u) = A^i u$ for some positive definite matrix $A^i \in \mathbb{R}^{d \times d}$, $y^i \in \mathbb{R}^d$ and we modify the definition of $J$ so that each term employs a different norm:

$$J(u) = \frac{1}{2} \sum_{i=1}^{d_z} |y^i - A^i u|_{A^i}^2.$$

We define

$$\overline{y} = \frac{1}{d_z} \sum_{i=1}^{d_z} y^i, \quad \overline{A} = \frac{1}{d_z} \sum_{i=1}^{d_z} A^i.$$

A straightforward calculation reveals that $\overline{A}$ is positive definite and $\mathsf{J}(u)$ has a unique minimizer $u^\star$ solving the equation $\overline{A}u^\star = \overline{y}$.

In this setting the analog of the algorithm from (3.13) becomes

$$u^{(\ell+1)} = u^{(\ell)} + \alpha_\ell \left( y^{i(\ell)} - A^{i(\ell)} u^{(\ell)} \right), \tag{3.14}$$

where $i(\ell)$ is chosen uniformly at random from $\{1, \ldots, d_z\}$ i.i.d. at every step, and independently from $u^{(\ell)}$. This gives an (in general inhomogeneous) Markov chain. Theorem 3.19 concerning stochastic gradient descent made the assumption that the time-step $\alpha_\ell$ decreases to zero with increasing $\ell$. Here we choose a fixed time-step $\alpha$ leading to a homogeneous Markov chain; we prove a positive result about the convergence of the algorithm in an average sense.

**Theorem 3.21** (Convergence of Stochastic Gradient Descent – Constant Step–Size)   *Let $\alpha_\ell = \alpha > 0$ and assume that, in (3.14), $\lim_{\ell \to \infty} \mathbb{E}\left[u^{(\ell)}\right]$ exists. Then the limit is given by $u^\star$.*

*Proof*   Take expectation in (3.14) conditional on knowing $u^{(\ell)}$ to obtain

$$\mathbb{E}\left[u^{(\ell+1)} | u^{(\ell)}\right] = u^{(\ell)} + \alpha \left( \mathbb{E}[y^{i(\ell)}] - \mathbb{E}[A^{i(\ell)} u^{(\ell)}] \right)$$
$$= u^{(\ell)} + \alpha \left( \overline{y} - \overline{A} u^{(\ell)} \right).$$

Taking expectation over $u^{(\ell)}$ gives

$$\mathbb{E}\left[u^{(\ell+1)}\right] = \mathbb{E}\left[u^{(\ell)}\right] + \alpha \left( \overline{y} - \overline{A}\, \mathbb{E}\left[u^{(\ell)}\right] \right).$$

Taking the limit $\ell \to \infty$ and assuming $\lim_{\ell \to \infty} \mathbb{E}\left[u^{(\ell)}\right]$ exists and is given by $u^\dagger$ yields

$$u^\dagger = u^\dagger + \alpha \left( \overline{y} - \overline{A} u^\dagger \right).$$

Hence $\overline{A} u^\dagger = \overline{y}$ and by the invertibility of $\overline{A}$ it follows that $u^\dagger = u^\star$.   □

## 3.5  Discussion and Bibliography

Standard textbooks on optimization include those of Nocedal and Wright (2006), Dennis Jr. and Schnabel (1996), and Boyd et al. (2004). The optimization perspective on inversion predates the development of the Bayesian approach as a computational tool, because it is typically far cheaper to implement. The subject of classical regularization techniques for inversion is discussed in Engl et al. (1996). The concept of MAP estimators, which links probability to optimization, is discussed in Kaipio and Somersalo (2006) and Tarantola (2015a) in the finite-dimensional setting. Dashti et al. (2013) studied this connection precisely: it defines the MAP estimator for infinite-dimensional Bayesian inverse problems, and the corresponding variational formulation, in the setting of Gaussian priors and Gaussian noise. Helin and Burger (2015) studied related ideas, but in the non-Gaussian setting, and Agapiou et al. (2017b) generalized the variational formulation of MAP estimators to non-Gaussian priors that are sparsity promoting. Recent work sets MAP estimators for PDE-based inverse problems within the existing framework of statistical estimation theory (Nickl et al., 2020), and also within the framework of $\Gamma$-convergence (Ayanbayev et al., 2021). Tarantola (2015b) gives an example of optimization-based inversion in a large-scale geophysical application.

A discussion of gradient-based descent in both continuous and discrete time may be found in Stuart and Humphries (1998). Stochastic analogs of (3.1) may be used to sample the probability distribution $\exp\bigl(-\beta J(u)\bigr)$ and an introduction to this subject may be found in Pavliotis (2014). The idea of using *stochastic approximation* for solving nonlinear equations defined via an expectation was introduced in Robbins and Monro (1951). The specific analysis in the case of such equations defined as a gradient, and in particular the statement and proof of a result closely related to Theorem 3.19, may be found in Kiefer and Wolfowitz (1952). The link to machine learning, described in Example 3.20, is overviewed in Goodfellow et al. (2016). Bottou et al. (2018) provides an accessible introduction to optimization methods for large-scale machine learning.

# 4

# Gaussian Approximation

Recall the inverse problem of finding $u$ from $y$ given by (1.1), and the Bayesian formulation which follows from Assumption 1.1. In the previous chapter we explored the idea of obtaining a point estimator using an optimization perspective arising from maximizing the posterior pdf. We related this idea to finding the center of a ball of radius $\delta$ with maximal probability in the limit $\delta \to 0^+$. Whilst the idea is intuitively appealing, and reduces the complexity of Bayesian inference from determination of a pdf to determination of a single point, the approach has a number of limitations, in particular for noisy, multi-peaked, or high-dimensional posterior distributions; the examples in the previous chapter illustrated these limitations.

In this chapter we again adopt an optimization approach to the problem of Bayesian inference, but instead seek a Gaussian distribution $p = \mathcal{N}(\mu, \Sigma)$ that minimizes some distance-like measure from the posterior $\pi^y(u)$. However, rather than using a metric to define the distance, we use the Kullback–Leibler divergence introduced in Section 4.1. Since this divergence is not symmetric, we obtain two distinct minimization problems described, in turn, in Sections 4.2 and 4.3. Both approaches are compared in Section 4.4. In Section 4.5 we show how Bayes' theorem itself can be formulated through a closely related minimization principle. The chapter closes in Section 4.6 with extensions and bibliographical remarks.

## 4.1 The Kullback–Leibler Divergence

**Definition 4.1**    Let $\pi$, $\pi' > 0$ be two pdfs on $\mathbb{R}^d$.[1] The *Kullback–Leibler divergence*, also known as *relative entropy* of $\pi$ with respect to $\pi'$ is defined by

$$
\begin{aligned}
d_{\mathrm{KL}}(\pi \| \pi') &:= \int_{\mathbb{R}^d} \log\left(\frac{\pi(u)}{\pi'(u)}\right) \pi(u)\, du \\
&= \mathbb{E}^{\pi}\left[\log\left(\frac{\pi}{\pi'}\right)\right] \\
&= \mathbb{E}^{\pi'}\left[\log\left(\frac{\pi}{\pi'}\right)\frac{\pi}{\pi'}\right].
\end{aligned}
$$

$\diamond$

Kullback–Leibler is a divergence in that $d_{\mathrm{KL}}(\pi \| \pi') \geq 0$, with equality if and only if $\pi = \pi'$. From the definition it is clear that $d_{\mathrm{KL}}(\pi \| \pi') = 0$ if $\pi = \pi'$; that it is otherwise strictly positive is proved in Lemma 4.3 below, as a consequence of the analogous property for the Hellinger or total variation distances. However, unlike Hellinger and total variation, it does not define a metric. In particular, the Kullback–Leibler divergence is not symmetric: in general,

$$
d_{\mathrm{KL}}(\pi \| \pi') \neq d_{\mathrm{KL}}(\pi' \| \pi),
$$

a fact that will be important in this chapter. Nevertheless, it is useful for at least four reasons: (1) it provides an upper bound for many distances, as illustrated in Lemma 4.3 below; (2) its logarithmic structure allows explicit computations that are difficult using actual distances; (3) it satisfies many convenient analytical properties such as being convex in both arguments and lower-semicontinuous in the topology of weak convergence; and (4) it has an information-theoretic and a physical interpretation.

**Example 4.2**    Consider two Gaussian densities $p_1$ and $p_2$ on $\mathbb{R}^d$ with means $\mu_1$, $\mu_2$ and positive-definite covariance matrices $\Sigma_1$, $\Sigma_2$. Then

$$
d_{\mathrm{KL}}(p_1 \| p_2) = \frac{1}{2}\left(\log\frac{\det \Sigma_2}{\det \Sigma_1} - d + |\mu_1 - \mu_2|_{\Sigma_2}^2 + \mathrm{Tr}(\Sigma_2^{-1}\Sigma_1)\right).
$$

$\diamond$

The following lemma establishes upper bounds on total variation and Hellinger distances in terms of the Kullback–Leibler divergence. Note that as a corollary we obtain a proof of the fact that $d_{\mathrm{KL}}(\pi \| \pi') > 0$ if $\pi \neq \pi'$.

---

[1] The definition extends to situations where the support of $\pi'$ is not the whole of $\mathbb{R}^d$, provided $\pi$ is absolutely continuous with respect to $\pi'$.

**Lemma 4.3** *The Kullback–Leibler divergence provides the following upper bounds for Hellinger and total variation distance:*

$$d_{\mathrm{H}}(\pi, \pi')^2 \leq \frac{1}{2} d_{\mathrm{KL}}(\pi\|\pi'), \quad d_{\mathrm{TV}}(\pi, \pi')^2 \leq d_{\mathrm{KL}}(\pi\|\pi').$$

*Proof* The second inequality follows from the first one by Lemma 1.9; thus we prove only the first inequality. Consider the function $\varphi \colon \mathbb{R}^+ \mapsto \mathbb{R}$ defined by

$$\varphi(x) = x - 1 - \log x.$$

Note that

$$\varphi'(x) = 1 - \frac{1}{x},$$
$$\varphi''(x) = \frac{1}{x^2},$$
$$\varphi(\infty) = \varphi(0) = \infty.$$

Thus, the function is convex on its domain. As the minimum of $\varphi$ is attained at $x = 1$, and as $\varphi(1) = 0$, we deduce that $\varphi(x) \geq 0$ for all $x \in (0, \infty)$. Hence,

$$x - 1 \geq \log x \qquad \text{for all } x \geq 0,$$
$$\sqrt{x} - 1 \geq \frac{1}{2} \log x \qquad \text{for all } x \geq 0.$$

We can use this last inequality to bound the Hellinger distance:

$$d_{\mathrm{H}}(\pi, \pi')^2 = \frac{1}{2} \int \left(1 - \sqrt{\frac{\pi'}{\pi}}\right)^2 \pi\, du$$
$$= \frac{1}{2} \int \left(1 + \frac{\pi'}{\pi} - 2\sqrt{\frac{\pi'}{\pi}}\right) \pi\, du$$
$$= \int \left(1 - \sqrt{\frac{\pi'}{\pi}}\right) \pi\, du \leq -\frac{1}{2} \int \log\left(\frac{\pi'}{\pi}\right) \pi\, du = \frac{1}{2} d_{\mathrm{KL}}(\pi\|\pi').$$

$\square$

## 4.2 Best Gaussian Fit by Minimizing $d_{\mathrm{KL}}(p\|\pi)$

In this section we prove the existence of a best Gaussian approximation $p = \mathcal{N}(\mu, \Sigma)$ to a given pdf $\pi$ in the sense that $d_{\mathrm{KL}}(p\|\pi)$ is minimized. As part of our analysis, we will show that Gaussian pdfs $p$ that minimize $d_{\mathrm{KL}}(p\|\pi)$ can be found by solving a stochastic optimization algorithm to determine optimal mean and covariance. Therefore, the stochastic gradient descent algorithm studied in Chapter 3 provides a natural method to find a best Gaussian fit. While the existence of a minimizer and the applicability of stochastic gradient descent apply more broadly, we focus our discussion on the case where $\pi = \pi^y$ is a posterior distribution satisfying the following assumption:

**Assumption 4.4** *The posterior distribution $\pi(u) = \frac{1}{Z} \exp(-\mathsf{L}(u)) \rho(u)$ satisfies:*

- *The loss function $\mathsf{L}(u)$ is non-negative and bounded above.*
- *The prior is a centered isotropic Gaussian: $\rho(u) = \mathcal{N}(0, \lambda^{-1} I)$.*

Let $\mathcal{G}$ be the set of Gaussian distributions on $\mathbb{R}^d$ with positive definite covariance,

$$\mathcal{G} = \{\mathcal{N}(\mu, \Sigma) : \mu \in \mathbb{R}^d, \Sigma \in \mathbb{R}^{d \times d} \text{ positive definite}\}.$$

We have the following theorem, which establishes the existence of a best Gaussian approximation. We remark, however, that minimizers need not be unique. Note that $\mathcal{G}$ is an open set since the set of positive definite matrices is open. It is thus implicit in the following theorem that the infimum is indeed attained with positive definite covariance.

**Theorem 4.5** (Best Gaussian Approximation)  *Under Assumption 4.4, there exists at least one probability distribution $p \in \mathcal{G}$ at which the infimum*

$$\inf_{p \in \mathcal{G}} d_{\mathrm{KL}}(p \| \pi)$$

*is attained.*

*Proof*  The Kullback–Leibler divergence can be computed explicitly as

$$d_{\mathrm{KL}}(p \| \pi) = \mathbb{E}^p \left[ \log p \right] - \mathbb{E}^p \left[ \log \pi \right]$$

$$= \mathbb{E}^p \left[ -\frac{1}{2} |u - \mu|^2_\Sigma - \frac{1}{2} \log\left( (2\pi)^d \det \Sigma \right) + \mathsf{L}(u) + \frac{\lambda}{2} |u|^2 + \log Z \right].$$

Note that $Z$ is the normalization constant for $\pi$ and is independent of $p$, and hence of $\mu$ and $\Sigma$. We can represent a random variable $u \sim p$ by writing $u = \mu + \Sigma^{1/2} \xi$, where $\xi \sim \mathcal{N}(0, I)$, and hence

$$|u|^2 = |\mu|^2 + |\Sigma^{1/2} \xi|^2 + 2\langle \mu, \Sigma^{1/2} \xi \rangle.$$

Using this we obtain

$$d_{\mathrm{KL}}(p \| \pi) = -\frac{d}{2} - \frac{d}{2} \log(2\pi) - \frac{1}{2} \log \det \Sigma + \mathbb{E}^p \left[ \mathsf{L}(u) \right]$$
$$+ \frac{\lambda}{2} |\mu|^2 + \frac{\lambda}{2} \mathrm{tr}(\Sigma) + \log Z.$$

Define

$$J(\mu, \Sigma) = \frac{\lambda}{2}|\mu|^2 + \frac{\lambda}{2}\mathrm{tr}(\Sigma) - \frac{1}{2}\log\det\Sigma + \mathbb{E}^p\big[\mathsf{L}(u)\big],$$

$$J_0(\mu, \Sigma) = \frac{\lambda}{2}|\mu|^2 + \frac{\lambda}{2}\mathrm{tr}(\Sigma) - \frac{1}{2}\log\det\Sigma.$$

Note that since $\mathsf{L}$ is assumed to be bounded above, $\mathsf{J} \to \infty$ if and only if $\mathsf{J}_0 \to \infty$. Furthermore, writing positive definite $\Sigma = QDQ^\top$ where $Q$ is orthogonal and $D$ is diagonal with non-negative entries $\{\sigma_i\}_{i=1}^d$, we find that

$$J(\mu, \Sigma) = \frac{\lambda}{2}|\mu|^2 + \frac{1}{2}\sum_{i=1}^d\Big(\lambda\sigma_i - \log(\sigma_i)\Big) + \mathbb{E}^p\big[\mathsf{L}(u)\big],$$

$$J_0(\mu, \Sigma) = \frac{\lambda}{2}|\mu|^2 + \frac{1}{2}\sum_{i=1}^d\Big(\lambda\sigma_i - \log(\sigma_i)\Big).$$

For any $\Sigma$, $\mathsf{J}_0(\mu, \Sigma) \to \infty$ (and hence $\mathsf{J}(\mu, \Sigma) \to \infty$) as $|\mu| \to \infty$. Furthermore, for any $\mu$ and any $i$, $\mathsf{J}_0(\mu, \Sigma) \to \infty$ (and hence $\mathsf{J}(\mu, \Sigma) \to \infty$) as $\sigma_i \to 0^+$ or $\sigma_i \to \infty$. Now define, for $\Sigma = QDQ^\top$ as above,

$$\tilde{\mathcal{G}} := \{(\mu, \Sigma) : \mu \in \mathbb{R}^d, Q \in \mathbb{R}^{d\times d} : Q^\top Q = I, \ |\mu| \le M, \ r \le \sigma_i \le R \text{ for all } i\}.$$

Note that $\mathsf{J}(0, I) < \infty$. Thus there are $M, r, R > 0$ such that the infimum of $\mathsf{J}(\mu, \Sigma)$ over $\mu \in \mathbb{R}^d$ and positive definite $\Sigma$ is equal to the infimum of $\mathsf{J}(\mu, \Sigma)$ over the closed and bounded set $\tilde{\mathcal{G}}$. Since $\mathsf{J}$ is continuous in $\tilde{\mathcal{G}}$ it achieves its infimum, and the proof is complete. □

**Remark 4.6** (Minimizing $d_{\mathrm{KL}}(p\|\pi)$ with Stochastic Gradient Descent) The proof of Theorem 4.5 shows that a best Gaussian approximation $p \in \mathcal{G}$ to $\pi$ can be found by minimizing the objective

$$J(\mu, \Sigma) = \mathbb{E}^{\xi\sim\mathcal{N}(0,I)}\Big[\frac{\lambda}{2}|\mu|^2 + \frac{\lambda}{2}\mathrm{tr}(\Sigma) - \frac{1}{2}\log\det\Sigma + \mathsf{L}(\mu + \Sigma^{1/2}\xi)\Big]$$

$$= \int_{\mathbb{R}^d} F(u, z)\zeta(z)\, dz,$$

where $u = (\mu, \Sigma)$, $\zeta = \mathcal{N}(0, I)$, and

$$F(u, z) = \frac{\lambda}{2}|\mu|^2 + \frac{\lambda}{2}\mathrm{tr}(\Sigma) - \frac{1}{2}\log\det\Sigma + \mathsf{L}(\mu + \Sigma^{1/2}z).$$

Thus, this optimization problem can be solved using the stochastic gradient descent algorithm described in Chapter 3. ◇

## 4.3 Best Gaussian Fit by Minimizing $d_{\mathrm{KL}}(\pi\|p)$

In this section we show that the best Gaussian approximation in Kullback–Leibler with respect to its second argument is unique and given by moment matching.

**Theorem 4.7** (Best Gaussian Approximation by Moment Matching) *Assume that $\overline{\mu} := \mathbb{E}^{\pi}[u]$ is finite and that $\overline{\Sigma} := \mathbb{E}^{\pi}[(u - \overline{\mu}) \otimes (u - \overline{\mu})]$ is positive definite. Then the infimum*

$$\inf_{p \in \mathcal{G}} d_{\mathrm{KL}}(\pi\|p)$$

*is attained at the element in $\mathcal{G}$ with mean $\overline{\mu}$ and covariance $\overline{\Sigma}$.*

*Proof*   By definition

$$d_{\mathrm{KL}}(\pi\|p) = -\mathbb{E}^{\pi}[\log p] + \mathbb{E}^{\pi}[\log \pi]. \tag{4.1}$$

Since the second term does not involve $p$, we study minimization of

$$-\mathbb{E}^{\pi}[\log p] = -\mathbb{E}^{\pi}\left[\log\left(\frac{1}{\sqrt{(2\pi)^d \det \Sigma}} \exp\left(-\frac{1}{2}|u - \mu|_{\Sigma}^2\right)\right)\right]$$

$$= \frac{1}{2}\mathbb{E}^{\pi}\left[|u - \mu|_{\Sigma}^2\right] + \frac{1}{2}\log\det\Sigma + \frac{d}{2}\log 2\pi.$$

Let $\Omega = \Sigma^{-1}$. Then our task is equivalent to minimizing the following function of $\mu$ and $\Omega$:

$$J(\mu, \Omega) = \frac{1}{2}\mathbb{E}^{\pi}[\langle u - \mu, \Omega(u - \mu)\rangle] - \frac{1}{2}\log\det\Omega.$$

First we find the critical points of $J$ by taking its first order partial derivative with respect to $\mu$ and $\Omega$ and setting both to zero:

$$\partial_{\mu}J = -\mathbb{E}^{\pi}[\Omega(u - \mu)] = 0;$$

$$\partial_{\Omega}J = \frac{1}{2}\partial_{\Omega}(\mathbb{E}^{\pi}[(u - \mu) \otimes (u - \mu) : \Omega]) - \frac{1}{2}\det\Omega\partial_{\Omega}\det\Omega$$

$$= \frac{1}{2}\mathbb{E}^{\pi}[(u - \mu) \otimes (u - \mu)] - \frac{1}{2}\Omega^{-1} = 0;$$

here we have used the relation $\partial_{\Omega}\det\Omega = \det\Omega \cdot \Omega^{-1}$. Solving the above two equations gives us the critical point, expressed in terms of mean and covariance,

$$(\overline{\mu}, \overline{\Sigma}) = (\mathbb{E}^{\pi}[u], \mathbb{E}^{\pi}[(u - \overline{\mu}) \otimes (u - \overline{\mu})]).$$

The fact that the critical point $(\overline{\mu}, \overline{\Sigma}^{-1})$ is a minimizer of $J$ follows because $J$ is convex. Indeed, note that $J$ is the sum of two convex functions: a positive definite quadratic form and a negative log-determinant. $\qquad\square$

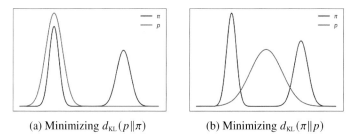

(a) Minimizing $d_{\mathrm{KL}}(p\|\pi)$        (b) Minimizing $d_{\mathrm{KL}}(\pi\|p)$

Figure 4.1 (a) Minimizing $d_{\mathrm{KL}}(p\|\pi)$ can lead to serious information loss while (b) minimizing $d_{\mathrm{KL}}(\pi\|p)$ ensures a comprehensive consideration of all components of $\pi$.

***Remark* 4.8** (Minimizing $d_{\mathrm{KL}}(\pi\|p)$ with Monte Carlo)   Theorem 4.7 shows that the Gaussian $p \in \mathcal{G}$ closest to $\pi$ in the sense of minimizing $d_{\mathrm{KL}}(\pi\|p)$ is the Gaussian with the same mean and covariance $(\overline{\mu}, \overline{\Sigma})$ as $\pi$. Both mean and covariance can be computed using Monte Carlo methods, a family of algorithms designed to compute expected values with respect to a given target distribution using samples. Monte Carlo algorithms will be studied in Chapter 5.     $\diamond$

## 4.4 Comparison Between $d_{\mathrm{KL}}(\pi\|p)$ and $d_{\mathrm{KL}}(p\|\pi)$

It is instructive to compare the two different minimization problems, both leading to a "best Gaussian," that we described in the preceding two sections. We write the two relevant divergences as follows and then explain the nomenclature:

$$d_{\mathrm{KL}}(p\|\pi) = \mathbb{E}^p\left[\log\left(\frac{p}{\pi}\right)\right] = \mathbb{E}^p\left[\log p\right] - \mathbb{E}^p\left[\log \pi\right], \quad \text{``Mode-seeking''}$$

$$d_{\mathrm{KL}}(\pi\|p) = \mathbb{E}^\pi\left[\log\left(\frac{\pi}{p}\right)\right] = \mathbb{E}^\pi\left[\log \pi\right] - \mathbb{E}^\pi\left[\log p\right]. \quad \text{``Mean-seeking''}$$

Note that when minimizing $d_{\mathrm{KL}}(p\|\pi)$ we want $\log\frac{p}{\pi}$ to be small in regions of high probability under $p$, which can happen when $p \simeq \pi$ or when $p$ is much smaller than $\pi$. This illustrates the fact that minimizing $d_{\mathrm{KL}}(p\|\pi)$ may miss out components of $\pi$. For example, in Figure 4.1(a) $\pi$ is a bimodal distribution but minimizing $d_{\mathrm{KL}}(p\|\pi)$ over Gaussians $p$ can only give a single mode approximation which is achieved by matching one of the modes; we may think of this as "mode-seeking." In contrast, when minimizing $d_{\mathrm{KL}}(\pi\|p)$ over Gaussians $p$ we want $\log\frac{\pi}{p}$ to be small where $p$ appears as the denominator. This implies that wherever $\pi$ has some mass we must let $p$ also have some mass there in order to keep $\frac{\pi}{p}$ as close as possible to one. Therefore, the minimization is carried out by allocating the mass of $p$ in a way such that on average the divergence between $p$ and $\pi$ attains its minimum, as shown in Figure 4.1(b); hence the label "mean-seeking." Different applications will favor different choices between the mean- and mode-seeking approaches to Gaussian approximation.

## 4.5 Variational Formulation of Bayes' Theorem

This chapter has been concerned with finding the best Gaussian approximation to a measure with respect to Kullback–Leibler divergences. Bayes' Theorem 1.2 itself can be formulated through a closely related minimization principle. Consider a posterior $\pi^y(u)$ in the following form:

$$\pi^y(u) = \frac{1}{Z} \exp(-\mathsf{L}(u))\rho(u),$$

where $\rho(u)$ is the prior, $\mathsf{L}(u)$ is the negative log-likelihood, and $Z$ the normalization constant. We assume here for exposition that all pdfs are positive. Dropping the superscript $y$ from $\pi^y$ for notational simplicity, we express $d_{\text{KL}}(p\|\pi)$ in terms of the prior as follows:

$$
\begin{aligned}
d_{\text{KL}}(p\|\pi) &= \int_{\mathbb{R}^d} \log\left(\frac{p}{\pi}\right) p \, du \\
&= \int_{\mathbb{R}^d} \log\left(\frac{p}{\rho}\frac{\rho}{\pi}\right) p \, du \\
&= \int_{\mathbb{R}^d} \log\left(\frac{p}{\rho} \exp(\mathsf{L}(u))Z\right) p \, du \\
&= d_{\text{KL}}(p\|\rho) + \mathbb{E}^p[\mathsf{L}(u)] + \log Z.
\end{aligned}
$$

If we define

$$\mathcal{J}(p) = d_{\text{KL}}(p\|\rho) + \mathbb{E}^p[\mathsf{L}(u)],$$

then we have the following:

**Theorem 4.9** (Bayes' Theorem as an Optimization Principle) *The posterior distribution $\pi$ is given by the following minimization principle:*

$$\pi = \text{argmin}_{p\in\mathscr{P}}\mathcal{J}(p),$$

*where $\mathscr{P}$ contains all pdfs on $\mathbb{R}^d$.*

*Proof* Note that

$$d_{\text{KL}}(p\|\pi) = \mathcal{J}(p) + \log Z.$$

Since $Z$ is the normalization constant for $\pi$ and is independent of $p$, the minimizer of $d_{\mathrm{KL}}(p\|\pi)$ over $p \in \mathscr{P}$ will also be the minimizer of $\mathcal{J}(p)$. Since the unique global minimizer of $d_{\mathrm{KL}}(p\|\pi)$ is attained at $p = \pi$, the result follows. $\qquad\square$

The posterior distribution $\pi$ is the minimizer of $\mathcal{J}(p)$ over all pdfs. However, we can approximate $\pi$ by minimizing $\mathcal{J}(p)$ over a subset of all pdfs. The following example of this connects to earlier parts of the chapter; further discussion on other computational methods and theoretical insights that stem from viewing Bayes theorem as an optimization problem may be found in the conclusion Section 4.6.

**Example 4.10** (Optimization over Gaussians)　If we approximate $\pi$ by minimizing $\mathcal{J}(p)$ over Gaussians then we obtain the method studied in Section 4.2.　$\diamond$

## 4.6　Discussion and Bibliography

The definition of the Kullback–Leibler divergence, and upper bounds in terms of probability metrics, can be found in Gibbs and Su (2002). For a basic introduction to variational Bayesian methods, including the moment-matching version of Gaussian approximation, see Bishop (2006). The idea of approximating a target distribution $\pi$ by minimizing the Kullback–Leibler divergence within a family of admissible distributions is popular in probabilistic machine learning. Variational Bayesian methods (Jordan et al., 1999; Wainwright and Jordan, 2008) minimize $d_{\mathrm{KL}}(p\|\pi)$; in contrast, expectation propagation methods (Minka, 2013), which seek a factorized approximate distribution, proceed by minimizing $d_{\mathrm{KL}}(\pi\|p)$. We refer to Wainwright and Jordan (2008) and Blei et al. (2017) for accessible introductions to variational Bayesian methods and further pointers to the literature.

In this chapter we have focused on Gaussian approximations, but other families of admissible distributions can be considered. The family of admissible distributions should in practice be large enough to allow for accurate approximation of the target distribution, while also allowing for efficient optimization. Gaussian approximations are useful in Bayesian inverse problems and are invoked by many data assimilation algorithms, as we shall see in Chapter 10. In probabilistic machine learning it is common to invoke mean-field rather than Gaussian approximations, and a variety of efficient optimization algorithms are available in this context (Bishop, 2006). Recent works that employ variational inference techniques for the solution of inverse problems include Agrawal et al. (2022) and Law and Zankin (2022).

The problem of finding a Gaussian approximation of a general finite-dimensional probability distribution is studied in Lu et al. (2017), and infinite-dimensional formulations are considered in Pinski et al. (2015b) and the companion paper Pinski et al. (2015a). Gaussian approximation of small noise diffusions are studied in Sanz-Alonso and Stuart (2017). The approximation in Theorem 4.5 consists of a single Gaussian distribution. If the posterior has more than one mode, a single Gaussian may not be appropriate. For an approximation composed of Gaussian mixtures, the reader is referred to Lu et al. (2017). Garcia Trillos et al. (2019) highlights how minimization of Kullback–Leibler divergence arises naturally in the optimization of local entropy and heat regularized costs in deep learning.

The formulation of Bayes' theorem as an optimization principle is well known; see the book of MacKay (2003) and the paper Bassiri et al. (2016) for clear expositions of this subject. There are at least three advantages of viewing Bayes' theorem as an optimization problem. First, the variational formulation provides a natural way to approximate the posterior by restricting the minimization problem to distributions satisfying some computationally desirable property. For instance, variational Bayesian methods often restrict the minimization to densities with a factorizable structure implied by independence with respect to the components of the unknown $u$; similarly, in Section 4.2 we have studied restriction to the class of Gaussian distributions. Second, variational formulations can be used to show convergence of posterior distributions indexed by some parameters using techniques from calculus of variations. For instance, Garcia Trillos et al. (2020) and Garcia Trillos and Sanz-Alonso (2018) exploit the variational formulation of Bayes' theorem to establish convergence of Bayesian procedures. Third, variational formulations provide natural paths, defined by a gradient flow, towards the posterior. Understanding these flows and their rates of convergence is helpful in the design and choice of sampling algorithms (Garcia Trillos and Sanz-Alonso, 2020).

For more information about the properties of the exponential family we refer to Nielsen and Garcia (2009), and for background on matrix calculations that were used in this chapter see Petersen and Pedersen (2008).

# 5

# Monte Carlo Sampling and Importance Sampling

In this chapter we introduce Monte Carlo sampling and importance sampling. These are two general techniques for estimating expectations with respect to a given pdf $\pi$. Monte Carlo generates independent samples from $\pi$ and combines them with equal weights, whilst importance sampling uses independent samples, weighted appropriately, from a different distribution. In quantifying the error in Monte Carlo and importance sampling, we will use a distance on random probability measures that reduces to total variation in the case of deterministic probability measures; and we will introduce the $\chi^2$ divergence.

In Bayesian inverse problems, we are typically unable to directly generate samples from the posterior distribution $\pi^y$ itself, so that Monte Carlo sampling is not viable; however, importance sampling may be used. For example, it is often possible to generate samples from the prior; importance sampling can then be used to reweight samples from the prior distribution, to approximate posterior expectations.

Recall that for any pdf $p$ and function $\varphi \colon \mathbb{R}^d \longrightarrow \mathbb{R}$, we denote

$$p(\varphi) = \mathbb{E}^p[\varphi(u)] = \int_{\mathbb{R}^d} \varphi(u)p(u)\, du. \tag{5.1}$$

Thus we view the pdf $p$ as a linear functional on the space of real-valued functions on $\mathbb{R}^d$. Our task in this chapter is to evaluate $\pi(f)$ for target distribution $\pi$ on $\mathbb{R}^d$ and for a given test function $f \colon \mathbb{R}^d \longrightarrow \mathbb{R}$. Thus, we are interested in computing

$$\pi(f) = \int_{\mathbb{R}^d} f(u)\pi(u)\, du. \tag{5.2}$$

Monte Carlo sampling approximates this integral using samples from $\pi$.

To describe importance sampling, we note that for any pdf $\rho$ such that the support of $\pi$ is contained in the support of $\rho$, equation (5.2) can be rewritten as

$$\pi(f) = \int_{\mathbb{R}^d} f(u)\left(\frac{\pi(u)}{\rho(u)}\right)\rho(u)\,du = \rho(fw), \tag{5.3}$$

where

$$w(u) = \frac{\pi(u)}{\rho(u)}.$$

We assume that the ratio $\pi(u)/\rho(u)$ is only known up to a normalization constant and write

$$w(u) = \frac{\pi(u)}{\rho(u)} = \frac{1}{Z}l(u), \tag{5.4}$$

where the unknown normalizing constant is defined by $Z = \rho(l)$. Noting that $w(u) = Z^{-1}l(u)$, we obtain from (5.3)

$$\pi(f) = \frac{\rho(fl)}{\rho(l)}. \tag{5.5}$$

Importance sampling methods are based on approximating the two integrals on the right-hand side of this identity with Monte Carlo, using samples from $\rho$. Note that it is not necessary to know $Z$ to implement this method.

A particular application of importance sampling in the context of Bayes' theorem is the setting where $\rho$ is the prior, $\pi$ the posterior and $g$ the likelihood. However, the importance sampling method is not restricted to this splitting of the posterior into a product of likelihood and prior; and indeed, depending on the specific test function $f$ of interest, the importance sampling method may be far from optimal if applied with this choice of $\rho$.

To summarize, Monte Carlo approximates $\pi(f)$ using (5.2) and samples from $\pi$; importance sampling approximates $\pi(f) = \rho(fw)$ using (5.5) and samples from $\rho$. Underlying the approximations of integrals are approximations of measures. For this reason, it is convenient in this chapter to generalize the concept of pdf to include Dirac mass distributions. A Dirac mass at $v$ will be viewed as having pdf $\delta(\cdot - v)$ where $\delta(\cdot)$ integrates to one and takes the value zero everywhere except at the origin. This Dirac mass is also sometimes written as $\delta_v(\cdot)$.

This chapter is organized as follows. We first introduce and analyze Monte Carlo sampling in Section 5.1. Importance sampling is then studied in Section 5.2. We close in Section 5.3 with pointers to the extant literature on this subject.

# 5.1 Monte Carlo Sampling

Monte Carlo sampling applies when it is possible to generate i.i.d. samples $u^{(n)} \sim \pi$, $1 \le n \le N$. The method approximates the target distribution $\pi$ by a sum of Dirac masses located at the samples $u^{(n)}$, each given equal weight $1/N$. This leads to the Monte Carlo estimator $\pi_{\text{MC}}^N$ of $\pi$ given by

$$\pi_{\text{MC}}^N := \frac{1}{N} \sum_{n=1}^{N} \delta(u - u^{(n)}). \tag{5.6}$$

We summarize this simple procedure in the following algorithm:

---

**Algorithm 5.1** Monte Carlo Sampling Algorithm

---

1: **Input**: Target distribution $\pi$, number of samples $N$.
2: **Samples From Target**: Sample $u^{(n)} \sim \pi$ i.i.d. $\quad n \in \{1, \dots, N\}$.
3: **Output**: Target approximation $\pi \approx \pi_{\text{MC}}^N := \frac{1}{N} \sum_{n=1}^{N} \delta(u - u^{(n)})$.

---

This algorithm leads to the following estimator of $\pi(f)$:

$$\pi_{\text{MC}}^N(f) = \frac{1}{N} \sum_{n=1}^{N} f(u^{(n)}), \ u^{(n)} \sim \pi \quad \text{i.i.d.}$$

We are interested in determining whether the estimator $\pi_{\text{MC}}^N(f)$ of $\pi(f)$ is accurate regardless of the specific test function $f$. For this reason, we seek to understand whether the Monte Carlo estimator $\pi_{\text{MC}}^N$ is a good approximation to $\pi$ in a suitable metric. This perspective will also be useful in analyzing importance sampling in this chapter, and when analyzing sequential methods for data assimilation in Chapters 11 and 12. Note that $\pi_{\text{MC}}^N$ is a *random* probability measure due to sampling, and so in order to formalize this question we need a distance between random probability measures. To this end, for random probability measures $\pi$ and $\pi'$, we define

$$d(\pi, \pi') = \sup_{|f|_\infty \le 1} \left( \mathbb{E}\left[ \left( \pi(f) - \pi'(f) \right)^2 \right] \right)^{1/2}, \tag{5.7}$$

where the expectation is taken over the random variable, in our case the randomness from sampling $\pi$. It is possible to show that $d(\cdot, \cdot)$ indeed defines a distance between random probability measures. Furthermore, when $\pi, \pi'$ are deterministic, then we have $d(\pi, \pi') = 2d_{\text{TV}}(\pi, \pi')$. Using this distance between random probability measures, we have the following result.

**Theorem 5.1** (Monte Carlo Error)    *For* $f \colon \mathbb{R}^d \longrightarrow \mathbb{R}$ *denote* $|f|_\infty := \sup_{u \in \mathbb{R}^d}$
$|f(u)|$. *We have*

$$\sup_{|f|_\infty \leq 1} \left| \mathbb{E} \left[ \pi_{\mathrm{MC}}^N(f) - \pi(f) \right] \right| = 0,$$

$$d(\pi_{\mathrm{MC}}^N, \pi)^2 \leq \frac{1}{N}.$$

*Proof*    To prove the first result, namely that the estimator is unbiased, we use
linearity of the expected value and that $u^{(n)} \sim \pi$:

$$\mathbb{E} \left[ \pi_{\mathrm{MC}}^N(f) \right] = \mathbb{E} \left[ \frac{1}{N} \sum_{n=1}^N f\left(u^{(n)}\right) \right]$$

$$= \frac{1}{N} N \pi(f) = \pi(f) = \mathbb{E} \left[ \pi(f) \right].$$

Therefore the supremum over $|f|_\infty \leq 1$ is a supremum over a quantity that is
zero, for any $f$, and the result follows.

For the second result, note that since $\pi_{\mathrm{MC}}^N(f)$ is unbiased, its variance agrees
with its mean squared error. Now using that the $u^{(n)} \sim \pi$ are independent we
deduce that

$$\mathrm{Var} \left[ \pi_{\mathrm{MC}}^N(f) \right] = \mathrm{Var} \left[ \frac{1}{N} \sum_{n=1}^N f\left(u^{(n)}\right) \right]$$

$$= \frac{1}{N^2} N \mathrm{Var}_\pi [f] = \frac{1}{N} \mathrm{Var}_\pi [f].$$

For $|f|_\infty \leq 1$, we have

$$\mathrm{Var}_\pi [f] = \pi(f^2) - \pi(f)^2 \leq \pi(f^2) \leq 1,$$

and therefore

$$\sup_{|f|_\infty \leq 1} \left| \mathbb{E} \left[ \left( \pi_{\mathrm{MC}}^N(f) - \pi(f) \right)^2 \right] \right| = \sup_{|f|_\infty \leq 1} \left| \frac{1}{N} \mathrm{Var}_\pi [f] \right| \leq \frac{1}{N}.$$

$\square$

The theorem shows that the Monte Carlo estimator $\pi_{\mathrm{MC}}^N$ is an unbiased approximation for the posterior $\pi$ and that, by choosing $N$ large enough, expectation
of any bounded function $f$ can in principle be approximated by Monte Carlo
sampling to arbitrary accuracy. Furthermore, although the convergence is slow
with respect to $N$ – the mean squared error decays like $N^{-1}$ so the typical error
only decays like $N^{-1/2}$ – there is no dependence on the dimension of the problem
or on the properties of $f$, other than its supremum. Moreover, the proof of
Theorem 5.1 shows that, in fact, the Monte Carlo error in the approximation of
$\pi(f)$ is determined by the variance of $f$ under $\pi$.

**Example 5.2** (Approximation of an Integral) Let $f : \mathbb{R} \longrightarrow \mathbb{R}$ be a sigmoid function defined on $\mathbb{R}$ and shown in Figure 5.1(a) below as the blue solid curve. For the target distribution $\pi$ we take a mixture of two Gaussians found by choosing from $\mathcal{N}(-5, 1)$ with probability $1/10$ and from $\mathcal{N}(5, 1)$ with probability $9/10$. We wish to approximate the expected value, under $\pi$, of $f(u) \times \mathbb{I}_{[a,b]}(u)$ where

$$
\mathbb{1}_{[a,b]}(u) = \begin{cases} 1 & \text{if } u \in [a, b], \\ 0 & \text{otherwise.} \end{cases}
$$

We use Monte Carlo sampling to generate $N$ random samples $u^{(1)}, \ldots, u^{(N)}$ and compute the error between the actual integral and the Monte Carlo estimator. The integral and estimator are in the form:

$$
\pi(f) = \int_a^b f(u)\pi(u)\,\mathrm{d}u,
$$

$$
\pi_{\mathrm{MC}}^N(f) = \frac{1}{N} \sum_{n=1}^{N} f(u^{(n)})\mathbb{1}_{[a,b]}(u^{(n)}).
$$

The results of a set of numerical experiments with $a = -5, b = 5$ and varying $N$ are shown in Figure 5.1(b). A randomly chosen subset of the samples used when $N = 100$ is displayed in Figure 5.1(a); only samples in $[-5, 5]$ are shown, since other samples do not contribute to the estimator in this case. $\diamond$

## 5.2 Importance Sampling

Monte Carlo sampling can only be used when it is possible to sample from the desired target distribution $\pi$. When it is not possible to sample from $\pi$, we can draw samples from another *proposal* distribution $\rho$ instead. Consider $\pi$ as in equation (5.4). Given a test function $f : \mathbb{R}^d \to \mathbb{R}$ we can rewrite its expectation with respect to $\pi$ in terms of expected values with respect to $\rho$ as in equation (5.5). Approximating the numerator and the denominator using Monte Carlo with samples from $\rho$ gives

$$
\pi(f) \approx \sum_{n=1}^{N} w^{(n)} f\left(u^{(n)}\right), \quad u^{(n)} \sim \rho \text{ i.i.d.}
$$

$$
= \pi_{\mathrm{IS}}^N(f),
$$

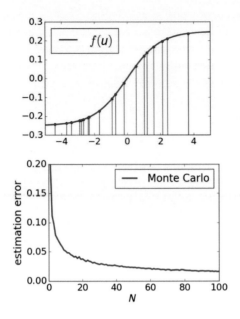

Figure 5.1 Large sample size $N$ reduces the estimation error by the Monte Carlo method.

where

$$w^{(n)} := \frac{\mathsf{l}(u^{(n)})}{\sum_{m=1}^{N} \mathsf{l}(u^{(m)})}, \qquad \pi_{\mathrm{IS}}^{N} := \sum_{n=1}^{N} w^{(n)} \delta(u - u^{(n)}).$$

Thus, given $N$ samples $u^{(1)}, \ldots, u^{(N)}$ generated i.i.d. according to $\rho$, we can estimate $\pi$ with the *particle approximation measure* $\pi_{\mathrm{IS}}^{N}$.

---

**Algorithm 5.2** Importance Sampling Algorithm

---

1: **Input**: Target distribution $\pi(u) = \frac{1}{Z}\mathsf{l}(u)\rho(u)$, proposal distribution $\rho$, number of samples $N$.

2: **Samples From Proposal**: Sample $u^{(n)} \sim \rho$ i.i.d.  $n \in \{1, \ldots, N\}$.

3: **Importance Weights**: Compute for $n \in \{1, \ldots, N\}$,

$$w^{(n)} := \frac{\mathsf{l}(u^{(n)})}{\sum_{m=1}^{N} \mathsf{l}(u^{(m)})}.$$

4: **Output**: Target approximation $\pi \approx \pi_{\mathrm{IS}}^{N} := \sum_{n=1}^{N} w^{(n)} \delta(u - u^{(n)})$.

---

We emphasize that implementation of this algorithm does not assume knowledge of the normalizing constant $Z$, but only that $g$ can be evaluated and that $\rho$ can be sampled from. In particular, note that the algorithm is invariant under $g \mapsto \lambda g$ for any scalar $\lambda$. Algorithm 5.2 leads to the following estimator of $\pi(f)$ :

$$\pi_{\text{IS}}^N (f) = \sum_{n=1}^N w^{(n)} f(u^{(n)}), \quad u^{(n)} \sim \rho \quad \text{i.i.d.}$$

**Example 5.3** (Change of Measurement)    We consider a similar set-up as in Example 5.2, integrating a sigmoid function, shown in blue in Figure 5.2, with respect to a pdf $\pi$ which is bimodal, shown in red in Figure 5.2; we again restrict the support of the desired integral. We estimate the integral using importance sampling based on $N$ random samples $u^{(1)}, \ldots, u^{(N)}$ from the measure $\rho = \mathcal{N}(\mu, \sigma^2)$, shown in green in Figure 5.2. The estimator of the integral is given by

$$\pi_{\text{IS}}^N (f) = \sum_{n=1}^N w^{(n)} f(u^{(n)}) \mathbb{1}_{[a,b]}(u^{(n)}),$$

$$w^{(n)} = \frac{\mathsf{l}(u^{(n)})}{\sum_{m=1}^N \mathsf{l}(u^{(m)})}.$$

Here $g$ is a function proportional to the ratio of the densities of $\pi$ and $\rho$. If $\pi(u^{(n)}) > \rho(u^{(n)})$, the samples should have been denser, so we raise the weight on $f(u^{(n)})$ in proportion to $\frac{\pi(u^{(n)})}{\rho(u^{(n)})} > 1$. If $\pi(u^{(n)}) < \rho(u^{(n)})$, the samples should have been less dense, so we lower the weight on $f(u^{(n)})$ in proportion to $\frac{\pi(u^{(n)})}{\rho(u^{(n)})} < 1$.    ◊

We now introduce the $\chi^2$ divergence between probability distributions, and discuss some of its properties, before going on to use it to quantify the accuracy of importance sampling.

**Definition 5.4**    Let $\pi, \pi' > 0$ be two pdfs on $\mathbb{R}^d$.[1] The $\chi^2$ *divergence* of $\pi$ with respect to $\pi'$ is

$$d_{\chi^2}(\pi \| \pi') := \int_{\mathbb{R}^d} \left( \frac{\pi(u)}{\pi'(u)} - 1 \right)^2 \pi'(u) \, du. \tag{5.8}$$

◊

The $\chi^2$ divergence is not a distance as it is, in general, not symmetric; it is, however, distance-like and captures the closeness of the two distributions; this is

---

[1] The definition extends to situations where the support of $\pi'$ is not the whole of $\mathbb{R}^d$, provided $\pi$ is absolutely continuous with respect to $\pi'$.

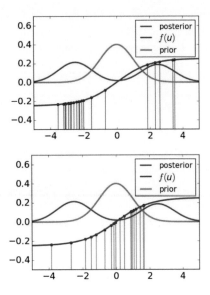

Figure 5.2 Importance sampling is a change of measure via the importance weights. The red curve shows a bimodal distribution $\pi$ and the green curve shows a Gaussian distribution $\rho$. The blue curve is the function to be integrated, on its support $[-5, 5]$. The upper figure shows samples from the posterior $\pi$ itself; these would be used for Monte Carlo sampling; the lower curve shows samples from the prior $\rho$, as used for importance sampling. The importance weights capture and compensate for the difference of sampling from these two distributions.

analogous to the Kullback–Leibler divergence defined in the preceding chapter. The next lemma shows that the $\chi^2$ divergence may be used to upper bound the Kullback–Leibler divergence and therefore, by Lemma 4.3, also the total variation and Hellinger distances.

**Lemma 5.5**   *The $\chi^2$ divergence provides the following upper bounds for the Kullback–Leibler divergence:*

$$d_{\mathrm{KL}}(\pi\|\pi') \leq \log\!\left(d_{\chi^2}(\pi\|\pi') + 1\right), \qquad d_{\mathrm{KL}}(\pi\|\pi') \leq d_{\chi^2}(\pi\|\pi').$$

*Proof*   The second inequality is a direct consequence of the first one, noting that, for $x \geq 0$, $\log(x + 1) \leq x$. To prove the first inequality note that by Jensen inequality,

$$d_{\mathrm{KL}}(\pi\|\pi') = \int_{\mathbb{R}^d} \log\left(\frac{\pi(u)}{\pi'(u)}\right)\pi(u)\,du$$

$$\leq \log\left(\int_{\mathbb{R}^d} \frac{\pi(u)}{\pi'(u)}\frac{\pi(u)}{\pi'(u)}\pi'(u)\,du\right)$$

$$= \log\left(d_{\chi^2}(\pi\|\pi') + 1\right),$$

where for the last equality we used that

$$d_{\chi^2}(\pi\|\pi') = \int_{\mathbb{R}^d}\left(\frac{\pi(u)}{\pi'(u)} - 1\right)^2\pi'(u)\,du$$

$$= \int_{\mathbb{R}^d}\left(\frac{\pi(u)}{\pi'(u)}\right)^2\pi'(u)\,du - 2\int_{\mathbb{R}^d}\left(\frac{\pi(u)}{\pi'(u)}\right)\pi'(u)\,du + \int_{\mathbb{R}^d}\pi'(u)\,du$$

$$= \int_{\mathbb{R}^d}\left(\frac{\pi(u)}{\pi'(u)}\right)^2\pi'(u)\,du - 1.$$

$\square$

The next result shows that, similarly as for Monte Carlo sampling, the mean squared error of $\pi_{\mathrm{IS}}^N(f)$ as an estimator of $\pi(f)$ is order $N^{-1}$. However, there are two main differences: the estimator is now biased, and the constant in the mean squared error depends on the $\chi^2$ divergence between the target and the proposal.

**Theorem 5.6** (Importance Sampling Error)  *We have*

$$\sup_{|f|_\infty \leq 1}\left|\mathbb{E}\left[\pi_{\mathrm{IS}}^N(f) - \pi(f)\right]\right| \leq 2\frac{1 + d_{\chi^2}(\pi\|\rho)}{N},$$

$$d(\pi_{\mathrm{IS}}^N, \pi)^2 \leq 4\frac{1 + d_{\chi^2}(\pi\|\rho)}{N}.$$

*Proof*  The proof of the first item (bias) uses the second item (variance). Nonetheless, we start with the proof for the bias, because bias and variance are often thought of, conceptually, in that order. Given

$$\pi(u) = \frac{1}{Z}\mathsf{I}(u)\rho(u) = \frac{1}{\rho(\mathsf{I})}\mathsf{I}(u)\rho(u),$$

the proof of Lemma 5.5 shows that

$$d_{\chi^2}(\pi\|\rho) = \frac{\rho(\mathsf{I}^2)}{\rho(\mathsf{I})^2} - 1.$$

To ease the notation we introduce

$$\zeta := \frac{\rho(\mathsf{I}^2)}{\rho(\mathsf{I})^2}.$$

We rewrite

$$\pi(f) = \frac{\rho(\mathsf{l}f)}{\rho(\mathsf{l})} \simeq \frac{\rho_{\mathrm{MC}}^N(\mathsf{l}f)}{\rho_{\mathrm{MC}}^N(\mathsf{l})} = \pi_{\mathrm{IS}}^N(f).$$

Then we have

$$
\begin{aligned}
\pi_{\mathrm{IS}}^N(f) - \pi(f) &= \pi_{\mathrm{IS}}^N(f) - \frac{\rho(\mathsf{l}f)}{\rho(\mathsf{l})} \\
&= \frac{\pi_{\mathrm{IS}}^N(f)\big(\rho(\mathsf{l}) - \rho_{\mathrm{MC}}^N(\mathsf{l})\big)}{\rho(\mathsf{l})} - \frac{\big(\rho(\mathsf{l}f) - \rho_{\mathrm{MC}}^N(\mathsf{l}f)\big)}{\rho(\mathsf{l})}.
\end{aligned}
\tag{5.9}
$$

The expectation of the second term is zero and hence

$$
\begin{aligned}
\big|\mathbb{E}\big[\pi_{\mathrm{IS}}^N(f) - \pi(f)\big]\big| &= \frac{1}{\rho(\mathsf{l})}\Big|\mathbb{E}\big[\pi_{\mathrm{IS}}^N(f)\big(\rho(\mathsf{l}) - \rho_{\mathrm{MC}}^N(\mathsf{l})\big)\big]\Big| \\
&\leq \frac{1}{\rho(\mathsf{l})}\Big|\mathbb{E}\big[\big(\pi_{\mathrm{IS}}^N(f) - \pi(f)\big)\big(\rho(\mathsf{l}) - \rho_{\mathrm{MC}}^N(\mathsf{l})\big)\big]\Big|,
\end{aligned}
$$

since $\mathbb{E}\big[\rho(\mathsf{l}) - \rho_{\mathrm{MC}}^N(\mathsf{l})\big] = 0$. Using the Cauchy–Schwarz inequality, the second result from this theorem (whose proof follows) and Theorem 5.1 we have, for all $|f|_\infty \leq 1$,

$$
\begin{aligned}
\big|\mathbb{E}\big[\pi_{\mathrm{IS}}^N(f) - \pi(f)\big]\big| &\leq \frac{1}{\rho(\mathsf{l})}\bigg(\mathbb{E}\Big[\big(\pi_{\mathrm{IS}}^N(f) - \pi(f)\big)^2\Big]\bigg)^{1/2}\bigg(\mathbb{E}\Big[\big(\rho(\mathsf{l}) - \rho_{\mathrm{MC}}^N(\mathsf{l})\big)^2\Big]\bigg)^{1/2} \\
&\leq \frac{1}{\rho(\mathsf{l})}\left(\frac{4\zeta}{N}\right)^{1/2}\left(\frac{\rho(\mathsf{l}^2)}{N}\right)^{1/2} = \frac{2\zeta}{N}.
\end{aligned}
$$

We now prove the second result. We use the splitting of $\pi_{\mathrm{IS}}^N(f) - \pi(f)$ into the sum of two terms as derived in equation (5.9). Using Theorem 5.1, the basic inequality $(a - b)^2 \leq 2(a^2 + b^2)$ and that for all $|f|_\infty \leq 1$, $|\pi_{\mathrm{IS}}^N(f)| \leq 1$, we have, for all $|f|_\infty \leq 1$,

$$\left| \mathbb{E}\left[ \left( \pi_{\mathrm{IS}}^N(f) - \pi(f) \right)^2 \right] \right|$$

$$\leq \frac{2}{\rho(\mathsf{l})^2} \left( \mathbb{E}\left[ \left( \pi_{\mathrm{IS}}^N(f) \right)^2 \left( \rho(\mathsf{l}) - \rho_{\mathrm{MC}}^N(\mathsf{l}) \right)^2 \right] + \mathbb{E}\left[ \left( \rho(\mathsf{l}f) - \rho_{\mathrm{MC}}^N(\mathsf{l}f) \right)^2 \right] \right)$$

$$\leq \frac{2}{\rho(\mathsf{l})^2} \left( \mathbb{E}\left[ \left( \rho(\mathsf{l}) - \rho_{\mathrm{MC}}^N(\mathsf{l}) \right)^2 \right] + \mathbb{E}\left[ \left( \rho(\mathsf{l}f) - \rho_{\mathrm{MC}}^N(\mathsf{l}f) \right)^2 \right] \right)$$

$$= \frac{2}{\rho(\mathsf{l})^2 N} \left( \mathrm{Var}_\rho[\mathsf{l}] + \mathrm{Var}_\rho[\mathsf{l}f] \right)$$

$$\leq \frac{2}{\rho(\mathsf{l})^2 N} \left( \mu(\mathsf{l}^2) + \mu(\mathsf{l}^2 f^2) \right)$$

$$\leq \frac{4\rho(\mathsf{l}^2)}{\rho(\mathsf{l})^2 N} = \frac{4\zeta}{N}.$$

Therefore,

$$d(\pi_{\mathrm{IS}}^N, \pi)^2 = \sup_{|f|_\infty \leq 1} \left| \mathbb{E}\left[ \left( \pi_{\mathrm{IS}}^N(f) - \pi(f) \right)^2 \right] \right| \leq \frac{4\zeta}{N}.$$

$\square$

**Remark 5.7** In Theorem 5.6 we measure the quality of $\pi_{\mathrm{IS}}^N$ as an approximation of the target $\pi$ by considering the worst-case bias and mean squared error over the class of bounded test functions $\{f \colon \mathbb{R}^d \to \mathbb{R} : |f|_\infty = 1\}$. We show that worst-case error upper bounds can be obtained in terms of the $\chi^2$ divergence between the target and the proposal, quantifying the intuitive fact that, over a broad of test functions, the performance of importance sampling depends on the closeness between target and proposal. Note, however, that for a *specific* function $f$ careful choice of $\rho$ in the importance sampling methodology may lead to considerable improvement over Monte Carlo sampling.

Unlike Monte Carlo, the importance sampling estimator $\pi_{\mathrm{IS}}^N(f)$ is biased for $\pi(f)$. The theorem shows, however, that the bias decays at a rate that is twice that of the standard deviation, and so for large $N$ the mean squared error is dominated by the variance. As for Monte Carlo, the rate of convergence of the variance is governed by the inverse of $N$, and the dimension $d$ does not directly appear in the upper-bound. However, for importance sampling to be accurate (with a limited number of samples $N$) it is important that target and proposal are close in $\chi^2$ divergence, a condition that will not be typically satisfied in high dimensions. $\diamond$

**Example 5.8** (Explicit Bound for a Linear-Gaussian Inverse Problem) Let

$a \in \mathbb{R}$ be given, and consider the one-dimensional inverse problem

$$y = au + \eta, \qquad \eta \sim \mathcal{N}(0, \gamma^2),$$

supplemented with a Gaussian prior $u \sim \rho(u) = \mathcal{N}(0, \widehat{c}^2)$. Defining

$$\mathsf{l}(u) := \exp\left(-\frac{a^2}{2\gamma^2}u^2 + \frac{ay}{\gamma^2}u\right)$$

we can write the posterior distribution $\pi(u)$ in the form (5.4), namely

$$\pi(u) = \frac{1}{Z}\mathsf{l}(u)\rho(u).$$

Setting $\delta^2 := a^2\widehat{c}^2/\gamma^2$ a direct calculation shows that

$$\rho(\mathsf{l}) = \frac{1}{\sqrt{\delta^2 + 1}}\exp\left(\frac{1}{2}\frac{\delta^2 y^2}{a^2\widehat{c}^2 + \gamma^2}\right),$$

$$\rho(\mathsf{l}^2) = \frac{1}{\sqrt{2\delta^2 + 1}}\exp\left(\frac{2\delta^2 y^2}{2a^2\widehat{c}^2 + \gamma^2}\right),$$

and so, noting that $\frac{y}{\sqrt{a^2\widehat{c}^2 + \gamma^2}} \sim \mathcal{N}(0, 1)$ under our model, we obtain that

$$\zeta = \frac{\rho(\mathsf{l}^2)}{\rho(\mathsf{l})^2}$$

$$= \frac{\delta^2 + 1}{\sqrt{2\delta^2 + 1}}\exp\left(\frac{\delta^2}{2\delta^2 + 1}z^2\right), \qquad z \sim \mathcal{N}(0, 1).$$

Theorem 5.6 then guarantees that

$$d(\pi_{\mathrm{IS}}^N, \pi)^2 \le \frac{4\zeta}{N}.$$

It is illustrative to note that $\zeta$ – and hence the $\chi^2$-divergence between the posterior and the prior – is an increasing function of $\delta^2 = a^2\widehat{c}^2/\gamma^2$. This is intuitive, since (i) larger $a$ and $\widehat{c}^2$ make the prior less informative; and (ii) smaller $\gamma$ makes the data more informative. In either of these two limiting regimes, we expect the posterior to become further away from the prior.                                                ◇


## 5.3 Discussion and Bibliography

A classic reference on the Monte Carlo method is Hammersley and Handscomb (1964). Recent textbooks covering both methodological and theoretical aspects of Monte Carlo methods include Liu (2008) and Robert and Casella (2013). In practice, a wide range of probabilities, integrals and summations can be approximated by the Monte Carlo method. An advantage of Monte Carlo methods is that the convergence rate is independent of the dimension of the vector space supporting the random variable; indeed, the $N^{-1/2}$ rate can be obtained for infinite-dimensional problems, in principle. A caveat of Monte Carlo methods is that they converge slowly. A faster convergence rate can be attained using quasi-random, low discrepancy sequences rather than random samples from the target. These quasi-random points can be suitably chosen in order to provide greater uniformity than random or pseudo-random sequences. The convergence theory, practical limitations, and scalability to high dimension of the resulting *quasi-Monte Carlo* methods are overviewed in Caflisch (1998), Dick et al. (2013), and Sloan and Woźniakowski (1998). The subject of multi-level Monte Carlo (MLMC) has made the use of Monte Carlo methods practical in new areas of application; see Giles (2015) for an overview. The methodology applies when approximating expectations over infinite-dimensional spaces, and distributes the computational budget over different levels of approximation, with the goal of optimizing the cost per unit error, noting that the latter balances sampling and approximation-based sources of error.

Importance sampling is reviewed in Tokdar et al. (2010). The methodology was first developed as an approach to reduce the variance of Monte Carlo integration (Kahn and Marshall, 1953; Kahn, 1955). The chapter notes Anderson (2014) give a comparison of Monte Carlo and importance sampling with examples. Early investigations of importance sampling focused on the following question: given a test function $f$, how should one choose the proposal $\rho$ so that the estimator $\pi_{\text{IS}}^N(f)$ of $\pi(f)$ has a small mean squared error? This question has led to a plethora of algorithms for simulation of rare events, which is still a very active area of research. The presentation in this chapter closely follows Agapiou et al. (2017a) and Sanz-Alonso and Wang (2021), which study importance sampling from the perspective of filtering and sequential importance resampling. In this context, it is important to guarantee the accuracy of the importance sampling estimator $\pi_{\text{IS}}^N(f) \approx \pi(f)$ for a variety of test functions. This can be achieved by ensuring that $\pi_{\text{IS}}^N$ is close to $\pi$, as shown in Theorem 5.6. In order for importance sampling to be accurate for a wide family of test functions, target and proposal need to be sufficiently close, since otherwise the *effective sample size* will be low (Agapiou et al., 2017a; Sanz-Alonso and Wang, 2021; Martino et al., 2017). Necessary sample size results for importance sampling in terms of several divergences between target and proposal are established in Sanz-Alonso (2018), and Chatterjee and Diaconis (2018). Bugallo et al. (2017) and Kawai (2017) consider advanced importance sampling via adaptive algorithms. Some recent adaptive methods are based on the idea of finding the proposal distribution within some parametric family that is closest to the target distribution in an appropriate sense (Ryu and Boyd, 2014; Akyildiz and Míguez, 2021; Deniz Akyildiz, 2022).

# 6

# Markov Chain Monte Carlo

In this chapter we study Markov chain Monte Carlo (MCMC), a methodology that delivers approximate samples from a given *target* distribution $\pi$. The methodology applies to settings in which $\pi$ is the posterior distribution in (1.2), but it is also widely used in numerous applications beyond Bayesian inference. As with Monte Carlo and importance sampling, MCMC may be viewed as approximating the target distribution by a sum of Dirac masses, thus allowing the approximation of expectations with respect to the target. Implementation of Monte Carlo presupposes that independent samples from the target can be obtained. Importance sampling and MCMC bypass this restrictive assumption: importance sampling by appropriately weighting independent samples from a proposal distribution, and MCMC by drawing correlated samples from a Markov kernel that has the target as invariant distribution.

The concepts of Markov kernel and invariant distribution will hence play a central role in this chapter, and we start in Section 6.1 with a recap of the elements of this theory needed in the remainder of the chapter. Then in Section 6.2 we provide a general discussion of Markov chain sampling, which assumes the existence of an ergodic Markov chain, with a kernel from which samples may be drawn iteratively, with invariant distribution equal to the target $\pi$. Following that, in Section 6.3 we discuss Metropolis–Hastings sampling which assumes the existence of a Markov kernel from which samples may readily be drawn, and then uses a correction mechanism to obtain a new Markov chain with invariant distribution equal to the target $\pi$. The relationship between Metropolis–Hastings sampling and Markov chain sampling is analogous to the relationship between importance sampling and Monte Carlo sampling. After introducing the general Metropolis–Hastings methodology, and showing its invariance with respect to the target distribution in Section 6.4, we will specify to the case where $\pi$ is a posterior distribution given via Bayes' theorem from the product of the likelihood function and the prior distribution. In this context, we will analyze in Section 6.5 the convergence of the pCN algorithm, which uses the prior and the likelihood separately as part of its design, and is prototypical of many useful Metropolis–Hastings methods, especially for high-dimensional sampling problems. The chapter closes in Section 6.6 with extensions and bibliographical remarks.

# 6.1  Markov Chains in $\mathbb{R}^d$

We recall that $p\colon \mathbb{R}^d \times \mathbb{R}^d \to \mathbb{R}$ is called a *Markov kernel* if,

(i)  $p(u,v) \geq 0$ for all $(u,v) \in \mathbb{R}^d \times \mathbb{R}^d$; and

(ii)  $\int_{\mathbb{R}^d} p(u,v)\, dv = 1$ for all $u \in \mathbb{R}^d$.

Thus if $p\colon \mathbb{R}^d \times \mathbb{R}^d \to \mathbb{R}$ is a Markov kernel, then $p(u,\cdot)\colon \mathbb{R}^d \to \mathbb{R}^+$ is a pdf on $\mathbb{R}^d$. We also recall that $\pi$ is an *invariant distribution* of the Markov kernel $p(u,v)$ if, for any $v \in \mathbb{R}^d$,

$$\int_{\mathbb{R}^d} \pi(u)p(u,v)\, du = \pi(v). \tag{6.1}$$

A *sample path* of the Markov chain generated by kernel $p$ is defined as follows: given initial distribution $\pi_0$, generate $\{u^{(n)}\}_{n \in \mathbb{Z}^+}$ inductively:

$$u^{(0)} \sim \pi_0,$$
$$u^{(n+1)} \sim p(u^{(n)}, \cdot), \quad n \in \mathbb{Z}^+.$$

Note that $\{u^{(n)}\}_{n \in \mathbb{Z}^+}$ is a random sequence and hence, for each $n \in \mathbb{Z}^+$, there is a marginal distribution on $u^{(n)}$, denoted $\pi_n$; in later discussions correlations between $u^{(n)}$ and $u^{(m)}$ for $n \neq m$ will also be relevant. The following result is fundamental.

**Lemma 6.1**  *Let $\pi$ be an invariant distribution of the Markov kernel $p$. Let $\{u^{(n)}\}_{n \in \mathbb{Z}^+}$ be a sample path generated with kernel $p$ and initial distribution $\pi_0 = \pi$. Then it follows that $u^{(n)} \sim \pi$ for all $n \in \mathbb{Z}^+$.*

*Proof*  By induction it suffices to show that if $\pi_n = \pi$ then $\pi_{n+1} = \pi$. Let $A$ denote an arbitrary subset in $\mathbb{R}^d$. We first note that

$$\mathbb{P}(u^{(n+1)} \in A \mid u^{(n)}) = \int_A p(u^{(n)}, v)\, dv.$$

Thus, using $\pi_n = \pi$, exchanging the order of integration and using the invariance of $\pi$ with respect to kernel $p$, we find that

$$
\begin{aligned}
\pi_{n+1}(A) &= \mathbb{P}(u^{(n+1)} \in A) \\
&= \mathbb{E}^{u^{(n)} \sim \pi_n} \left[ \mathbb{P}\left(u^{(n+1)} \in A \mid u^{(n)}\right) \right] \\
&= \int_{\mathbb{R}^d} \pi_n(u) \left( \int_A p(u, v) \, dv \right) du \\
&= \int_{\mathbb{R}^d} \pi(u) \left( \int_A p(u, v) \, dv \right) du \\
&= \int_A \left( \int_{\mathbb{R}^d} \pi(u) p(u, v) \, du \right) dv \\
&= \int_A \pi(v) \, dv \\
&= \pi(A).
\end{aligned}
$$

Since $A$ is arbitrary the proof is complete. $\qquad\square$

In the following it will be useful to compute expectations with respect to the distribution on sample paths $u = \{u^{(n)}\}_{n \in \mathbb{Z}^+}$ implied by the Markov kernel $p$ and initial distribution $\pi_0$. To this end we let $\mathbb{E}$ denote expectation with respect to the distribution on sample paths and define, for real-valued functions $f$ and $g$ on the sample paths,

$$
\begin{aligned}
\operatorname{Var}(f(u)) &:= \mathbb{E}\left[ (f(u) - \mathbb{E}(f))^2 \right], \\
\operatorname{Cov}(f(u), g(u)) &:= \mathbb{E}\left[ (f(u) - \mathbb{E}(f))(g(u) - \mathbb{E}(g)) \right].
\end{aligned}
$$

We will be particularly interested in the case in which the initial distribution of the Markov chain is $\pi$; the preceding lemma shows that each element $u^{(n)}$ of the sample path $u$ is then distributed according to $\pi$. We then write $\mathbb{E}^{u^{(0)} \sim \pi}$. If, abusing notation, $f$ and $g$ depend only on a single element $u^{(n)}$ of $u$, then we have

$$
\begin{aligned}
\operatorname{Var}(f(u^{(n)})) &:= \operatorname{Var}_\pi(f(u)) := \pi\left((f(u) - \pi(f))^2\right), \\
\operatorname{Cov}(f(u^{(n)}), g(u^{(m)})) &:= \mathbb{E}^{u^{(0)} \sim \pi}\left[ (f(u^{(n)}) - \pi(f))(g(u^{(m)}) - \pi(g)) \right].
\end{aligned}
$$

## 6.2 Markov Chain Sampling

The idea of MCMC is simple to state: given a target distribution $\pi$, find a Markov kernel that can be sampled from and has $\pi$ as its invariant distribution. Samples $\{u^{(n)}\}_{n=1}^N$ drawn iteratively from the kernel may be used to approximate posterior expectations. The samples are given uniform weights $1/N$ but, in contrast to standard Monte Carlo, they are not independent and they are not drawn exactly from the target $\pi$. However, if the chain is guaranteed to satisfy *sample path ergodicity*, then the resulting estimator for $\pi(f)$ is asymptotically unbiased and satisfies a central limit theorem for suitable test functions $f$. We display the algorithm, define the estimator and then state a theorem summarizing convergence.

---

**Algorithm 6.1** Markov Chain Sampling Algorithm

---

1: **Input**: Target distribution $\pi$, initial distribution $\pi_0$, Markov kernel $q(u,v)$ with invariant distribution $\pi$, number of samples $N$.

2: **Initial Draw**: Draw initial sample $u^{(0)} \sim \pi_0$.

3: **Subsequent Samples**: For $n = 0, 1, \ldots, N-1$ do:

   1 Sample $u^{(n+1)} \sim q(u^{(n)}, \cdot)$.

4: **Output**: Target approximation $\pi \approx \pi_{\text{MCMC}}^N := \frac{1}{N} \sum_{n=1}^N \delta(u - u^{(n)})$.

---

The estimator for $\pi(f)$ resulting from Algorithm 6.1 is then

$$\pi_{\text{MCMC}}^N(f) = \frac{1}{N} \sum_{n=1}^N f(u^{(n)}).$$

Recall the notation Var, Cov and $\mathbb{E}^{u^{(0)} \sim \pi}$ from the previous section. We then have the following result concerning the error in this estimator.

**Theorem 6.2** (MCMC Error)   *Let $f: \mathbb{R}^d \longrightarrow \mathbb{R}$ satisfy $\text{Var}_\pi[f] = 1$. We have*

$$\mathbb{E}^{u^{(0)} \sim \pi}\left[\pi_{\text{MCMC}}^N(f) - \pi(f)\right] = 0,$$

$$\mathbb{E}^{u^{(0)} \sim \pi}\left[\left(\pi_{\text{MCMC}}^N(f) - \pi(f)\right)^2\right] = \frac{\tau_N^2(f)}{N},$$

*where*

$$\tau_N^2(f) = 1 + 2 \sum_{m=1}^{N-1} \frac{N-m}{N} \text{Cov}\left(f(u^{(0)}), f(u^{(m)})\right).$$

*In particular,*

$$\lim_{N \to \infty} N \, \mathbb{E}^{u^{(0)} \sim \pi}\left[\left(\pi_{\text{MCMC}}^N(f) - \pi(f)\right)^2\right] = \tau^2(f),$$

*where*

$$\tau^2(f) = 1 + 2 \sum_{m=1}^{\infty} \mathrm{Cov}\big(f(u^{(0)}), f(u^{(m)})\big),$$

*provided that the series converges.*

*Proof* First note that, under the assumptions that $u^{(0)} \sim \pi$ and that the kernel $q$ has invariant distribution $\pi$, it follows that $u^{(n)} \sim \pi$ for all $n \geq 1$. Therefore, $\pi_{\mathrm{MCMC}}^N$ is unbiased for $\pi(f)$ by linearity of expectation. Now we characterize the mean squared error of $\pi_{\mathrm{MCMC}}^N$, which agrees with its variance:

$$\mathbb{E}^{u^{(0)} \sim \pi}\left[\left(\pi_{\mathrm{MCMC}}^N(f) - \pi(f)\right)^2\right] = \mathrm{Var}[\pi_{\mathrm{MCMC}}^N(f)]$$

$$= \frac{1}{N^2}\left[\sum_{n=1}^{N} \mathrm{Var}[f(u^{(n)})]\right.$$

$$\left. + 2 \sum_{n=1}^{N-1} \sum_{m>n} \mathrm{Cov}\big(f(u^{(n)}), f(u^{(m)})\big)\right]$$

$$= \frac{1}{N^2}\left[N + 2 \sum_{n=1}^{N-1}\sum_{m=1}^{N-n} \mathrm{Cov}\big(f(u^{(n)}), f(u^{(n+m)})\big)\right]$$

$$= \frac{1}{N}\left[1 + \frac{2}{N} \sum_{m=1}^{N-1}\sum_{n=1}^{N-m} \mathrm{Cov}\big(f(u^{(n)}), f(u^{(n+m)})\big)\right]$$

$$= \frac{1}{N}\left[1 + \frac{2}{N} \sum_{m=1}^{N-1}\sum_{n=1}^{N-m} \mathrm{Cov}\big(f(u^{(0)}), f(u^{(m)})\big)\right]$$

$$= \frac{1}{N}\left[1 + 2 \sum_{m=1}^{N-1} \frac{N-m}{N} \mathrm{Cov}\big(f(u^{(0)}), f(u^{(m)})\big)\right]$$

$$= \frac{\tau_N^2(f)}{N}.$$

The final result follows by the dominated convergence theorem. $\square$

***Remark* 6.3** Suppose that $\mathrm{Var}_\pi[f] = 1$. If, for $1 \leq n \leq N$, $u^{(n)} \sim \pi$ are independent, then we have that

$$\mathrm{Var}\left[\frac{1}{N} \sum_{n=1}^{N} f(u^{(n)})\right] = \frac{1}{N},$$

as we saw in the proof of Theorem 5.1 for standard Monte Carlo. Thus, if the *auto-correlations* $\mathrm{Cov}\big(f(u^{(0)}), f(u^{(m)})\big)$ are positive, then the ergodic average will be less accurate than estimated from an i.i.d. sample. This is because positively correlated random variables have redundant information so are less informative than i.i.d. random variables. On the other hand, if the correlations are negative ergodic averages may be more accurate than a direct Monte Carlo estimator with i.i.d. samples.

The theorem is stated in the idealized (and unrealistic) setting in which the Markov chain starts at the desired target distribution. In general, ergodicity is needed to ensure that chains initialized far from stationarity will converge to the desired target. Controlling the size of $\tau^2(f)$ and ensuring rapid convergence to stationarity are the two primary design goals when constructing Markov chains invariant with respect to $\pi$. ◇

Addressing the design and analysis of MCMC methods in generality and depth is beyond the scope of a single chapter; entire books are devoted to this subject! We will restrict our discussion to a particular class of MCMC methods, known as Metropolis–Hastings algorithms. We will prove that the desired target distribution is invariant for the Metropolis–Hastings kernel, and we will show *geometric ergodicity* of the pCN Metropolis–Hastings algorithm, meaning that the distribution $\pi_n$ of the $n$th sample approaches the invariant distribution exponentially fast in total variation distance. The idea is illustrated in Figure 6.1: after an initial number of *burn-in* steps, the samples from the chain start to concentrate in regions where the target distribution has the greatest mass. We will not discuss sample path ergodicity, noting simply that a general abstract theory exists to deduce it from geometric ergodicity.

Figure 6.1 The Markov chain samples points from distribution $\pi_n$ at step $n$, and the sampling distribution converges towards the target distribution $\pi$ whose high density regions are represented by the dashed circles.

## 6.3 Metropolis–Hastings Sampling

Here we outline the Metropolis–Hastings algorithm. The algorithm has two ingredients: a *proposal kernel* $q(u, v)$, which is a Markov transition kernel; and an acceptance probability $a(u, v)$ that will be used to convert the proposal kernel into a kernel $p_{\mathrm{MH}}(u, v)$ for which the given target $\pi$ is an invariant distribution. Given the $n$th sample $u^{(n)}$, we generate $u^{(n+1)}$ by drawing $v^\star$ from the distribution $q(u^{(n)}, \cdot)$. The result is accepted, which means setting $u^{(n+1)} = v^\star$, with probability $a(u^{(n)}, v^\star)$; it is rejected, meaning $u^{(n+1)} = u^{(n)}$, with the remaining probability $1 - a(u^{(n)}, v^\star)$. The acceptance probability is given by

$$a(u, v) = \min\left(\frac{\pi(v)q(v, u)}{\pi(u)q(u, v)}, 1\right). \tag{6.2}$$

---

**Algorithm 6.2** Metropolis–Hastings Algorithm

---

1: **Input**: Target distribution $\pi$, initial distribution $\pi_0$, Markov kernel $q(u, v)$, number of samples $N$.

2: **Initial Draw**: Draw initial sample $u^{(0)} \sim \pi_0$.

3: **Subsequent Samples**: For $n = 0, 1, \ldots, N - 1$ do:

   1 Sample $v^\star \sim q(u^{(n)}, \cdot)$.
   2 Calculate the acceptance probability $a_n := a(u^{(n)}, v^\star)$.
   3 Update

$$u^{(n+1)} = \begin{cases} v^\star, & \text{with probability } a_n, \\ u^{(n)}, & \text{with probability } 1 - a_n. \end{cases}$$

4: **Output**: Target approximation $\pi \approx \pi_{\text{MH}}^N := \frac{1}{N} \sum_{n=1}^{N} \delta(u - u^{(n)})$.

---

The estimator resulting from Algorithm 6.2 for $\pi(f)$ is then

$$\pi_{\text{MH}}^N(f) = \frac{1}{N} \sum_{n=1}^{N} f(u^{(n)}).$$

The Metropolis–Hastings algorithm implicitly defines a Markov kernel $p_{\text{MH}}(u, \cdot)$ which specifies the density of the $(n + 1)$th sample given that the $n$th sample is located at $u$. For $u \neq v$, the Metropolis–Hastings kernel has the following simple expression in terms of the proposal kernel and the acceptance probability

$$p_{\text{MH}}(u, v) = a(u, v)q(u, v); \tag{6.3}$$

this expression may be deduced noting that in order to move from $u$ to a new location $v$, the move needs to be proposed and accepted.

**Remark 6.4**   We note the following on the Metropolis–Hastings algorithm.

- In order to implement the Metropolis–Hastings algorithm one needs to be able to sample from the proposal kernel $q(u, \cdot)$ and evaluate the acceptance probability $a(u, v)$. Importantly, the target distribution only appears in the acceptance probability $a(u, v)$, and only the ratio $\pi(v)/\pi(u)$ is involved. Therefore, the Metropolis–Hastings algorithm may be implemented for target distributions that are only specified up to an unknown normalizing constant.

- If $q(u, v) = q(v, u)$ the acceptance probability simplifies to $\min\left(1, \pi(v)/\pi(u)\right)$. This is the setting in which the original *Metropolis algorithm* was introduced. In such a case, moves to regions of higher target density are always accepted, while moves to regions of smaller but non-zero target density are accepted with positive probability in order to ensure exploration of the target space. The quantity $\pi(u)q(u, v)$ should be viewed as a joint distribution on the pair $(u, v)$ with $u$ distributed according to the invariant distribution and $v \mid u$ then defined by the Markov kernel. In the general *Metropolis–Hastings algorithm setting*, when $q$ is not necessarily symmetric, the method favors moves that are easier to be reversed, in the sense that $\pi(v)q(v, u) > \pi(u)q(u, v)$.

- The Metropolis–Hastings algorithm is extremely flexible due to the freedom in the choice of proposal kernel $q(u, v)$. For this algorithm the ergodic behavior, and size of $\tau^2(\cdot)$, is heavily dependent on the choice of proposal kernel.

- The accept–reject step may be implemented by drawing, independently from the proposal, a uniformly distributed random variable $\theta_n$ in the interval $[0, 1]$. Recall $a_n$ as defined in Algorithm 6.1. If $\theta_n \in [0, a_n)$, then the proposal is accepted ($u^{(n+1)} = v^\star$); it is rejected ($u^{(n+1)} = u^{(n)}$) otherwise.

$\diamond$

## 6.4 Invariance of the Target Distribution $\pi$

In this section we show that the target $\pi$ is an invariant distribution for the Metropolis–Hastings kernel. We start by introducing the notion of detailed balance and showing that it implies invariance. We then prove that the Metropolis–Hastings kernel satisfies detailed balance with respect to $\pi$, and hence $\pi$ is invariant.

### 6.4.1 Detailed Balance and Its Implication

A Markov kernel $p(u, v)$ satisfies *detailed balance* with respect to $\pi$ if, for any $u, v \in \mathbb{R}^d$,

$$\pi(u)p(u, v) = \pi(v)p(v, u).$$

Detailed balance of $p(u, v)$ with respect to $\pi$ implies that $\pi$ is an invariant distribution for $p(u, v)$. To see this, note that if $p(u, v)$ satisfies detailed balance with respect to $\pi$, then

$$\int_{\mathbb{R}^d} \pi(u)p(u,v)\,du = \pi(v)\int_{\mathbb{R}^d} p(v,u)\,du = \pi(v).$$

Invariance guarantees that, if the chain is distributed according to $\pi$ at a given step, then it will also be distributed according to $\pi$ in the following step. Detailed balance guarantees that the in/out probability flux between any two states is preserved; this is a stronger condition, which implies invariance.

### 6.4.2 Detailed Balance and the Metropolis–Hastings Algorithm

The following theorem establishes the detailed balance of the Metropolis–Hastings kernel with respect to the target $\pi$; it implies, as a consequence, that the target is an invariant distribution for the Metropolis–Hastings kernel.

**Theorem 6.5** (Metropolis–Hastings and Detailed Balance)  *The Metropolis–Hastings kernel satisfies detailed balance with respect to the distribution* $\pi$.

*Proof*  We need to show that, for any $u,v \in \mathbb{R}^d$,

$$\pi(u)p_{\mathrm{MH}}(u,v) = \pi(v)p_{\mathrm{MH}}(v,u). \tag{6.4}$$

We let $v^\star$ denote the point proposed from kernel $q(u,\cdot)$, calculate the joint probability distribution of $(u, v^\star, v)$ and then integrate out $v^\star$ in order to identify $\pi(u)p_{\mathrm{MH}}(u,v)$. We first note that the random variable $v \mid (u, v^\star)$ has density

$$\delta_{v^\star}(v)a(u,v^\star) + \delta_u(v)\big(1 - a(u,v^\star)\big). \tag{6.5}$$

The density of $(u, v^\star)$ is found from the product of the density of $v^\star \mid u$ and the density of $u$ and is hence given by

$$q(u,v^\star)\pi(u). \tag{6.6}$$

Multiplying (6.5) and (6.6) gives the density of $(u, v^\star, v)$ and integrating out $v^\star$ gives the density of $(u,v)$, namely

$$\pi(u)p_{\mathrm{MH}}(u,v) = \pi(u)q(u,v)a(u,v) + \pi(u)\delta_u(v)\beta(u),$$

$$\beta(u) = \int_{\mathbb{R}^d}\big(1 - a(u,v^\star)\big)q(u,v^\star)dv^\star.$$

Now note that

$$q(u,v)a(u,v) = \min\!\left(\frac{\pi(v)q(v,u)}{\pi(u)q(u,v)}, 1\right)q(u,v)$$

$$= \frac{1}{\pi(u)} \times \min\!\big(\pi(u)q(u,v), \pi(v)q(v,u)\big).$$

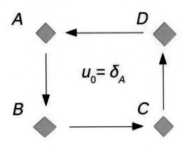

Figure 6.2 The arrows represent transitions with probability one in a four-state Markov chain. The invariant distribution is the uniform distribution but for $\pi_0 = \delta_A$, we have $\pi_1 = \delta_B$, $\pi_2 = \delta_C$, $\pi_3 = \delta_D$, $\pi_4 = \delta_A$, etc. Here $\pi_n$ does not converge to a limit distribution.

Thus, invoking symmetry,

$$\pi(u)q(u,v)a(u,v) = \min\big(\pi(u)q(u,v), \pi(v)q(v,u)\big) = \pi(v)q(v,u)a(v,u).$$

It is then apparent that $\pi(u)p_{\mathrm{MH}}(u,v)$ is symmetric with respect to the pair $(u,v)$, establishing (6.4) and completing the proof. □

Invariance of the Metropolis–Hastings kernel $p_{\mathrm{MH}}$ with respect to $\pi$ implies that if the initial sample is drawn from the target ($\pi_0 = \pi$), then all subsequent samples are also distributed according to the target ($\pi_n = \pi$).

## 6.5 Convergence to the Target Distribution

In the previous section we showed that if we initialize the Metropolis–Hastings algorithm with distribution $\pi$, all samples produced by the algorithm will be distributed according to $\pi$. But the motivation for the Metropolis–Hastings algorithm is that we are not able to directly sample from $\pi$. Our aim in this section is to show that, for certain Metropolis–Hastings methods, the law $\pi_n$ of the $n$th sample converges to $\pi$ regardless of the initial distribution $\pi_0$. This is a strong form of *ergodic* behavior which does not hold in general, as illustrated by the chain depicted in Figure 6.2.

In order to understand the mechanisms behind ergodicity we will first consider Markov chains with finite state-space. We then study a specific Metropolis–Hastings algorithm, known as the pCN (for *preconditioned Crank–Nicolson*) method, which applies to targets $\pi$ defined by their density with respect to a Gaussian distribution.

### 6.5.1 Finite State-Space

We consider a Markov chain on the finite state-space $S = \{1, \ldots, d\}$. The Markov kernel described earlier becomes a $d \times d$ *transition matrix* $P$ with non-negative entries $p(i, j)$ satisfying

$$\sum_{j \in S} p(i, j) = 1.$$

The invariant distribution becomes $d \times 1$ column vector $\pi$, with non-negative entries which sum to one, satisfying

$$\pi^\top = \pi^\top P. \tag{6.7}$$

Such an invariant distribution always exists but is not, in general, unique. The distribution at each step of the Markov chain is the $d \times 1$ column vector $\pi_n$ satisfying

$$\pi_{n+1}^\top = \pi_n^\top P, \tag{6.8}$$

where $\pi_0$ is the initial distribution of the chain. Ergodicity may be defined as convergence of the sequence $\pi_n$ to limit $\pi$ as $n \to \infty$; this is related to the eigenvalue 1 of $P$ having algebraic and geometric multiplicity one. We now illustrate a *coupling* approach to proving ergodicity and then, in the next subsection, generalize the methodology to study the pCN method on the continuous state-space $\mathbb{R}^d$.

**Theorem 6.6** (Ergodicity in Finite State-Space) *Let $\{u^{(n)}\}_{n \in \mathbb{Z}^+}$ be a Markov chain with state-space $S = \{1, \ldots, d\}$, transition matrix $P$ and initial distribution $\pi_0$. Assume that there is $\varepsilon > 0$ such that*

$$\min_{(i,j) \in S \times S} p(i, j) \geq \frac{\varepsilon}{d}. \tag{6.9}$$

*Then there is a unique solution $\pi$ to (6.7) within the class of probability vectors on $S$. Furthermore, the following convergence result holds for iteration (6.8):*

$$d_{\text{TV}}(\pi_n, \pi) \leq (1 - \varepsilon)^n. \tag{6.10}$$

*Proof* First note that the Markov matrix $P$ is a continuous map from the space of probability distributions on $S$ into itself; it thus continuously maps a compact, convex set into itself. By Brouwer's fixed point theorem it follows that $P$ has a fixed point in this space, ensuring that an invariant distribution $\pi$ solving (6.7) exists. We will now show that for any invariant distribution $\pi$ equation (6.10) holds, which also implies the uniqueness of the invariant distribution within the class of probability vectors.

Let $\pi$ be an invariant distribution, a probability vector on $S$. Proving convergence to equilibrium amounts to "forgetting the past," to show that the long-time behavior of the Markov chain does not depend on the initial distribution $\pi_0$ and in fact converges to $\pi$. In general, $u^{(n+1)}$ will be strongly dependent on $u^{(n)}$, but the condition given in (6.9) implies that there is always some residual chance that the chain jumps to any new state, at each step, independently of where it is currently located, $u^{(n)}$. This residual probability of the chain to make a "totally random" move will be shown to diminish the stochastic dependence on $u^{(0)}$ as $n$ increases.

To formalize this idea, let $b_n$ be i.i.d. Bernoulli random variables with $\mathbb{P}(b_n = 1) = \varepsilon$ and $\mathbb{P}(b_n = 0) = 1 - \varepsilon$; furthermore assume that the sequence $\{b_n\}$ is independent of the randomness defining draws from $\{p(u^{(n)}, \cdot)\}$. Define $r$ to be the uniform transition kernel with equal probability of transitioning to each state in $S : r(i, j) = d^{-1}$ for all $(i, j) \in S \times S$.

Using the lower bound on $p$ we may define a new Markov chain $\{w^{(n)}\}_{n \in \mathbb{Z}^+}$ as follows:

$$w^{(n+1)} \sim \begin{cases} s(w^{(n)}, \cdot), \text{ for } b_n = 0, \\ r(w^{(n)}, \cdot), \text{ for } b_n = 1, \end{cases} \tag{6.11}$$

where

$$s(i, j) := \frac{p(i, j) - \varepsilon r(i, j)}{1 - \varepsilon}.$$

We make two observations about this construction. First, the lower bound of $\varepsilon/d$ on $p(i, j)$ means that the probability transition matrix $s$ is well defined; second, the fact that $r(i, j)$ is independent of $i$ is key, as it means that sampling explicitly forgets the current state whenever $b_n = 1$. We may now compute

$$\mathbb{P}\left(w^{(n+1)} = j \mid w^{(n)} = i\right) = \varepsilon \, \mathbb{P}\left(w^{(n+1)} = j \mid w^{(n)} = i, b_n = 1\right)$$
$$+ (1 - \varepsilon) \, \mathbb{P}\left(w^{(n+1)} = j \mid w^{(n)} = i, b_n = 0\right)$$
$$= \varepsilon r(i, j) + p(i, j) - \varepsilon r(i, j)$$
$$= p(i, j).$$

Thus the kernel defined by (6.11) is equivalent in law to that defined by matrix $P$. However, by introducing the ancillary random variables $b_n$, we have made explicit the concept of "forgetting the past entirely, with a small probability" at every step. We may now use this to complete the proof. Let $f : S \mapsto \mathbb{R}$ be an arbitrary test function with $|f|_\infty \leq 1$ and $\tau := \min(n \in \mathbb{N} : b_n = 1)$. Then, regardless of how $w^{(0)}$ is initialized,

$$\mathbb{E}\left[f\left(w^{(n)}\right)\right] = \mathbb{E}\left[f\left(w^{(n)}\right) \mid \tau \geq n\right]\mathbb{P}(\tau \geq n) + \sum_{l=0}^{n-1}\mathbb{E}\left[f\left(w^{(n)}\right) \mid \tau = l\right]\mathbb{P}(\tau = l)$$

$$= \underbrace{\mathbb{E}\left[f\left(w^{(n)}\right) \mid \tau \geq n\right]\mathbb{P}(\tau \geq n)}_{|\cdot| \leq (1-\varepsilon)^n} + \underbrace{\sum_{l=0}^{n-1}\mathbb{E}^{w^{(0)} \sim \mathfrak{u}(\cdot)}\left[f\left(w^{(n-l)}\right)\right]\mathbb{P}(\tau=l)}_{\text{independent of original initial distribution}},$$

where $\mathfrak{u}$ denotes the uniform distribution on $S$.

Now consider two Markov chains $\{w^{(n)}\}$ and $\{w^{(n)'}\}$ with kernel (6.11), the first initialized from $\pi_0$ and the second from an invariant distribution $\pi$; denote their distributions at time $n$ by $\pi_n$ and $\pi_n'$, respectively. The law of $w^{(n)}$ agrees with the law $\pi_n$ of the original chain $u^{(n)}$ when initialized at $\pi_0$; on the other hand, for the second chain it follows from invariance that $\pi_n' = \pi$. We will use the variational characterization of the total variation distance established in Lemma 1.10. Employing the preceding identity and noting that the contribution which is independent of the initial distribution will cancel in the two different Markov chains, we obtain

$$d_{\text{TV}}(\pi_n, \pi_n') = \frac{1}{2}\sup_{|f|_\infty \leq 1}\left|\mathbb{E}^{\pi_n}[f(u)] - \mathbb{E}^{\pi_n'}[f(u)]\right| \leq (1-\varepsilon)^n.$$

Since $\pi_n' = \pi$ the desired result follows. $\qquad\square$

Before extending the above argument to a setting with continuous state-space, we make two remarks:

**Remark 6.7** The coupling proof we have just exhibited may be generalized in a number of ways; in particular:

- The distribution $r$ does not need to be uniform; it was only chosen so for convenience. What is important is that $r(i, j)$ is lower bounded, independently of $i$, for all $j$. Adapting $r$ to the matrix $P$ at hand, might in some cases greatly improve the above bound – a larger $\varepsilon$ might be identified.
- Convergence to equilibrium can also be shown if condition (6.9) holds with $P$ replaced by the $n$-step transition Markov matrix $P^n$. Again, for some chains this may yield faster bounds on the convergence to equilibrium.

$\diamond$

### 6.5.2 The pCN Method

The coupling argument used in the previous subsection for Markov chains with finite state-space may also be employed to study ergodicity of Markov chains on a continuous state-space. To illustrate this, we consider a particular Metropolis–Hastings algorithm, the pCN method, applied to a specific Bayesian inverse problem setting. Before we get into the details of this setting, we describe the idea behind the pCN method at a high level. The idea is this. If the desired target distribution has the form

$$\pi(u) = \frac{1}{Z}\tilde{l}(u)\tilde{\rho}(u) \tag{6.12}$$

and if the Metropolis–Hastings proposal kernel $q$ satisfies detailed balance with respect to $\tilde{\rho}$, then (6.2) simplifies to give

$$a(u, v) = \min\left(\frac{\tilde{\rho}(v)\tilde{l}(v)q(v, u)}{\tilde{\rho}(u)\,\tilde{l}(u)q(u, v)}, 1\right) = \min\left(\frac{\tilde{l}(v)}{\tilde{l}(u)}, 1\right). \tag{6.13}$$

We will apply and study this idea in the case where $\tilde{\rho}$ is a Gaussian distribution, in which case it is straightforward to construct a proposal kernel that satisfies detailed balance with respect to $\tilde{\rho}$. This scenario arises naturally in Bayesian inverse problems where the prior is either a Gaussian, or it is naturally expressed via density which is the product of a Gaussian with another function. We now formalize the inverse problem setting that we consider by imposing certain assumptions on the likelihood and the prior, and then relate both to the functions $\tilde{l}$ and $\tilde{\rho}$ in equation (6.12).

**Assumption 6.8**   *We make the following assumptions on the Bayesian inverse problem:*

- *Bounded likelihood: there are* $l^-, l^+ > 0$ *such that, for all* $u \in \mathbb{R}^d$,

$$0 < l^- < l(u) < l^+.$$

- *Truncated Gaussian prior: there is a compact set* $B \subset \mathbb{R}^d$ *of positive Lebesgue measure such that* $\rho(u) \propto \mathbb{1}_B(u)z(u)$, *where* $z$ *is the pdf of Gaussian* $\mathcal{N}(0, \widehat{C})$.

  Under Assumption 6.8 we obtain for the posterior density

$$\pi(u) \propto l(u)\mathbb{1}_B(u)z(u),$$

which is of the form in equation (6.12) with $\tilde{l}(u) = l(u)\mathbb{1}_B(u)$ and $\tilde{\rho}(u) = z(u)$. The pCN method is a Metropolis–Hastings algorithm with proposal kernel

$$q(u, \cdot) \sim \mathcal{N}\left((1 - \beta^2)^{1/2}u, \beta^2\widehat{C}\right), \tag{6.14}$$

where $\beta \in (0, 1]$ is a user-specified parameter that should be tuned to obtain an acceptance probability that, on average, stays away from 0 or $1$ – for example one that is approximately $1/2$. Thus, given the sample $u^{(n)}$, the pCN proposes a new sample

$$v^{\star} \sim \left(1 - \beta^2\right)^{1/2} u^{(n)} + \beta \xi^{(n)}, \quad \xi^{(n)} \sim \mathcal{N}(0, \widehat{C}),$$

which only requires to sample a Gaussian. Note that

$$\mathbb{E}\left[v^{\star}(v^{\star})^{\top}\right] = (1 - \beta^2) \, \mathbb{E}\left[u^{(n)}(u^{(n)})^{\top}\right] + \beta^2 \widehat{C},$$

demonstrating that if $u^{(n)} \sim \mathcal{N}(0, \widehat{C})$ then the proposal satisfies $v^{\star} \sim \mathcal{N}(0, \widehat{C})$ as well. The following lemma shows the stronger result that the proposal kernel satisfies detailed balance with respect to $z$.

**Lemma 6.9** *The proposal kernel* (6.14) *satisfies detailed balance with respect to the pdf $z$ of Gaussian $\mathcal{N}(0, \widehat{C})$.*

*Proof* Recall the notation for the covariance-weighted inner product and resulting norm described in the introduction to these notes. We need to show that $z(v)q(v, u)$ is symmetric in $u$ and $v$. By direct calculation,

$$
\begin{aligned}
-\log\big(z(v)q(v, u)\big) &= \frac{1}{2}|v|_{\widehat{C}}^2 + \frac{1}{2\beta^2}\left|u - \left(1 - \beta^2\right)^{1/2} v\right|_{\widehat{C}}^2 \\
&= \left(\frac{1}{2} + \frac{(1 - \beta^2)}{2\beta^2}\right)|v|_{\widehat{C}}^2 + \frac{1}{2\beta^2}|u|_{\widehat{C}}^2 - \frac{(1 - \beta^2)^{1/2}}{\beta^2}\langle u, v\rangle_{\widehat{C}} \\
&= \frac{1}{2\beta^2}\left(|v|_{\widehat{C}}^2 + |u|_{\widehat{C}}^2\right) - \frac{(1 - \beta^2)^{1/2}}{\beta^2}\langle u, v\rangle_{\widehat{C}}.
\end{aligned}
$$

$\square$

We now display the pCN algorithm applied in the setting of Assumption 6.8 and describe how it leads to an estimator of $\pi(f)$. The expression for the acceptance probability in Algorithm 6.3 follows from equation (6.13) using Lemma 6.9 and noting that $\pi_0$ being supported on $B$ implies that $u^{(n)} \in B$ for all $n$, as any proposed move out of $B$ will be rejected. Thus, $\mathbb{1}_B(u)$ may be dropped from the formula for the acceptance probability in equation (6.13).

---

**Algorithm 6.3** pCN Algorithm

---

1: **Input**: Tuning parameter $\beta \in (0, 1)$, covariance $\widehat{C}$, bounded set $B$, likelihood function $g$, initial distribution $\pi_0$ supported on $B$, number of samples $N$.

2: **Initial Draw**: Draw initial sample $u^{(0)} \sim \pi_0$.

3: **Subsequent Samples**: For $n = 0, 1, \ldots, N - 1$ do:

   1 Sample $v^\star \sim \mathcal{N}\left((1 - \beta^2)^{1/2} u^{(n)}, \beta^2 \widehat{C}\right)$.

   2 Calculate the acceptance probability $a_n := a(u^{(n)}, v^\star)$ where

$$a(u, v) = \min\left(\frac{\mathsf{l}(v)}{\mathsf{l}(u)} \mathbb{1}_B(v), 1\right).$$

   3 Update

$$u^{(n+1)} = \begin{cases} v^\star, & \text{with probability } a_n, \\ u^{(n)}, & \text{with probability } 1 - a_n. \end{cases}$$

4: **Output**: Target approximation $\pi \approx \pi_{\text{pCN}}^N := \frac{1}{N} \sum_{n=1}^N \delta(u - u^{(n)})$.

---

The estimator for $\pi(f)$ resulting from Algorithm 6.3 is then

$$\pi_{\text{pCN}}^N(f) = \frac{1}{N} \sum_{n=1}^N f(u^{(n)}).$$

We can now prove ergodicity using similar techniques to those employed in the previous subsection in the finite state-space setting. The main idea is that, restricted to the bounded set $B$, the probability density of the transition kernel is bounded away from zero by some $\varepsilon$. Splitting off a "forgetful part" that is triggered with probability $\varepsilon$ then yields the result.

**Theorem 6.10** (Ergodicity for pCN Method) *Assume that we apply the pCN method to sample from a posterior density $\pi$ arising from Assumptions 6.8 with initial condition drawn from any density supported on $B$. Then there exists a constant $\varepsilon \in (0, 1)$ such that*

$$d_{\text{TV}}(\pi_n, \pi) \leq (1 - \varepsilon)^n,$$

*where $\pi_n$ is the law of the $n$th sample from the pCN Metropolis–Hastings algorithm.*

*Proof of Theorem 6.10* Note again that since $u^{(0)} \in B$ we have $u^{(n)} \in B$ for all $n \geq 1$. Note further that since $B$ is compact and $q$ is continuous in both of its arguments, there is $q^- > 0$ such that, for any $u, v \in B$,

$$q(u, v) \geq q^-.$$

Let $p$ be the Markov kernel defined by the pCN Metropolis–Hastings algorithm. It follows that, for $u, v \in B$,

$$p(u, v) \geq q(u, v)a(u, v)$$

$$\geq q^- \frac{g^-}{g^+} =: \varepsilon \text{Leb}(B),$$

where the last equation defines $\varepsilon$ and $\text{Leb}(B)$ denotes the Lebesgue measure of $B$ (which is assumed to be positive). Analogously to the discrete proof, we now define $b_n$ to be i.i.d. Bernoulli random variables with $\mathbb{P}(b_n = 1) = \varepsilon$, independently of all other randomness, and consider the transition rule

$$u^{(n+1)} \sim \begin{cases} s(u^{(n)}, \cdot), & \text{for } b_n = 0, \\ r(\cdot), & \text{for } b_n = 1, \end{cases}$$

where $r$ denotes the uniform distribution on $B$ and, for $A \subset B$ and $u \in B$,

$$s(u, A) := \frac{p(u, A) - \varepsilon r(A)}{1 - \varepsilon}.$$

Just as in the discrete case, one can check that the resulting Markov kernel is equal to the pCN Metropolis–Hastings kernel $p(\cdot, \cdot)$. Furthermore, exponential convergence is then deduced in exactly the same way as in the discrete case. □

## 6.6 Discussion and Bibliography

The idea of sampling a target distribution $\pi$ by means of a $\pi$-invariant Markov chain was introduced in the statistical physics community in Metropolis et al. (1953), where a symmetric proposal kernel was used. A powerful generalization of the method was given by Hastings (1970) which allowed for asymmetric proposal kernels. The Bayesian methodology (Gelman et al., 2013), and in particular MCMC-based exploration of the posterior, became practical as a result of advances in computer power and were widely adopted for many sampling problems arising in science and engineering.

Gamerman and Lopes (2006) is a useful basic introduction to MCMC and Brooks et al. (2011) presents state of the art as of 2010. Cotter et al. (2013) overviews the pCN method and related MCMC algorithms specifically designed for inverse problems and other sampling problems in high-dimensional state-spaces. Lindvall (2002) describes the coupling method in a general setting. The book of Meyn and Tweedie (2012) contains a wide-ranging presentation of Markov chains, and their long-time behavior, including ergodicity and coupling. Furthermore, it describes the general framework for going from convergence of expectations in (possibly weighted) total variation distances to sample path ergodicity and almost-sure convergence of time averages, a topic we did not cover in this chapter. Mattingly et al. (2002) describes the coupling technique in the context of stochastic differential equations and their approximations.

The tuning of parameters in MCMC, such as the parameter $\beta$ appearing in the pCN method, is key to their success. If the goal of the MCMC sampling method is to approximate the expectation of a given test function $f$, then the aim of parameter tuning is to minimize the integrated auto-correlation $\tau^2(f)$ defined in Theorem 6.2. In general different $f$ will lead to different optimal proposal parameter choices; however, for a wide class of high-dimensional target distributions and specific proposal kernels there are generic rules of thumb, independent of $f$, for tuning parameters in the proposal (Roberts et al., 2001). This universality often arises from using suboptimal algorithms and, for specific problems, can be circumvented by using tailored proposals. For example, for target measures that have a density with respect to a Gaussian, the pCN proposal is preferable to the random walk Metropolis proposal, as demonstrated in Cotter et al. (2013), Hairer et al. (2014), and Garcia Trillos et al. (2020). Stochastic Newton MCMC methods for sampling posterior distributions in function space Bayesian inverse problems are studied in Petra et al. (2014).

# Exercises for Part I

**Exercise 1** (Hellinger Distance between Gaussians)  Recall the Hellinger distance $d_{\mathrm{H}}$ between two probability densities introduced in Definition 1.7. Consider two Gaussian densities on $\mathbb{R}$: $p_1 = \mathcal{N}(\mu_1, \sigma_1^2)$ and $p_2 = \mathcal{N}(\mu_2, \sigma_2^2)$. Show that the squared Hellinger distance between them is given by

$$d_{\mathrm{H}}(p_1, p_2)^2 = 1 - \sqrt{\exp\left(-\frac{(\mu_1 - \mu_2)^2}{2(\sigma_1^2 + \sigma_2^2)}\right)\frac{2\sigma_1\sigma_2}{(\sigma_1^2 + \sigma_2^2)}}\,.$$

**Exercise 2** (Kullback–Leibler Divergence between Gaussians)  Recall the Kullback–Leibler divergence $d_{\mathrm{KL}}$ introduced in Definition 4.1. Does $d_{\mathrm{KL}}$ define a metric on probability measures? Justify your answer. Consider two Gaussian densities on $\mathbb{R}$: $p_1 = \mathcal{N}(\mu_1, \sigma_1^2)$ and $p_2 = \mathcal{N}(\mu_2, \sigma_2^2)$. Show that the Kullback–Leibler divergence between them is given by

$$d_{\mathrm{KL}}(p_1 \| p_2) = \log\left(\frac{\sigma_2}{\sigma_1}\right) + \frac{1}{2}\left(\frac{\sigma_1^2}{\sigma_2^2} - 1\right) + \frac{(\mu_2 - \mu_1)^2}{2\sigma_2^2}\,.$$

Generalize this result to Gaussians $p_1 = \mathcal{N}(\mu_1, \Sigma_1)$ and $p_2 = \mathcal{N}(\mu_2, \Sigma_2)$ in $d$ dimensions, with positive definite $\Sigma_1$ and $\Sigma_2$, to obtain the formula in Example 4.2.

**Exercise 3** (Bound between Hellinger and Kullback–Leibler)  Verify the inequality

$$d_{\mathrm{H}}(p_1, p_2)^2 \leq \frac{1}{2}d_{\mathrm{KL}}(p_1 \| p_2)$$

for the one-dimensional Gaussian examples in the two previous exercises.

**Exercise 4** (Well-Posedness of Inverse Problem under Data Perturbation)  Consider the inverse problem $y = G(u) + \eta$ and noise $\eta \sim \mathcal{N}(0, \gamma^2 I_k)$. Suppose that there is $G^+$ such that $|G(u)| \leq G^+$ for any $u \in \mathbb{R}^d$. Let $y, y'$ with $|y|, |y'| \leq r$ be two instances of the data and let $\pi^y$ and $\pi^{y'}$ be the two corresponding posterior distributions with the same prior $\rho = \mathcal{N}(0, \lambda^{-1}I_d)$. Show that there is $c > 0$ such that $d_{\mathrm{H}}(\pi^y, \pi^{y'}) \leq c|y - y'|$.

**Exercise 5** (Randomized Maximum Likelihood)   Let $u_0^{(n)} \sim \mathcal{N}(\widehat{m}, \widehat{C})$ i.i.d. with $\widehat{C}$ positive definite. Let $u^{(n)}$ be the minimizer of

$$\mathsf{J}^{(n)}(u) := \frac{1}{2}|u - u_0^{(n)}|_{\widehat{C}}^2 + \frac{1}{2}|y + \Gamma^{1/2}\xi^{(n)} - Au|_{\Gamma}^2, \qquad \xi^{(n)} \sim \mathcal{N}(0, I) \text{ i.i.d.}$$

Assume also that $\{u_0^{(n)}\}$ and $\{\xi^{(n)}\}$ are mutually independent i.i.d. sequences. Show that $u^{(n)} \sim \mathcal{N}(m, C)$ i.i.d., where $m$ and $C$ are defined by

$$m := \widehat{m} + K(y - A\widehat{m}),$$
$$C := (I - KA)\widehat{C},$$

and

$$K := \widehat{C}A^\top(A\widehat{C}A^\top + \Gamma)^{-1}.$$

**Exercise 6** (Convergence of Gradient Descent)

(i) Suppose that $\mathsf{J}\colon \mathbb{R}^d \to \mathbb{R}$ has $r$-Lipschitz gradient. Show that, for any $u, v \in \mathbb{R}^d$, it holds that

$$\mathsf{J}(v) \leq \mathsf{J}(u) + \langle D\mathsf{J}(u), v - u \rangle + \frac{r}{2}|v - u|^2.$$

(ii) Let $r > 0$ be a real number. We say that $\mathsf{J}$ satisfies an $r$-Polyak–Lojasiewicz ($r$-PL) condition if, for all $u \in \mathbb{R}^d$, it holds that $r(\mathsf{J}(u) - \mathsf{J}^\star) \leq \frac{1}{2}|D\mathsf{J}(u)|^2$. Suppose that $\mathsf{J}$ has an $r$-Lipschitz gradient, satisfies a $c$-PL condition with $0 < c < r$, and achieves its infimum $\mathsf{J}^\star$. Show that the gradient descent algorithm with step-size $r^{-1}$ given by

$$u_{\ell+1} = u_\ell - r^{-1}D\mathsf{J}(u_\ell), \quad \ell = 0, 1, \ldots$$

has a linear convergence rate. More precisely, show that

$$\mathsf{J}(u_\ell) - \mathsf{J}^\star \leq \left(1 - \frac{c}{r}\right)^\ell \left(\mathsf{J}(u_0) - \mathsf{J}^\star\right).$$

(iii) We say that $\mathsf{J}$ is $r$-strongly convex if, for all $u, v \in \mathbb{R}^d$, it holds that

$$\mathsf{J}(v) \geq \mathsf{J}(u) + \langle \nabla\mathsf{J}(u), v - u \rangle + \frac{r}{2}|v - u|^2.$$

Show that $r$-strong convexity implies an $r$-PL condition.

**Exercise 7** (Best Gaussian Approximation)   Consider the inverse problem of recovering $u \in \mathbb{R}$ from data $y \in \mathbb{R}$ related by

$$y = u + 0.1u^3 + \eta, \qquad \eta \sim \mathcal{N}(0, 0.4).$$

Assume a Gaussian prior $\rho(u) = \mathcal{N}(0.5, 1)$, and that the observed data is $y = 1.1$. Write down the posterior pdf $\pi$ of $u$ given $y$ (up to a normalizing constant) and plot it. Propose an algorithm to find the best Gaussian approximation $d_{\mathrm{KL}}(p\|\pi)$ and an algorithm to find the best Gaussian approximation $d_{\mathrm{KL}}(\pi\|p)$. Implement your proposed algorithms and report your results by writing the means and variances that your algorithms output, and plotting the corresponding Gaussian pdfs along with the posterior $\pi$.

**Exercise 8** (Inferring Correlation from Data)   In this problem you will invent an MCMC algorithm for a simple inference problem with Gaussians. Specifically, we will infer the correlation between two Gaussian random variables. Consider the model $(y, z) \sim \mathcal{N}(\mu, \Sigma)$, with:

$$\mu = \begin{bmatrix} 0 \\ 0 \end{bmatrix}; \qquad \Sigma = \Sigma(u) = \begin{bmatrix} 1 & u \\ u & 1 \end{bmatrix}.$$

Draw $N = 1000$ i.i.d. samples from the distribution $(y, z) \sim \mathcal{N}(\mu, \Sigma(0)) = \mathcal{N}(0, I_2)$; henceforth we refer to this as the data. You will develop a Metropolis–Hastings MCMC algorithm to find the posterior distribution of $u$, given the data; you already know that the data was generated using $u = 0$ which provides intuition as you develop the algorithm. There are multiple aspects to developing this algorithm: finding the likelihood, constructing a prior, specifying a proposal distribution, and determining the acceptance function. In the next few parts, you will be stepped through developing each ingredient.

(i)  Show that the likelihood $\mathbb{P}(\{y^{(i)}, z^{(i)}\}_{i=1}^{N} \mid u)$ is given by:

$$\prod_{i=1}^{N} \mathbb{P}(y^{(i)}, z^{(i)} \mid u) = \prod_{i=1}^{N} \frac{1}{2\pi\sqrt{1 - u^2}}$$
$$\times \exp\left( -\frac{1}{2(1 - u^2)} \left[ (y^{(i)})^2 - 2u y^{(i)} z^{(i)} + (z^{(i)})^2 \right] \right).$$

(ii)  Consider Jeffreys prior $\mathbb{P}(u) = \frac{1/\pi}{|\det(\Sigma(u))|^{1/2}}$. Show that this defines a probability distribution and, for our specific choice of $\Sigma(u)$, has a closed form expression equal to $1/\{\pi(1 - u^2)^{1/2}\}$.

(iii)  Consider the posterior distribution $\mathbb{P}(u \mid \{y^{(i)}, z^{(i)}\}_{i=1}^{N})$.

(iv)  Consider the proposal distribution

$$v^{\star} \sim \mathrm{Uniform}\left( u^{(n)} - 0.1, u^{(n)} + 0.1 \right).$$

This proposal distribution is symmetric with respect to $u^{(n)}$, meaning that there is equal probability of moving in either direction of $u^{(n)}$. The Metropolis–Hastings algorithms with these types of proposal distributions are often referred to as *random walk Metropolis algorithms*. Using this proposal distribution, find the acceptance probability function. Starting from $u^{(0)} = 0.1$ and after a burn-in time of $10^4$ samples, execute the Markov chain to generate $\overline{N} = 10^3$ samples. Keep a running sample mean and variance in the burn-in period. Plot the sample mean and variance as a function of $n$. Discuss your findings.

*Observation 1*: The running sample mean and variance are often used as a diagnosis for the convergence of the Markov chain.

*Observation 2*: Note that an on-line method for computing the running sample mean and running sample variance is given by:

$$m^{(n+1)} = \frac{n\, m^{(n)} + u^{(n+1)}}{n+1} \qquad c^{(n+1)} = \frac{(n-1)\, c^{(n)} + (u^{(n+1)} - m^{(n+1)})^2}{n}.$$

(v) Repeat the previous experiment but with the step-size of the proposal distribution changed from 0.1 to 0.4. That is, consider the proposal $v^\star \sim$ Uniform$(u^{(n)} - 0.4, u^{(n)} + 0.4)$. What do you observe about the convergence rate of the MCMC algorithm?

**Exercise 9** (Gibbs Sampling)    In this problem we consider Gibbs sampling, an MCMC algorithm for generating approximate samples from a multivariate distribution. Gibbs sampling is used when the conditional distribution of a variable conditioned on the rest is tractable (you will see an example in the next problem). In particular, for a discrete random vector $y = (y_1, y_2, \ldots, y_p) \in \mathbb{R}^p$, the Gibbs sampling algorithm is given by:

---
**Algorithm  Gibbs Sampling**
---
1: **Input**: joint distribution $\pi_0$ among collection of $p$ random variables.
2: **Initial Sample**: some initial value $y^{(0)} \sim \pi_0 \in \mathbb{R}^p$.
3: **Subsequent Samples**: For $n = 1, \ldots, N$,

$\vdots$

4: **Output**: sample $y^{(N)}$.

---

There is an intimate connection between Gibbs sampling and the Metropolis–Hastings algorithm as we now show, through two steps.

(i) First, consider the state $\left(y_1^{(n-1)}, y_2^{(n-1)}, \ldots, y_p^{(n-1)}\right)$. Let

$$v^\star \sim \mathbb{P}\left(y_1 \mid y_2^{(n-1)}, \ldots, y_p^{(n-1)}\right).$$

According to the Gibbs sampling algorithm, with probability 1, we transition to the state $\left(v^\star, y_2^{(n-1)}, \ldots, y_p^{(n-1)}\right)$. Show that this choice of proposal kernel for $v^\star$ satisfies the detailed balance equation with respect to the joint distribution.

(ii) Prove that with this choice of Markov kernel, the acceptance function in the Metropolis–Hastings algorithm reduces to 1. Hence, Gibbs sampling is indeed a special case of the Metropolis–Hastings algorithm.

**Exercise 10** (The Ising Model)   Graphical models are a family of multivariate distributions which are Markov in accordance to a particular undirected graph. Each node in the graph $i \in V$ is associated to a random variable. The set of edges $E \subset \binom{V}{2}$ encodes the conditional dependency relationships: a variable conditioned on its neighbors is independent of the remaining variables.

In this problem we focus on the setting where the collection of random variables $\{y_i\}_{i=1}^P$ take on discrete values $\pm 1$. This is known as the Ising model and is described with the following joint distribution over the variables $y$:

$$\mathbb{P}(y) = \frac{1}{Z} \exp\left( \sum_{\{s,t\} \in E} u_{s,t} y_s y_t \right).$$

Here $u \in \mathbb{R}^{P \times P}$ encodes the graph structure. (We set the diagonal elements of $u$ to be zero.) In particular, $u_{s,t}$ is non-zero if variables $s$ and $t$ are connected via an edge.

(i) Suppose that you were tasked with sampling from this joint distribution. One possible approach would be to use importance sampling, a technique that is based on sampling from another distribution, and reweighting the samples based on the likelihood of the original joint distribution. While this is a natural approach, it becomes intractable in the setting where the number of variables $p$ is large (say $p = 20$). Why?

(ii) Show that the conditional distribution of a variable $y_r$ given the rest $(y_{V \setminus r})$ is given by:

$$\mathbb{P}(y_r \mid y_{V \setminus r}) = \frac{\exp(2y_r \sum_{t \in V \setminus r} u_{rt} y_t)}{\exp(2y_r \sum_{t \in V \setminus r} u_{rt} y_t) + 1}.$$

*Observation:* Notice that sampling from the conditional distribution is tractable. Why? This suggests that Gibbs sampling could be used to draw samples from the joint distribution.

(iii) We consider a specific example to showcase the use of Gibbs sampling for this problem. Consider a collection of $y \in \mathbb{R}^5$ discrete variables specified by the following $u^\star \in \mathbb{R}^{5\times5}$:

$$u^\star = \begin{bmatrix} 0 & 0.5 & 0 & 0.5 & 0 \\ 0.5 & 0 & 0.5 & 0 & 0.5 \\ 0 & 0.5 & 0 & 0.5 & 0 \\ 0.5 & 0 & 0.5 & 0 & 0 \\ 0 & 0.5 & 0 & 0 & 0 \end{bmatrix}.$$

Using a Gibbs sampler with initialization $y^{(0)} = \begin{pmatrix} 1 & -1 & -1 & 1 & 1 \end{pmatrix}^\mathsf{T}$ and burn-in period of 5000 samples, draw $N = 1000$ samples from the joint distribution. Report the sample mean and sample variance for each of the variables. From your samples, compute a correlation matrix of all the five variables and plot an image of the correlation values. Do you see a pattern? Does this confirm the validity of the sampling technique?

(iv) You will now reverse engineer $u$ from the samples you generated! You will use the Metropolis–Hastings algorithm to get the posterior distribution $\mathbb{P}(u \mid \{y^{(i)}\}_{i=1}^N)$. Notice that $u$ is symmetric and has zeros on the diagonal, meaning that there are $p(p - 1)/2$ free parameters. Hence we work with a vector $\tilde{u} \in \mathbb{R}^{p(p-1)/2}$ containing all the degrees of freedom of $u$. Recall that for Metropolis–Hastings, we need to construct a prior on $\tilde{u}$ and a proposal distribution. Since we expect the graph structure to be sparse (i.e. $\tilde{u}$ sparse), a natural prior on each element of $\tilde{u}_i$ is the Laplace distribution $\tilde{u}_i \sim \text{Laplace}(0, \lambda)$ i.i.d. Further, we use a random-walk proposal distribution:

$$v^\star \sim \tilde{u}^{(n)} + \mathcal{N}(0, \sigma^2 I),$$

with $\sigma^2 = 0.1$. With $\lambda = 0.2$ and a burn-in time of $10\,000$ samples, use Metropolis–Hastings to generate $\overline{N} = 1000$ samples from the posterior $\mathbb{P}(u \mid \{y^{(i)}\}_{i=1}^N)$. Compute and report the sample mean and variance of these samples. Do your findings match the underlying $u^\star$?

*Observation*: The acceptance probability function in the Metropolis–Hastings algorithm often removes the normalization constant in the target probability distribution. In this scenario, this does not happen. Why? What does this say about this method for large $p$?

(v) Suppose that the likelihood $\mathbb{P}(y_1, y_2, \ldots, y_p \mid u)$ is well approximated by:

$$\mathbb{P}(y_1, y_2, \ldots, y_p \mid u) \approx \prod_{r=1}^p \mathbb{P}(y_r \mid y_{V \setminus r}, u).$$

The expression on the right is sometimes referred to as the pseudo log-likelihood. Show that with this approximation, the MAP estimator of $u$ is given by:

$$\arg\min_{\substack{u,\, u=u^\top \\ \operatorname{diag}(u)=0}} \sum_{i=1}^{N}\sum_{r=1}^{p} -\log\left(\mathbb{P}(y_r^{(i)} \mid y_{V\setminus r}^{(i)}, u)\right) + \frac{1}{\lambda}\|\tilde{u}\|_{\ell_1}.$$

# PART II

## DATA ASSIMILATION

# 7

# Filtering and Smoothing Problems and Well-Posedness

In this chapter we introduce data assimilation problems in which the model of interest, and the data associated with it, have a time-ordered nature. We distinguish between the filtering problem (on-line) in which the data is incorporated sequentially as it comes in, and the smoothing problem (off-line) which is a specific instance of the inverse problems that have been the subject of the preceding chapters. We formulate the filtering and smoothing problems in Section 7.1. After that, we focus on the smoothing problem in Section 7.2 and describe its interpretation as an inverse problem. This interpretation will allow us to seamlessly apply to the smoothing problem the well-posedness theory for inverse problems developed in Chapter 1. Section 7.3 is concerned with the on-line filtering problem. We will establish well-posedness of the filtering problem in total variation distance as a corollary of the well-posedness of the smoothing problem. We will also provide a roadmap for filtering methods that will be introduced in subsequent chapters, highlighting the settings in which they will be presented. Section 7.4 closes with extensions and bibliographical remarks.

## 7.1 Formulation of Filtering and Smoothing Problems

Consider the *stochastic dynamics model* given by

$$v_{j+1} = \Psi(v_j) + \xi_j, \ j \in \mathbb{Z}^+,$$
$$v_0 \sim \mathcal{N}(m_0, C_0), \ \xi_j \sim \mathcal{N}(0, \Sigma) \text{ i.i.d.,}$$

where we assume that $v_0$ is independent of the sequence $\{\xi_j\}$; this is often written as $v_0 \perp \{\xi_j\}$. Now we add the *data model* given by

$$y_{j+1} = h(v_{j+1}) + \eta_{j+1}, \ j \in \mathbb{Z}^+,$$
$$\eta_j \sim \mathcal{N}(0, \Gamma) \text{ i.i.d.},$$

where we assume that $\{\eta_j\} \perp v_0$ for all $j$ and $\eta_k \perp \xi_j$ for all $j, k$. The following will be assumed in the remainder of these notes.

**Assumption 7.1**   *The matrices $C_0$, $\Sigma$ and $\Gamma$ are positive definite. Further, we have $\Psi \in C(\mathbb{R}^d, \mathbb{R}^d)$ and $h \in C(\mathbb{R}^d, \mathbb{R}^k)$.*

We define, for a given and fixed integer $J$,

$$V := \{v_0, \ldots, v_J\}, \ Y := \{y_1, \ldots, y_J\}, \text{ and } Y_j := \{y_1, \ldots, y_j\}.$$

The sequence $V$ is often termed the *signal* and the sequence $Y$ the *data*.

**Definition 7.2**   The *smoothing problem* is to find the probability density $\Pi(V) := \mathbb{P}(V \mid Y) = \mathbb{P}(\{v_0, \ldots, v_J\} \mid \{y_1, \ldots, y_J\})$ on $\mathbb{R}^{d(J+1)}$ for some fixed integer $J$. We refer to $\Pi$ as the *smoothing distribution*.     ◇

**Definition 7.3**   The *filtering problem* is to find, and update sequentially in $j$, the probability densities $\pi_j(v_j) := \mathbb{P}(v_j \mid Y_j) = \mathbb{P}(v_j \mid \{y_1, \ldots, y_j\})$ on $\mathbb{R}^d$ for $j = 1, \ldots, J$. We refer to $\pi_j$ as the *filtering distribution at time $j$*.     ◇

The key conceptual issue to appreciate concerning the filtering problem, in comparison with the smoothing problem, is that interest is focused on characterizing, or approximating, a sequence of probability distributions, defined in an iterative fashion as the data is acquired sequentially.

**Remark 7.4**   We note the following identity:

$$\int \Pi(v_0, \ldots, v_J) \, dv_0 dv_1 \cdots dv_{J-1} = \pi_J(v_J).$$

This expresses the fact that the marginal of the smoothing distribution at time $J$ corresponds to the filtering distribution at time $J$. Note also that, for $j < J$, in general

$$\int \Pi(v_0, \ldots, v_J) \, dv_0 \cdots dv_{j-1} dv_{j+1} \cdots dv_J \neq \pi_j(v_j),$$

since the expression on the left-hand side of the equation depends on data $Y_J$, whereas that on the right-hand side depends only on $Y_j$, and $j < J$.     ◇

## 7.2 The Smoothing Problem

### 7.2.1 Formulation as an Inverse Problem

If we define

$$\eta := \{\eta_1, \ldots, \eta_J\}$$

and

$$G(V) := \{h(v_1), \ldots, h(v_J)\},$$

then the data model can be written in the form of the inverse problem (1.1):

$$Y = G(V) + \eta.$$

The stochastic dynamics model provides a prior probabilistic description of $V$, which may then be used to formulate a Bayesian version of the inverse problem of finding $V$ from $Y$.

### 7.2.2 Formula for pdf of the Smoothing Problem

The smoothing distribution can be found by combining a prior on $v$ and a likelihood function using Bayes' theorem. The prior is the probability distribution on $v$ implied by the distribution of $v_0$ and the stochastic dynamics model; the likelihood function is defined by the data model. We now derive the prior and the likelihood separately.

The prior distribution can be derived as follows:

$$\begin{aligned} \mathbb{P}(V) &= \mathbb{P}(v_J, v_{J-1}, \ldots, v_0) \\ &= \mathbb{P}(v_J | v_{J-1}, \ldots, v_0)\, \mathbb{P}(v_{J-1}, \ldots, v_0) \\ &= \mathbb{P}(v_J | v_{J-1})\, \mathbb{P}(v_{J-1}, \ldots, v_0). \end{aligned}$$

The third equality comes from the Markov, or memoryless, property which follows from the independence of the elements of the sequence $\{\xi_j\}$. By induction, we have

$$\mathbb{P}(V) = \mathbb{P}(v_0) \prod_{j=0}^{J-1} \mathbb{P}(v_{j+1} | v_j)$$

$$= \frac{1}{Z_\rho} \exp\bigl(-\mathsf{R}(V)\bigr)$$

$$=: \rho(V),$$

where $Z_\rho > 0$ is a normalizing constant and

$$R(V) := \frac{1}{2}|v_0 - m_0|_{C_0}^2 + \frac{1}{2}\sum_{j=0}^{J-1}|v_{j+1} - \Psi(v_j)|_\Sigma^2.$$

The likelihood function, which incorporates the measurements gathered from observing the system, depends only on the measurement model and may be derived as follows:

$$\mathbb{P}(Y|V) = \prod_{j=0}^{J-1}\mathbb{P}(y_{j+1}|v_0,\ldots,v_J)$$

$$= \prod_{j=0}^{J-1}\mathbb{P}(y_{j+1}|v_{j+1})$$

$$\propto \exp\big(-\mathsf{L}(V;Y)\big),$$

where the loss function is given by

$$\mathsf{L}(V;Y) := \frac{1}{2}\sum_{j=0}^{J-1}|y_{j+1} - h(v_{j+1})|_\Gamma^2.$$

The factorization of $\mathbb{P}(Y \mid V)$ in terms of the product of the $\mathbb{P}(y_{j+1} \mid v_{j+1})$ follows from the independence of the elements of $\{\eta_j\}$ and the fact that the observation at time $j + 1$ depends only on the state at time $j + 1$.

Using Bayes' Theorem 1.2 we find the smoothing distribution by combining the likelihood and prior

$$\Pi(V) \propto \mathbb{P}(Y \mid V)\,\mathbb{P}(V)$$

$$= \frac{1}{Z}\exp\big(-\mathsf{R}(V) - \mathsf{L}(V;Y)\big).$$

Note that $V \in \mathbb{R}^{d(J+1)}$ and $Y \in \mathbb{R}^{kJ}$.

### 7.2.3 Well-Posedness of the Smoothing Problem

Now we study the well-posedness of the smoothing problem with respect to perturbations in the data. To this end, we consider two smoothing distributions corresponding to different observed data sequences $Y, Y'$:

$$\Pi(V) := \mathbb{P}(V \mid Y) = \frac{1}{Z}\exp\big(-\mathsf{R}(V) - \mathsf{L}(V;Y)\big),$$

$$\Pi'(V) := \mathbb{P}(V \mid Y') = \frac{1}{Z'}\exp\big(-\mathsf{R}(V) - \mathsf{L}(V;Y')\big).$$

We make the following assumptions:

**Assumption 7.5** *There is a finite non-negative constant R such that the data Y, Y' and the observation function h satisfy:*

- $|Y|, |Y'| \le R$;
- *letting* $\varphi(V) := \left( \sum_{j=1}^{J} (|h(v_j)|^2) \right)^{1/2}$, *it holds that* $\mathbb{E}^\rho[\varphi^2(V)] < \infty$.

The following theorem shows well-posedness of the smoothing problem.

**Theorem 7.6** (Well-Posedness of Smoothing) *Under Assumption 7.5, there is $\kappa \in [0, \infty)$ independent of Y and Y' such that*

$$d_{\mathrm{H}}(\Pi, \Pi') \le \kappa |Y - Y'|.$$

*Proof* We show that the proof of Theorem 1.15, which established well-posedness for Bayesian inverse problems under Assumption 1.13, applies in the smoothing context as well. To do so, we rewrite the problem in the same notation used in Chapter 1, and show that Assumption 7.5 above implies Assumption 1.13. Write

$$\Pi(V) = \frac{1}{Z} \exp\big(-\mathsf{L}(V; Y)\big) \rho(V) = \frac{1}{Z} \mathsf{I}(V; Y) \rho(V),$$

$$\Pi'(V) = \frac{1}{Z'} \exp\big(-\mathsf{L}(V; Y')\big) \rho(V) = \frac{1}{Z'} \mathsf{I}(V; Y') \rho(V),$$

where $Z, Z' > 0$ are normalization constants. Here $|Y - Y'|$ plays the role of $\delta$ in Theorem 1.15. Since the likelihood $\mathsf{I}(V; Y) := \exp\big(-\mathsf{L}(V; Y)\big)$ and $\mathsf{L}(V; Y)$ is positive, we have that

$$\sup_v \left| \sqrt{\mathsf{I}(V; Y)} \right| + \left| \sqrt{\mathsf{I}(V; Y')} \right| \le 2,$$

and so Assumption 1.13 (ii) is satisfied. To see that Assumption 1.13 (i) is also satisfied, note that $e^{-x}$ is Lipschitz-1. Therefore, using the Cauchy–Schwarz inequality and some algebraic manipulations, there is $\kappa$ independent of $Y$ and $Y'$ such that

$$\left| \sqrt{\mathsf{I}(V, Y)} - \sqrt{\mathsf{I}(V; Y')} \right| \le \frac{1}{2} \left| \mathsf{L}(V; Y) - \mathsf{L}(V; Y') \right|$$

$$= \frac{1}{2} \left| \sum_{j=0}^{J-1} \frac{1}{2} \left( |y_{j+1} - h(v_{j+1})|_\Gamma^2 - |y'_{j+1} - h(v_{j+1})|_\Gamma^2 \right) \right|$$

$$\le \kappa \sum_{j=0}^{J-1} |y_{j+1} - y'_{j+1}|_\Gamma |y_{j+1} + y'_{j+1} - 2h(v_{j+1})|_\Gamma$$

$$\le \kappa |Y - Y'| \varphi(V),$$

where $\varphi$ is defined in Assumption 7.5. This shows that under Assumption 7.5

the likelihood function of the smoothing problem satisfies Assumption 1.13 with $\delta = |Y - Y'|$; Theorem 7.6 follows from Theorem 1.15. ☐

## 7.3 The Filtering Problem

### 7.3.1 Formula for pdf of the Filtering Problem

Filtering concerns the iterative updating of distributions, as new data arrives. We recall that we denote the filtering distribution at time $j$ by $\pi_j = \mathbb{P}(v_j|Y_j)$, and we now introduce $\widehat{\pi}_{j+1} = \mathbb{P}(v_{j+1}|Y_j)$. Then, we decompose in two steps the updating of the filtering distribution from time $j$ to time $j + 1$:

$$
\begin{aligned}
\textbf{Prediction Step:} \quad & \widehat{\pi}_{j+1} = \mathcal{P}\pi_j. \\
\textbf{Analysis Step:} \quad & \pi_{j+1} = \mathcal{A}_j\widehat{\pi}_{j+1}.
\end{aligned}
\tag{7.1}
$$

The combination of the prediction and analysis steps is shown schematically in Figure 7.1 and leads to the update

$$
\pi_{j+1} = \mathcal{A}_j\mathcal{P}\pi_j,
$$

where $\mathcal{P}$ is a Markov map and $\mathcal{A}_j$ is a likelihood map (Bayes' theorem) that we define in what follows.

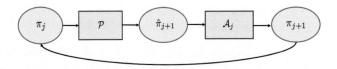

Figure 7.1 Prediction and analysis steps combined.

We first derive the map $\mathcal{P}$, which is sometimes termed *prediction*. By the

Markov property of the stochastic dynamics model, we have

$$\widehat{\pi}_{j+1}(v_{j+1}) = \mathbb{P}(v_{j+1} \mid Y_j)$$

$$= \int_{\mathbb{R}^d} \mathbb{P}(v_{j+1} \mid Y_j, v_j) \, \mathbb{P}(v_j \mid Y_j) \, dv_j$$

$$= \int_{\mathbb{R}^d} \mathbb{P}(v_{j+1} \mid v_j) \, \mathbb{P}(v_j \mid Y_j) \, dv_j$$

$$= \int_{\mathbb{R}^d} \mathbb{P}(v_{j+1} \mid v_j) \pi_j(v_j) \, dv_j$$

$$= \frac{1}{(2\pi)^{d/2}(\det \Sigma)^{1/2}} \int_{\mathbb{R}^d} \exp\left(-\frac{1}{2}|v_{j+1} - \Psi(v_j)|_{\Sigma}^2\right) \pi_j(v_j) \, dv_j.$$

$$(7.2)$$

This defines the operator $\mathcal{P}$; the prediction step is shown schematically in Figure 7.2. Note that $\mathcal{P}$ is independent of step $j$ because the Markov chain defined by the stochastic dynamics model is time-homogeneous. In the absence of data, the distribution of $v_j$ simply evolves through repeated application of $\mathcal{P}$.

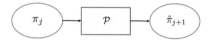

Figure 7.2 Prediction step.

Now we derive the likelihood map $\mathcal{A}_j$, which is sometimes called *analysis*. Note that the prediction step does not make use of the new observation $y_{j+1}$, which is assimilated in the analysis step through application of Bayes' theorem, as follows:

$$\pi_{j+1}(v_{j+1}) = \mathbb{P}(v_{j+1}|Y_{j+1})$$

$$= \mathbb{P}(v_{j+1}|Y_j, y_{j+1})$$

$$= \frac{\mathbb{P}(y_{j+1}|v_{j+1}, Y_j) \, \mathbb{P}(v_{j+1}|Y_j)}{\mathbb{P}(y_{j+1}|Y_j)}$$

$$= \frac{\mathbb{P}(y_{j+1}|v_{j+1}) \, \mathbb{P}(v_{j+1}|Y_j)}{\mathbb{P}(y_{j+1}|Y_j)}$$

$$= \frac{\exp(-\frac{1}{2}|y_{j+1} - h(v_{j+1})|_{\Gamma}^2)\widehat{\pi}_{j+1}(v_{j+1})}{\int_{\mathbb{R}^d} \exp(-\frac{1}{2}|y_{j+1} - h(v_{j+1})|_{\Gamma}^2)\widehat{\pi}_{j+1}(v_{j+1}) \, dv_{j+1}}.$$

$$(7.3)$$

This defines the map $\mathcal{A}_j$ through multiplication by the likelihood, and then normalization to a probability measure. The analysis update is shown schematically in Figure 7.3. It depends on $j$ because the data $y_{j+1}$ appears in the equation, and this will change with each set of measurements.

Figure 7.3  Update step.

## 7.3.2 Well-Posedness of the Filtering Problem

Now we establish the well-posedness of the filtering problem. We let

$$\pi_J = \mathbb{P}(v_J|Y), \qquad \pi'_J = \mathbb{P}(v_J|Y')$$

be two filtering distributions arising from observed data $Y = Y_J$ and $Y' = Y'_J$. As noted in Remark 7.4, the filtering distribution at time $J$ is the $J$th marginal of the smoothing distribution; using this observation, the well-posedness of the filtering problem is a direct consequence of the well-posedness of the smoothing problem in the Hellinger distance. However, for the filtering problem this approach only gives well-posedness in the (weaker) total variation distance.

**Corollary 7.7** (Well-Posedness of Filtering)   *Under Assumption 7.5, there exists $\kappa = \kappa(R)$ such that $d_{\mathrm{TV}}(\pi_J, \pi'_J) \le \kappa|Y - Y'|$.*

*Proof*   Let $\Pi, \Pi'$ be the smoothing distributions $\Pi = \mathbb{P}(V \mid Y)$ and $\Pi' = \mathbb{P}(V \mid Y')$. We note that there exists $\kappa$ such that $d_{\mathrm{TV}}(\Pi, \Pi') \le \kappa|Y - Y'|$ by Theorem 7.6 and by the fact that the Hellinger distance bounds the total variation distance (Lemma 1.9). Let $f: \mathbb{R}^d \to \mathbb{R}$ and $F: \mathbb{R}^{d(J+1)} \to \mathbb{R}$. Then

$$
\begin{aligned}
d_{\mathrm{TV}}(\pi_J, \pi'_J) &= \frac{1}{2} \sup_{|f|_\infty \le 1} \left| \mathbb{E}^{\pi_J}[f(v_J)] - \mathbb{E}^{\pi_{J}'}[f(v_J)] \right| \\
&= \frac{1}{2} \sup_{|f|_\infty \le 1} \left| \mathbb{E}^{\Pi}[f(v_J)] - \mathbb{E}^{\Pi'}[f(v_J)] \right| \\
&\le \frac{1}{2} \sup_{|F|_\infty \le 1} \left| \mathbb{E}^{\Pi}[F(V)] - \mathbb{E}^{\Pi'}[F(V)] \right| \\
&= d_{\mathrm{TV}}(\Pi, \Pi') \\
&\le \kappa|Y - Y'|.
\end{aligned}
$$

Here the first inequality follows from the fact that $\{|f| \le 1\}$ can be viewed as a subset of $\{|F| \le 1\}$.   □

| Kalman Filter | $\Psi(\cdot) = M\cdot$ | $h(\cdot) = H\cdot$ | **P** | Chapter 8 |
|---|---|---|---|---|
| 3DVAR | General $\Psi$ | $h(\cdot) = H\cdot$ | **S** | Chapter 9 |
| Extended Kalman Filter | General $\Psi$ | $h(\cdot) = H\cdot$ | **S** | Chapter 10 |
| Ensemble Kalman Filter | General $\Psi$ | $h(\cdot) = H\cdot$ | **S** | Chapter 10 |
| Bootstrap Particle Filter | General $\Psi$ | General $h$ | **P** | Chapter 11 |
| Optimal Particle Filter | General $\Psi$ | $h(\cdot) = H\cdot$ | **P** | Chapter 12 |

Table 7.1 *Summary of the filtering methods considered in the following chapters, along with the settings in which they will be presented.*

### 7.3.3 Roadmap to Discrete Filtering Methods

There are several filtering methods for performing the prediction and analysis steps. Some methods can be applied generally to nonlinear problems. However, others require a linear dynamics model ($\Psi(\cdot) = M\cdot$) and/or linear observations ($h(\cdot) = H\cdot$). Some of the methods provably approximate the filtering distributions, while some just estimate the state using covariance information to weight the relative importance of predictions based on the dynamics model and on the data model.

The applicability of the methods that will be studied in the following chapters is summarized in Table 7.1, with respect to linearity/nonlinearity of the dynamics and the observation model. Furthermore, **P** is used to denote methods which provably approximate the filtering distributions $\pi_j$ in certain large particle limit; **S** denotes methods which only attempt to estimate the state using the data. Some of these constraints on the setting in which they apply can be relaxed, but the list above describes the methods as will be presented in these notes. Furthermore, extended and ensemble Kalman filters are observed to accurately represent the filtering distributions in situations where approximate Gaussianity holds; this may be induced by small noise and/or by large data.

## 7.4 Discussion and Bibliography

Law et al. (2015) gives a mathematical introduction to data assimilation; for further information on the smoothing problem as presented here, see Section 2.3 in that book; for further information on the filtering problem as presented here, see Section 2.4. Our notes present new perspectives on data assimilation, different from those emphasized in Law et al. (2015), including their formulation as random dynamical systems, detailed discussion of both the bootstrap and optimal particle filters, and the use of data assimilation in the solution of inverse problems; on the other hand, Law et al. (2015) links the pseudocode to downloadable code, a resource that usefully complements our notes.

The books of Abarbanel (2013), Reich and Cotter (2015), Asch et al. (2016), Särkkä (2013), Bain and Crisan (2008), Crisan and Rozovskii (2011), and Evensen et al. (2022) and the review by Reich (2019) give alternative foundational presentations of the subject of data assimilation. The books of Kalnay (2003), Oliver et al. (2008), Majda and Harlim (2012), and Carrassi et al. (2018) study data assimilation in the context of weather forecasting, oil reservoir simulation, turbulence modeling, and geophysical sciences, respectively.

In this chapter, we have assumed throughout that $\Sigma$, the model covariance, is positive definite. In applications, the stochastic dynamics model can be interpreted as arising from discretization of a stochastic differential equation governing the evolution of the state. Even if the underlying signal is governed by a deterministic map $\Psi$, the use of a *stochastic* dynamics model can help account for errors in the modeling of this deterministic map. However, the case where $\Sigma \equiv 0$ is also of interest as it corresponds to deterministic dynamics without model error. In this case we again define

$$\eta := \{\eta_1, \ldots, \eta_J\}$$

and then define

$$G_0(v_0) := \left\{ h\big(\Psi^{(1)}(v_0)\big), h\big(\Psi^{(2)}(v_0)\big), \ldots, h\big(\Psi^{(J)} v_0\big) \right\},$$

where $\Psi^{(j)}$ denotes $\Psi$ composed with itself $j$ times. Then the data model can be written in the form of the following inverse problem for the determination of the initial condition of the dynamical system:

$$Y = G_0(v_0) + \eta.$$

The Gaussian assumption $v_0 \sim \mathcal{N}(m_0, C_0)$ provides a prior model for a Bayesian formulation of this problem. We refer to Hairer et al. (2011) for the derivation of the posterior distribution in other related settings, including dynamical systems defined by ordinary and stochastic differential equations with discrete and continuous observations.

To streamline the presentation, throughout Part II of these notes we assume to have access to maps $\Psi$ and $h$, and covariance matrices $C_0$, $\Sigma$, and $\Gamma$ defining the dynamics and data models. In practice, however, models only reflect imperfectly the evolution of the system and the relationship between signal and data. For this reason, an important challenge in data assimilation is the identification and correction of model errors, and the estimation of model parameters, along with the state, from data. Several recent efforts that leverage machine learning to address model error in dynamical systems are reviewed in Levine and Stuart (2022). Relatedly, several recent frameworks are emerging to blend data assimilation with machine learning to obtain model corrections or surrogate models for the dynamics, including Chen et al. (2022), Bocquet et al. (2020), Brajard et al. (2020), Gottwald and Reich (2021), Krishnan et al. (2017).

# 8

# The Kalman Filter and Smoother

Recall the stochastic dynamics and data models introduced in the previous chapter:

$$
\begin{aligned}
v_{j+1} &= \Psi(v_j) + \xi_j, & \xi_j &\sim \mathcal{N}(0, \Sigma) \text{ i.i.d.}, \\
y_{j+1} &= h(v_{j+1}) + \eta_{j+1}, & \eta_j &\sim \mathcal{N}(0, \Gamma) \text{ i.i.d.},
\end{aligned}
\tag{8.1}
$$

with $v_0 \sim \mathcal{N}(m_0, C_0)$, $C_0, \Sigma$, and $\Gamma$ positive definite and $v_0 \perp \{\xi_j\} \perp \{\eta_j\}$. Here we study the filtering and smoothing problems under the assumption that both the state-transition function $\Psi(\cdot)$ and the observation function $h(\cdot)$ are linear. Throughout, we will assume the following:

**Assumption 8.1** *The stochastic dynamics and the data models defined by equation (8.1) hold with linear $\Psi(\cdot)$ and $h(\cdot)$:*

- *Linear dynamics: $v_{j+1} = M v_j + \xi_j$ for some $M \in \mathbb{R}^{d \times d}$.*
- *Linear observation: $y_{j+1} = H v_{j+1} + \eta_{j+1}$ for some $H \in \mathbb{R}^{k \times d}$.*

We will be mostly concerned with the case where $d > k$. Under the *linear-Gaussian* assumption, the filtering and smoothing distributions are Gaussian and therefore are fully characterized by their mean and covariance. We consider first the *Kalman filter* in Section 8.1, which gives explicit formulae for the iterative update of the mean and covariance of the filtering distribution, and then in Section 8.2 the *Kalman smoother*, which characterizes the smoothing distribution. Section 8.3 closes this chapter with bibliographical remarks. While the Kalman filter and the Kalman smoother only characterize the filtering and smoothing distributions in the linear-Gaussian setting, their importance extends beyond this setting, as will be demonstrated in the next two chapters.

# 8.1 Kalman Filter

The *filtering problem* is to estimate the state at time $j$ given the data from the past up to the present time $j$. That is, we want to determine the pdf $\pi_j = \mathbb{P}(v_j \mid Y_j)$, where $Y_j := \{y_1, \ldots, y_j\}$. We define $\widehat{\pi}_{j+1} = \mathbb{P}(v_{j+1} \mid Y_j)$ and recall the evolution

$$\pi_{j+1} = \mathcal{A}_j \mathcal{P} \pi_j, \quad \pi_0 = \mathcal{N}(m_0, C_0),$$

which can be decomposed in terms of the prediction and analysis steps (7.1). Note that $\mathcal{P}$ does not depend on $j$ because the same Markov chain defined by the state dynamics governs each prediction step, whereas $\mathcal{A}_j$ depends on $j$ because at each step $j$ the likelihood sees different data. The linear dynamics assumption implies that applying the operator $\mathcal{P}$ to a Gaussian distribution gives again a Gaussian, and the linear observation assumption implies that applying the operator $\mathcal{A}_j$ to a Gaussian gives again a Gaussian. Therefore, we have the following:

**Theorem 8.2** (Gaussianity of Filtering Distributions)   *Under Assumption 8.1, $\pi_0$, $\{\pi_{j+1}\}_{j \in \mathbb{Z}^+}$, and $\{\widehat{\pi}_{j+1}\}_{j \in \mathbb{Z}^+}$ are all Gaussian distributions.*

As a consequence, the filtering distributions can be entirely characterized by their mean and covariance. We write

$$\widehat{\pi}_{j+1} = \mathbb{P}(v_{j+1} \mid Y_j) = \mathcal{N}(\widehat{m}_{j+1}, \widehat{C}_{j+1}), \qquad \text{(prediction)}$$
$$\pi_{j+1} = \mathbb{P}(v_{j+1} \mid Y_{j+1}) = \mathcal{N}(m_{j+1}, C_{j+1}), \qquad \text{(analysis)}$$

and aim to find update formulae for these means and covariances. The Kalman filter achieves this.

**Theorem 8.3** (Characterization of the Kalman Filter)   *Suppose that Assumption 8.1 holds. Then, for all $j \in \mathbb{Z}^+$, $C_j$ is positive definite and*

$$\widehat{m}_{j+1} = M m_j, \tag{8.2a}$$
$$\widehat{C}_{j+1} = M C_j M^\top + \Sigma, \tag{8.2b}$$
$$C_{j+1}^{-1} = (M C_j M^\top + \Sigma)^{-1} + H^\top \Gamma^{-1} H, \tag{8.2c}$$
$$C_{j+1}^{-1} m_{j+1} = (M C_j M^\top + \Sigma)^{-1} M m_j + H^\top \Gamma^{-1} y_{j+1}. \tag{8.2d}$$

*Proof*   The proof proceeds by breaking the Kalman filter step above into the prediction and the analysis steps. We first derive the update formulae, assuming that $C_j$ and $\widehat{C}_{j+1}$ are positive definite; we conclude with an inductive proof that this is indeed the case.

**Prediction:** The mean and variance of the prediction step may be calculated as follows. The mean is given by:

$$\widehat{m}_{j+1} = \mathbb{E}\left[v_{j+1} \mid Y_j\right]$$
$$= \mathbb{E}\left[Mv_j + \xi_j \mid Y_j\right]$$
$$= M\,\mathbb{E}\left[v_j \mid Y_j\right] + \mathbb{E}\left[\xi_j \mid Y_j\right]$$
$$= Mm_j,$$

where we used that $\xi_j$ and $Y_j$ are independent. The covariance is given by

$$\widehat{C}_{j+1} = \mathbb{E}\left[(v_{j+1} - \widehat{m}_{j+1}) \otimes (v_{j+1} - \widehat{m}_{j+1}) \mid Y_j\right]$$
$$= \mathbb{E}\left[M(v_j - m_j) \otimes M(v_j - m_j) \mid Y_j\right] + \mathbb{E}\left[\xi_j \otimes \xi_j \mid Y_j\right]$$
$$+ \mathbb{E}\left[\xi_j \otimes M(v_j - m_j) \mid Y_j\right] + \mathbb{E}\left[M(v_j - m_j) \otimes \xi_j \mid Y_j\right]$$
$$= M\,\mathbb{E}\left[(v_j - m_j) \otimes (v_j - m_j) \mid Y_j\right]M^\top + \Sigma$$
$$= MC_jM^\top + \Sigma,$$

where we used that $\xi_j$ and $v_j$ are independent. Thus, in the linear-Gaussian setting, the prediction operator $\mathcal{P}$ from $\pi_j = \mathcal{N}(m_j, C_j)$ to $\widehat{\pi}_{j+1} = \mathcal{N}(\widehat{m}_{j+1}, \widehat{C}_{j+1})$ is given by

$$\widehat{m}_{j+1} = Mm_j,$$
$$\widehat{C}_{j+1} = MC_jM^\top + \Sigma.$$

**Analysis:** The analysis step may be derived as follows, using Bayes' Theorem 1.2:

$$\mathbb{P}(v_{j+1} \mid Y_{j+1}) = \mathbb{P}(v_{j+1} \mid y_{j+1}, Y_j)$$
$$\propto \mathbb{P}(y_{j+1} \mid v_{j+1}, Y_j)\,\mathbb{P}(v_{j+1} \mid Y_j)$$
$$= \mathbb{P}(y_{j+1} \mid v_{j+1})\,\mathbb{P}(v_{j+1} \mid Y_j).$$

This gives

$$\mathbb{P}(v_{j+1} \mid Y_{j+1}) \propto \exp\left(-\frac{1}{2}|v_{j+1} - m_{j+1}|^2_{C_{j+1}}\right)$$
$$\propto \exp\left(-\frac{1}{2}|y_{j+1} - Hv_{j+1}|^2_\Gamma\right)\exp\left(-\frac{1}{2}|v_{j+1} - \widehat{m}_{j+1}|^2_{\widehat{C}_{j+1}}\right) \quad (8.3)$$
$$= \exp\left(-\frac{1}{2}|y_{j+1} - Hv_{j+1}|^2_\Gamma - \frac{1}{2}|v_{j+1} - \widehat{m}_{j+1}|^2_{\widehat{C}_{j+1}}\right).$$

Taking logarithms and matching quadratic and linear terms in $v_{j+1}$ from either side of this identity gives the update operator $\mathcal{A}_j$ from $\widehat{\pi}_{j+1} = \mathcal{N}(\widehat{m}_{j+1}, \widehat{C}_{j+1})$

to $\pi_{j+1} = \mathcal{N}(m_{j+1}, C_{j+1})$:

$$C_{j+1}^{-1} = \widehat{C}_{j+1}^{-1} + H^\top \Gamma^{-1} H,$$
$$C_{j+1}^{-1} m_{j+1} = \widehat{C}_{j+1}^{-1} \widehat{m}_{j+1} + H^\top \Gamma^{-1} y_{j+1}.$$

Combining the prediction operator $\mathcal{P}$ and update operator $\mathcal{A}_j$ yields the desired update formulae.

**Positive-definiteness:** It remains to show that $C_j > 0$ for all $j \in \mathbb{Z}^+$. We will use induction. By assumption the result holds true for $j = 0$. Assume that it is true for $C_j$. For the prediction operator $\mathcal{P}$ we have, for $u \neq 0$,

$$\langle u, \widehat{C}_{j+1} u \rangle = \langle u, M C_j M^\top u \rangle + \langle u, \Sigma u \rangle$$
$$= \langle M^\top u, C_j M^\top u \rangle + \langle u, \Sigma u \rangle$$
$$\geq \langle u, \Sigma u \rangle$$
$$> 0,$$

where we used that $C_j > 0$ and $\Sigma > 0$. Therefore $\widehat{C}_{j+1}, \widehat{C}_{j+1}^{-1} > 0$. Then for the update operator $\mathcal{A}_j$:

$$\langle u, C_{j+1}^{-1} u \rangle = \langle u, \widehat{C}_{j+1}^{-1} u \rangle + \langle u, H^\top \Gamma^{-1} H u \rangle$$
$$= \langle u, \widehat{C}_{j+1}^{-1} u \rangle + \langle H u, \Gamma^{-1} H u \rangle$$
$$\geq \langle u, \widehat{C}_{j+1}^{-1} u \rangle$$
$$> 0,$$

where we used that $\Gamma > 0$. Therefore, $C_{j+1}, C_{j+1}^{-1} > 0$, which concludes the proof. $\qquad\square$

**Remark 8.4** The previous proof reveals two interesting facts about the structure of the Kalman filter updates. The first is that the covariance update does not involve the observed data; this can be thought of as a consequence of the fact that the posterior covariance in the linear-Gaussian setting for inverse problems does not depend on the observed data, as noted in Chapter 2. The second is that the update formulae for the covariance are affine in the prediction step, but nonlinear in the analysis step; specifically, the analysis step is linear in the precisions (inverse covariances). $\qquad\diamond$

### 8.1.1 Kalman Filter: Algorithmic Implementation

We now rewrite the Kalman filter in an alternative form, which can be advantageous for algorithmic implementation. This formulation is summarized in

Algorithm 8.1 below, and it is written in terms of covariance matrices instead of precision matrices.

---

**Algorithm 8.1** Kalman Filter Algorithm

---

1: **Input**: Initial distribution $\pi_0 = \mathcal{N}(m_0, C_0)$ with $m_0 \in \mathbb{R}^d$, $C_0 \in \mathbb{R}^{d \times d}$.

2: For $j = 0, 1, \ldots, J - 1$ do the following prediction and analysis steps:

3: **Prediction**:

$$\widehat{m}_{j+1} = M m_j, \tag{8.4}$$

$$\widehat{C}_{j+1} = M C_j M^\top + \Sigma, \tag{8.5}$$

4: **Analysis**:

$$\begin{aligned} m_{j+1} &= \widehat{m}_{j+1} + K_{j+1} d_{j+1}, \\ C_{j+1} &= (I - K_{j+1} H) \widehat{C}_{j+1}, \end{aligned} \tag{8.6}$$

where

$$\begin{aligned} d_{j+1} &= y_{j+1} - H \widehat{m}_{j+1}, \\ S_{j+1} &= H \widehat{C}_{j+1} H^\top + \Gamma, \\ K_{j+1} &= \widehat{C}_{j+1} H^\top S_{j+1}^{-1}. \end{aligned} \tag{8.7}$$

5: **Output**: Predicted distributions $\widehat{\pi}_{j+1} = \mathcal{N}(\widehat{m}_{j+1}, \widehat{C}_{j+1})$ and filtering distributions $\pi_{j+1} = \mathcal{N}(m_{j+1}, C_{j+1})$, $j = 0, 1, \ldots, J - 1$.

---

Importantly, the formulation in Theorem 8.3 involves a matrix inversion in the state-space $\mathbb{R}^d$ while the one given in Algorithm 8.1 requires only inversion in the data space $\mathbb{R}^k$ to compute $S_{j+1}^{-1}$. In many applications the observation space dimension is much smaller than the state-space dimension ($k \ll d$), and then the formulation given in Algorithm 8.1 leads to much cheaper computations than the one given in Theorem 8.3.

The vector $d_{j+1}$ is known as the *innovation* and the matrix $K_{j+1}$ as the *Kalman gain*. Note that $d_{j+1}$ measures the mismatch of the predicted state from the given data.

Combining the form of $d_{j+1}$ and $\widehat{m}_{j+1}$ shows that the update formula for the Kalman mean can be written as

$$m_{j+1} = (I - K_{j+1} H) \widehat{m}_{j+1} + K_{j+1} y_{j+1}, \quad \widehat{m}_{j+1} = M m_j. \tag{8.8}$$

This update formula has the very natural interpretation that the mean update is formed as a linear combination of the evolution of the noise-free dynamics and of the data. Equations (8.6) and (8.8) show that the Kalman gain $K_{j+1}$ determines the weight given to the new observation $y_{j+1}$ in the state estimation. The update formula (8.8) may also be derived from an optimization perspective, the topic of the next subsection.

The fact that the analysis update given by Algorithm 8.1 agrees with the one derived in Theorem 8.3 can be established using the following lemma:

**Lemma 8.5** (Woodbury Matrix Identity)  *Let $A \in \mathbb{R}^{p \times p}$, $U \in \mathbb{R}^{p \times q}$, $B \in \mathbb{R}^{q \times q}$, $V \in \mathbb{R}^{q \times p}$. If $A, B > 0$, then $A + UBV$ is invertible and*

$$(A + UDV)^{-1} = A^{-1} - A^{-1}U(B^{-1} + VA^{-1}U)^{-1}VA^{-1},$$

Now, to see the agreement between the characterization in terms of precision matrices in Theorem 8.3 and the covariance characterization in (8.6) and (8.7), note that Lemma 8.5 applied to (8.2c) gives

$$
\begin{aligned}
C_{j+1} &= \widehat{C}_{j+1} - \widehat{C}_{j+1}H^\top (\Gamma + H\widehat{C}_{j+1}H^\top)^{-1}H\widehat{C}_{j+1} \\
&= \left(I - \widehat{C}_{j+1}H^\top (\Gamma + H\widehat{C}_{j+1}H^\top)^{-1}H\right)\widehat{C}_{j+1} \\
&= (I - \widehat{C}_{j+1}H^\top S_{j+1}^{-1}H)\widehat{C}_{j+1} \\
&= (I - K_{j+1}H)\widehat{C}_{j+1},
\end{aligned}
$$

as desired.

## 8.1.2 Optimization Perspective: Mean of Kalman Filter

Since $\pi_{j+1}$ is Gaussian, its mean agrees with its mode. Thus, formulae (8.3) implies that

$$
\begin{aligned}
m_{j+1} &= \mathrm{argmax}_v\, \pi_{j+1}(v) \\
&= \mathrm{argmin}_v\, J(v),
\end{aligned}
$$

where

$$J(v) := \frac{1}{2}|y_{j+1} - Hv|_\Gamma^2 + \frac{1}{2}|v - \widehat{m}_{j+1}|_{\widehat{C}_{j+1}}^2.$$

In other words, $m_{j+1}$ is chosen to fit both the observed data $y_{j+1}$ and the predictions $\widehat{m}_{j+1}$ as well as possible. The covariances $\Gamma$ and $\widehat{C}_{j+1}$ determine the relative weighting between the two quadratic terms. The solution of the minimization problem is given by (8.8), as may be verified by direct differentiation of J.

An alternative derivation which is helpful in more sophisticated contexts is to cast the problem in terms of constrained minimization. Write $v' = v - \widehat{m}_{j+1}$,

$y' = y_{j+1} - H\widehat{m}_{j+1}$, and $C' = \widehat{C}_{j+1}$. Then minimization of J may be reformulated as

$$m_{j+1} = \widehat{m}_{j+1} + \mathrm{argmin}_{v'}\left(\frac{1}{2}|y' - Hv'|_{\Gamma}^2 + \frac{1}{2}\langle v', b\rangle\right),$$

where the minimization is now subject to the constraint $C'b = v'$. Using Lagrange multipliers we write

$$\mathsf{I}(v') = \frac{1}{2}|y' - Hv'|_{\Gamma}^2 + \frac{1}{2}\langle v', b\rangle + \langle \lambda, C'b - v'\rangle; \qquad (8.9)$$

computing the derivative and setting to zero gives

$$-H^{\top}\Gamma^{-1}(y' - Hv') + \frac{1}{2}b - \lambda = 0,$$

$$\frac{1}{2}v' + C'\lambda = 0,$$

$$v' - C'b = 0.$$

The last two equations imply that $C'(2\lambda + b) = 0$. Thus we set $\lambda = -\frac{1}{2}b$ and drop the second equation, replacing the first by

$$-H^{\top}\Gamma^{-1}(y' - HC'b) + b = 0.$$

Solving for $b$ gives

$$\begin{aligned}
v &= \widehat{m}_{j+1} + v'\\
&= \widehat{m}_{j+1} + C'b\\
&= \widehat{m}_{j+1} + C'(H^{\top}\Gamma^{-1}HC' + I)^{-1}H^{\top}\Gamma^{-1}y'\\
&= \widehat{m}_{j+1} + C'(H^{\top}\Gamma^{-1}HC' + I)^{-1}H^{\top}\Gamma^{-1}(y_{j+1} - H\widehat{m}_{j+1})\\
&= (I - K_{j+1}H)\widehat{m}_{j+1} + K_{j+1}y_{j+1},
\end{aligned}$$

where we have defined

$$K_{j+1} = C'(H^{\top}\Gamma^{-1}HC' + I)^{-1}H^{\top}\Gamma^{-1}.$$

It remains to show that $K_{j+1}$ agrees with the definition given in (8.7). To see this we note that if we choose $S$ to be any matrix satisfying $K_{j+1} = C'H^{\top}S^{-1}$, then

$$H^{\top}S^{-1} = (H^{\top}\Gamma^{-1}HC' + I)^{-1}H^{\top}\Gamma^{-1}$$

so that

$$(H^{\top}\Gamma^{-1}HC' + I)H^{\top} = H^{\top}\Gamma^{-1}S.$$

Thus

$$H^{\top}\Gamma^{-1}HC'H^{\top} + H^{\top} = H^{\top}\Gamma^{-1}S,$$

which may be achieved by choosing any $S$ so that

$$\Gamma^{-1}(HC'H^{\top} + \Gamma) = \Gamma^{-1}S$$

and multiplication by $\Gamma$ gives the desired formula for $S$.

### 8.1.3 Optimality of Kalman Filter

The following theorem states that the Kalman filter gives the best estimator of the mean in an on-line setting. In the following, $\mathbb{E}$ denotes expectation with respect to all randomness present in the problem statement, through the initial condition, the noisy dynamical evolution, and the noisy data. Furthermore, $\mathbb{E}[\cdot \mid Y_j]$ denotes conditional expectation, given the data $Y_j$ up to time $j$.

**Theorem 8.6** (Optimality of Kalman Filter)   *Let $\{m_j\}$ be the sequence computed using the Kalman filter, and $\{z_j\}$ be any sequence in $\mathbb{R}^d$ such that $z_j$ is $Y_j$ measurable.[1] Then, for all $j \in \mathbb{N}$,*

$$\mathbb{E}\left[|v_j - m_j|^2 \,\middle|\, Y_j\right] \leq \mathbb{E}\left[|v_j - z_j|^2 \,\middle|\, Y_j\right].$$

*Proof*   Note that $m_j$ and $z_j$ are fixed and non-random, given $Y_j$. Thus, we have:

$$\begin{aligned}
\mathbb{E}\left[|v_j - z_j|^2 \mid Y_j\right] &= \mathbb{E}\left[|v_j - m_j + m_j - z_j|^2 \mid Y_j\right] \\
&= \mathbb{E}\left[|v_j - m_j|^2 + 2\langle v_j - m_j, m_j - z_j\rangle + |m_j - z_j|^2 \mid Y_j\right] \\
&= \mathbb{E}\left[|v_j - m_j|^2 \mid Y_j\right] + 2\langle \mathbb{E}\left[v_j - m_j \mid Y_j\right], m_j - z_j\rangle \\
&\quad + |m_j - z_j|^2 \\
&= \mathbb{E}\left[|v_j - m_j|^2 \mid Y_j\right] + 2\langle \mathbb{E}\left[v_j \mid Y_j\right] - m_j, m_j - z_j\rangle \\
&\quad + |m_j - z_j|^2 \\
&= \mathbb{E}\left[|v_j - m_j|^2 \mid Y_j\right] + 0 + |m_j - z_j|^2 \\
&\geq \mathbb{E}\left[|v_j - m_j|^2 \mid Y_j\right].
\end{aligned}$$

The fifth step follows since $m_j = \mathbb{E}\left[v_j \mid Y_j\right]$.   □

## 8.2  Kalman Smoother

We next discuss the Kalman smoother, which refers to the smoothing problem in the linear-Gaussian setting of Assumption 8.1. As with the Kalman filter, it

[1]  For practical purposes, this means $z_j$ is a fixed non-random function of given observed $Y_j$.

is possible to solve the problem explicitly because the smoothing distribution is itself a Gaussian. The explicit formulae computed help to build intuition about the smoothing distribution more generally. We recall Remark 7.4, which implies that the filtering distribution at time $j = J$ determines the marginal of the Kalman smoother on its last coordinate. However, the filtering distributions do not determine the Kalman smoother in its entirety.

### 8.2.1  Defining Linear System

Let $V = \{v_0, \ldots, v_J\}$ and $Y = \{y_1, \ldots, y_J\}$. Using Bayes' Theorem 1.2 and the fact that $\{\xi_j\}$, $\{\eta_j\}$ are mutually independent i.i.d. sequences, independent of $v_0$, we have

$$\mathbb{P}(V \mid Y) \propto \mathbb{P}(Y \mid V)\, \mathbb{P}(V) = \prod_{j=1}^{J} \mathbb{P}(y_j \mid v_j) \times \prod_{j=0}^{J-1} \mathbb{P}(v_{j+1} \mid v_j) \times \mathbb{P}(v_0).$$

Noting that

$$v_{j+1} \mid v_j \sim \mathcal{N}(Mv_j, \Sigma), \quad y_j \mid v_j \sim \mathcal{N}(Hv_j, \Gamma)$$

the smoothing distribution can be expressed as

$$\mathbb{P}(V \mid Y) \propto \exp(-\mathsf{J}(V)), \tag{8.10}$$

where

$$\mathsf{J}(V) := \frac{1}{2}|v_0 - m_0|_{C_0}^2 + \frac{1}{2}\sum_{j=0}^{J-1}|v_{j+1} - Mv_j|_{\Sigma}^2 + \frac{1}{2}\sum_{j=0}^{J-1}|y_{j+1} - Hv_{j+1}|_{\Gamma}^2. \tag{8.11}$$

**Theorem 8.7** (Characterization of the Kalman Smoother)  *Suppose that Assumption 8.1 holds. Then $\mathbb{P}(V \mid Y)$ is Gaussian with a block tridiagonal precision matrix $\Omega > 0$ and mean $m$ solving $\Omega m = r$, where*

$$\Omega = \begin{bmatrix} \Omega_{0,0} & \Omega_{0,1} & & & \\ \Omega_{1,0} & \Omega_{1,1} & \cdots & & 0 \\ 0 & \cdots & \cdots & & \\ & 0 & \cdots & \cdots & \cdots \\ & & \cdots & \Omega_{J-1,J-1} & \Omega_{J-1,J} \\ & & & \Omega_{J,J-1} & \Omega_{J,J} \end{bmatrix} \tag{8.12}$$

*with*

$$\Omega_{0,0} = C_0^{-1} + M^\top \Sigma^{-1} M,$$
$$\Omega_{j,j} = \Sigma^{-1} + M^\top \Sigma^{-1} M + H^\top \Gamma^{-1} H, \quad 1 \le j \le J-1,$$
$$\Omega_{J,J} = \Sigma^{-1} + H^\top \Gamma^{-1} H,$$
$$\Omega_{j,j+1} = -\Sigma^{-1} M, \quad 0 \le j \le J-1,$$
$$r_0 = C_0^{-1} m_0,$$
$$r_j = H^\top \Gamma^{-1} y_j, \quad 1 \le j \le J.$$

*Proof* We may write $J(V) = \frac{1}{2} |\Omega^{1/2}(V-m)|^2 + q$ with $q$ independent of $V$, by definition. Note that $\Omega$ is then the Hessian of $J(V)$, and differentiating in equation (8.11) we obtain that

$$\Omega_{0,0} = \partial_{v_0}^2 J(V) = C_0^{-1} + M^\top \Sigma^{-1} M,$$
$$\Omega_{j,j} = \partial_{v_j}^2 J(V) = \Sigma^{-1} + M^\top \Sigma^{-1} M + H^\top \Gamma^{-1} H,$$
$$\Omega_{J,J} = \partial_{v_J}^2 J(V) = \Sigma^{-1} + H^\top \Gamma^{-1} H,$$
$$\Omega_{j-1,j} = \partial_{v_{j-1}, v_j}^2 J(V) = -\Sigma^{-1} M.$$

Otherwise, for all other values of indices $\{k, l\}$, $\Omega_{k,l} = 0$. This proves that the matrix $\Omega$ has a block tridiagonal structure.

Now we focus on finding $m$. We have that $\nabla_V J(V) = \Omega(V-m)$, so that $-\nabla_V J(V)|_{V=0} = \Omega m$. Thus, we find $r$ as

$$r_0 = -\nabla_{v_0} J(V)|_{V=0} = -(-C_0^{-1} m_0) = C_0^{-1} m_0,$$
$$r_j = -\nabla_{v_j} J(V)|_{V=0} = -(-H^\top \Gamma^{-1} y_j) = H^\top \Gamma^{-1} y_j.$$

We have shown that $\Omega$ is symmetric and that $\Omega \ge 0$; to prove that $\Omega$ is a precision matrix, we need to show that $\Omega > 0$. Take, for the sake of argument, $Y = 0$ and $m_0 = 0$ in equation (8.11), so that every term in the expansion of $J(V)$ involves $V$. It is evident that in such case $J(V) = V^\top \Omega V$. Suppose that $V^\top \Omega V = 0$ for some nonzero $V$. Then by positive-definiteness of $C_0, \Sigma$, and $\Gamma$, it must be that $v_0 = 0$ and $v_{j+1} = M v_j$ for $j = 0, 1, \ldots, J$. Thus, we must have $V = 0$. This proves that $\Omega$ is positive definite. □

**Remark 8.8** Since the smoothing distribution in the linear-Gaussian setting is itself Gaussian, its mean agrees with its mode. Therefore, the posterior mean found above is the unique minimizer of $J(V)$; that is, the MAP estimator. ◊

### 8.2.2 Kalman Smoother: Solution of the Linear System

The mean of the Kalman smoother may be obtained by Gaussian elimination, as summarized in the following algorithm.

---

**Algorithm 8.2** Kalman Smoother by Gaussian Elimination

---

1: **Input**: Initial distribution $\pi_0 = \mathcal{N}(m_0, C_0)$ with $m_0 \in \mathbb{R}^d$, $C_0 \in \mathbb{R}^{d \times d}$.

2: **Row reduction**: Define a matrix sequence $\{\Omega_j\}$:

$$\Omega_0 = \Omega_{0,0},$$
$$\Omega_{j+1} = \Omega_{j+1,j+1} - M^\top \Sigma^{-1} \Omega_j^{-1} \Sigma^{-1} M, \quad j = 0, \ldots, J-1; \tag{8.13}$$

and vector sequence $\{z_j\}$:

$$z_0 = C_0^{-1} m_0,$$
$$z_{j+1} = \Pi^\top \Gamma^{-1} y_{j+1} - M^\top \Sigma^{-1} \Omega_j^{-1} z_j.$$

3: **Back-substitution**: Read off $m_J$ by solving the equation $\Omega_J m_J = z_J$. Perform back-substitution to obtain

$$\Omega_j m_j = z_j - \Omega_{j,j+1} m_{j+1}, \quad j = J-1, \ldots, 1.$$

4: **Output**: Mean $m = \{m_j\}_{j=0}^J$ of the Kalman smoother.

---

Note that $m_J$ found this way coincides with the mean of the Kalman filter at $j = J$. The rest of this chapter is devoted to proving the following proposition:

**Proposition 8.9**  *The matrices $\{\Omega_j\}$ in (8.13) are positive definite.*

*Proof*  The proof of this theorem relies on the following two lemmas:

**Lemma 8.10**  *If*

$$X := \begin{bmatrix} X_1 & \times & \times & \times \\ \times & X_2 & \times & \times \\ \times & \times & \cdots & \times \\ \times & \times & \times & X_d \end{bmatrix}$$

*is positive definite, then $X_i$ is positive definite for all $i \in \{1, \ldots, d\}$.*

**Lemma 8.11**  *Let $B$ be a block lower (or upper) triangular matrix with identity on the diagonal. Then $B$ is an invertible matrix.*

Using Lemma 8.10, we deduce that $\Omega_0 = \Omega_{0,0}$ is positive definite. Consider the matrix $B \in \mathbb{R}^{d(J+1) \times d(J+1)}$ defined as

$$B = \begin{bmatrix} I & 0 & & 0 \\ -\Omega_{1,0}\Omega_0^{-1} & I & \cdots & \cdots \\ 0 & & \cdots & 0 \\ & 0 & & I \end{bmatrix}.$$

We compute

$$
B\Omega B^\top =
\begin{bmatrix}
\Omega_0 & 0 & & & & 0 \\
0 & \Omega_1 & \Omega_{1,2} & \cdots & & 0 \\
& \Omega_{2,1} & \Omega_{2,2} & \cdots & & \\
& & & & & \\
0 & & & \Omega_{J-1,J-1} & \Omega_{J-1,J} \\
0 & & & \Omega_{J,J-1} & \Omega_{J,J}
\end{bmatrix}.
$$

By Lemma 8.10, the matrix

$$
\tilde{\Omega} =
\begin{bmatrix}
\Omega_1 & \Omega_{1,2} & \cdots & & 0 \\
\Omega_{2,1} & \Omega_{2,2} & \cdots & & \\
& & & & \\
& & \Omega_{J-1,J-1} & \Omega_{J-1,J} \\
& & \Omega_{J,J-1} & \Omega_{J,J}
\end{bmatrix}
$$

is positive definite, and so is $\Omega_0$.

Lemma 8.10 and the positive-definiteness of $\tilde{\Omega}$ imply that $\Omega_1$ is positive definite. Therefore, by Lemma 8.11 the matrix

$$
B_2 =
\begin{bmatrix}
I & 0 & & 0 \\
-\Omega_{2,1}\Omega_1^{-1} & I & \cdots & \cdots \\
& & \cdots & 0 \\
0 & & & I
\end{bmatrix}
$$

is invertible. Thus, we have

$$
B_2\tilde{\Omega}B_2^\top =
\begin{bmatrix}
\Omega_1 & 0 & & & & 0 \\
0 & \Omega_2 & \Omega_{2,3} & \cdots & & \\
& \Omega_{3,2} & \Omega_{3,3} & & & 0 \\
& & & & & \\
& & & \Omega_{J-1,J-1} & \Omega_{J-1,J} \\
0 & & & \Omega_{J,J-1} & \Omega_{J,J}
\end{bmatrix},
$$

giving the positive-definiteness of $\Omega_2$. Iterating the argument shows that all the $\Omega_j$ are positive definite. □

## 8.3 Discussion and Bibliography

The original paper of Kalman (1960) in which the Kalman filter is derived, is arguably the first systematic presentation of a methodology for combining predictive models with data; it is noteworthy that Kalman did not employ the

Bayesian perspective to derive the filter which bears his name, but rather invoked a minimum variance hypothesis. The continuous time analog of the Kalman filter, which goes by the name Kalman–Bucy filter and applies to stochastic differential equations, may be found in Kalman and Bucy (1961). We refer to Rauch et al. (1965), Gelb et al. (1974), Anderson and Moore (1979), Law et al. (2015), Reich and Cotter (2015), Asch et al. (2016), and Särkkä (2013) for further background on the linear-Gaussian setting and for alternative derivations and expressions of the Kalman update formulae. Kalman filters and smoothers are the cornerstones of numerous data assimilation algorithms for filtering and smoothing, some of which will be studied in the next two chapters. Harvey (1964) overviews the subject in the context of time-series analysis and economics. The optimality of the Kalman filter is described in Anderson and Moore (1979). Sanz-Alonso and Stuart (2015) contains an application of the optimality property of the Kalman filter (which applies beyond the linear-Gaussian setting to the mean of the filtering distribution in quite general settings). A link between the standard implementation of the Kalman smoother and Gauss–Newton methods for MAP estimation is made in Bell (1994). For further details on the Kalman smoother, in both discrete and continuous time, see Law et al. (2015) and Hairer et al. (2013). We refer to Krishnan et al. (2017) for a machine learning approach to learning linear (and nonlinear) dynamics and data models using deep learning.

# 9

# Optimization for Filtering and Smoothing: 3DVAR and 4DVAR

This chapter demonstrates the use of optimization, namely the 3DVAR and 4DVAR methodologies, to obtain information from the filtering and smoothing distributions. We emphasize that the methods we present in this chapter do not provide approximations of the filtering and smoothing distributions; they simply provide estimates of the signal, given data, in the filtering (on-line) and smoothing (off-line) data scenarios. Their relationship to the filtering and smoothing distributions is analogous to the relationship of MAP estimation to the full Bayesian posterior distribution. In the previous chapter we showed how the mean of the Kalman filter could be derived through an optimization principle, once the predictive covariance is known; this idea is generalized to nonlinear forward models to obtain 3DVAR. On the other hand, 4DVAR is defined directly as a MAP estimator.

Here "VAR" refers to variational, and encodes the concept of optimization. The 3D and 4D, respectively, refer to three Euclidean spatial dimensions and to three Euclidean spatial dimensions plus a time dimension; this nomenclature reflects the historical derivation of these problems in the geophysical sciences, but the specific structure of fields over three-dimensional Euclidean space plays no role in the generalized form of the methods described here. The key distinction is that 3DVAR solves a sequence of optimization problems at each point in time (hence is an on-line filtering method); in contrast, 4DVAR solves an optimization problem which involves data distributed over time (and is an off-line smoothing method).

This chapter is organized as follows. We introduce the problem setting in Section 9.1. 3DVAR and 4DVAR are considered, in turn, in Sections 9.2 and 9.3. Section 9.4 closes with extensions and bibliographical remarks.

|  Kalman Filter | 3DVAR |
| --- | --- |
| $m_{j+1} = \arg \min_v J(v)$ | $m_{j+1} = \arg \min_v J(v)$ |
| $J(v) = \frac{1}{2}\|y_{j+1} - Hv\|_\Gamma^2 + \frac{1}{2}\|v - \widehat{m}_{j+1}\|_{\widehat{C}_{j+1}}^2$ | $J(v) = \frac{1}{2}\|y_{j+1} - Hv\|_\Gamma^2 + \frac{1}{2}\|v - \widehat{m}_{j+1}\|_{\widehat{C}}^2$ |
| $\widehat{m}_{j+1} = Mm_j$ | $\widehat{m}_{j+1} = \Psi(m_j)$ |
| $m_{j+1} = (I - K_{j+1}H)\widehat{m}_{j+1} + K_{j+1}y_{j+1}$ | $m_{j+1} = (I - KH)\widehat{m}_{j+1} + Ky_{j+1}$ |

Table 9.1 *Comparison of Kalman filter and 3DVAR update formulae.*

## 9.1 The Setting

3DVAR borrows from the Kalman filter optimization principle outlined in Subsection 8.1.2, but substitutes a fixed given covariance for the predictive covariance. Throughout we consider the setting, commonly occurring in applications, in which the dynamics model is nonlinear, but the observation function is linear. We thus have a discrete-time dynamical system with noisy state transitions and noisy observations given by

Stochastic Dynamics Model:  $v_{j+1} = \Psi(v_j) + \xi_j, \quad j \in \mathbb{Z}^+.$

Data Model:  $y_{j+1} = Hv_{j+1} + \eta_{j+1}, \quad j \in \mathbb{Z}^+,$ for some $H \in \mathbb{R}^{k \times d}.$

Probabilistic Structure:  $v_0 \sim \mathcal{N}(m_0, C_0), \quad \xi_j \sim \mathcal{N}(0, \Sigma), \quad \eta_j \sim \mathcal{N}(0, \Gamma).$

Probabilistic Structure:  $v_0 \perp \{\xi_j\} \perp \{\eta_j\}$ independent.

## 9.2 3DVAR

We introduce 3DVAR by analogy with the update formula (8.8) for the Kalman filter, and its derivation through optimization from Subsection 8.1.2. The primary differences between 3DVAR and the Kalman filter mean update are that $\Psi(\cdot)$ can be nonlinear for 3DVAR, and that for 3DVAR we have no closed update formula for the covariances. To deal with this second issue, 3DVAR uses a fixed predicted covariance, independent of time $j$, and pre-specified. The resulting minimization problem, and its solution, is described in Table 9.1, making the analogy with the Kalman filter.

Note that the minimization itself is of a quadratic functional, and so may be solved by means of linear algebra. The constraint formulation used for the

Kalman filter, in Subsection 8.1.2, may also be applied and used to derive the mean update formula.

### 9.2.1 3DVAR: Algorithmic Implementation

The 3DVAR filtering method is fully described in the following algorithm.

---

**Algorithm 9.1** 3DVAR

---

1: **Input**: Initial mean $m_0 \in \mathbb{R}^d$ and fixed predictive covariance $\widehat{C} \in \mathbb{R}^{d \times d}$.
2: For $j = 0, 1, \ldots, J - 1$ do the following prediction and analysis steps:
3: **Prediction**:

$$\widehat{m}_{j+1} = \Psi(m_j). \tag{9.1}$$

4: **Analysis**:

$$m_{j+1} = (I - KH)\widehat{m}_{j+1} + K y_{j+1}. \tag{9.2}$$

5: **Output**: Estimates $\{m_j\}_{j=1}^{J}$ of the signal.

---

The Kalman gain $K$ for 3DVAR is fixed, because the predicted covariance $\widehat{C}$ is fixed. Precisely we have, by analogy with the Kalman filter, the following formulae for the 3DVAR gain matrix $K$ :

$$S = H\widehat{C}H^\top + \Gamma,$$
$$K = \widehat{C}H^\top S^{-1}.$$

The method also delivers an implied analysis covariance $C = (I - KH)\widehat{C}$. Note that the resulting algorithm which maps $m_j$ to $m_{j+1}$ may be specified directly in terms of the gain $K$, without need to introduce $\widehat{C}, C$, and $S$. In the remainder of this section we simply view $K$ as fixed and given. In this setting we show that the 3DVAR algorithm produces accurate state estimation under vanishing noise assumptions in the dynamics/data model.

### 9.2.2 3DVAR: Long-Time Accuracy

We will make the following assumptions on the dynamics/data model:

**Assumption 9.1** *Consider the dynamics/data model under the assumptions that $\xi_j \equiv 0, \Gamma = \gamma^2 \Gamma_0, |\Gamma_0| = 1$ and assume that the data $y_{j+1}$ used in the 3DVAR* *algorithm is found from observing a true signal $v_j^\dagger$ given by*

$$\text{Dynamics Model:} \quad v_{j+1}^\dagger = \Psi(v_j^\dagger), \quad j \in \mathbb{Z}^+.$$

$$\text{Data Model:} \quad y_{j+1} = Hv_{j+1}^\dagger + \gamma\eta_{j+1,0}^\dagger, \quad j \in \mathbb{Z}^+.$$

With this assumption of noise-free dynamics ($\xi_j \equiv 0$) we deduce that the 3DVAR filter produces output which, asymptotically, has an error of the same size as the observational noise error $\gamma$. The key additional assumption in the theorem that allows this deduction is a relationship between the Kalman gain $K$ and the derivative $D\Psi(\cdot)$ of the dynamics model. Encoded in the assumption are two ingredients: that the observation function $H$ is rich enough in principle to learn enough components of the system to synchronize the whole system; and that $K$ is designed cleverly enough to effect this synchronization. The proof of the theorem is simply using these two ingredients and then controlling the small stochastic perturbations, arising from noisy observations in Assumption 9.1.

**Theorem 9.2** (Accuracy of 3DVAR)    *Let Assumption 9.1 hold with $\eta_{j,0}^\dagger \sim \mathcal{N}(0, \Gamma_0)$ an i.i.d. sequence. Assume that, for the gain matrix $K$ appearing in the 3DVAR method, there exists a norm $\|\cdot\|$ on $\mathbb{R}^d$ and constant $\lambda \in (0, 1)$ such that, for all $v \in \mathbb{R}^d$,*

$$\|(I - KH)D\Psi(v)\| \le \lambda.$$

*Then, there is a constant $c > 0$ such that the 3DVAR algorithm satisfies the following large-time asymptotic error bound:*

$$\limsup_{j \to \infty} \mathbb{E}[\|m_j - v_j^\dagger\|] \le \frac{c\gamma}{1 - \lambda},$$

*where the expectation is taken with respect to the sequence $\{\eta_{j,0}^\dagger\}$.*

*Proof*    We have

$$v_{j+1}^\dagger = \Psi(v_j^\dagger),$$
$$m_{j+1} = (I - KH)\Psi(m_j) + Ky_{j+1},$$

and hence that

$$v_{j+1}^\dagger = (I - KH)\Psi(v_j^\dagger) + KH\Psi(v_j^\dagger),$$
$$m_{j+1} = (I - KH)\Psi(m_j) + KH\Psi(v_j^\dagger) + \gamma K\eta_{j+1,0}^\dagger.$$

Define $e_j = m_j - v_j^\dagger$. By subtracting the evolution equation for $v_j^\dagger$ from that for

$m_j$ we obtain, using the mean value theorem,

$$e_{j+1} = m_{j+1} - v_{j+1}^{\dagger}$$
$$= (I - KH)\big(\Psi(m_j) - \Psi(v_j^{\dagger})\big) + \gamma K\eta_{j+1,0}^{\dagger}$$
$$= \left((I - KH)\int_0^1 D\Psi\big(sm_j + (1-s)v_j^{\dagger}\big)ds\right)e_j + \gamma K\eta_{j+1,0}^{\dagger}.$$

As a result, by the triangle inequality,

$$\|e_{j+1}\| \le \left\|\left(\int_0^1 (I - KH)D\Psi\big(sm_j + (1-s)v_j^{\dagger}\big)ds\right)e_j\right\| + \|\gamma K\eta_{j+1,0}^{\dagger}\|$$
$$\le \left(\int_0^1 \left\|(I - KH)D\Psi\big(sm_j + (1-s)v_j^{\dagger}\big)\right\|ds\right)\|e_j\| + \|\gamma K\eta_{j+1,0}^{\dagger}\|$$
$$\le \lambda\|e_j\| + \gamma\|K\eta_{j+1,0}^{\dagger}\|.$$

Taking expectations on both sides, we obtain, for $c := \mathbb{E}[\|K\eta_{j+1,0}^{\dagger}\|] > 0$,

$$\mathbb{E}[\|e_{j+1}\|] \le \lambda\,\mathbb{E}[\|e_j\|] + \gamma\,\mathbb{E}[\|K\eta_{j+1,0}^{\dagger}\|]$$
$$\le \lambda\,\mathbb{E}[\|e_j\|] + \gamma c. \tag{9.3}$$

Using the discrete Gronwall inequality of Theorem 1.19, we have that

$$\mathbb{E}[\|e_j\|] \le \lambda^j\,\mathbb{E}[\|e_0\|] + \sum_{i=0}^{j-1} c\lambda^i \gamma$$
$$\le \lambda^j\,\mathbb{E}[\|e_0\|] + c\gamma\frac{1 - \lambda^j}{1 - \lambda}, \tag{9.4}$$

where $e_0 = m_0 - v_0$. Since $\lambda < 1$, the desired statement follows. $\qquad\square$

## 9.3 4DVAR

Recall that 3DVAR differs from 4DVAR because, whilst also based on an optimization principle, 4DVAR is applied in a distributed fashion over all data in the time interval $j = 1, \ldots, J$; in contrast 3DVAR is applied sequentially from time $j - 1$ to time $j$, for $j = 1, \ldots, J$. We consider two forms of the methodology: *weak constraint 4DVAR (w4DVAR)*, in which the fact that the dynamics model contains randomness is accounted for in the optimization; and *4DVAR* (sometimes known as *strong constraint 4DVAR*), which can be derived from w4DVAR in the limit of $\Sigma \to 0$ (no randomness in the dynamics).

The objective function minimized in w4DVAR is

$$J(V) = \frac{1}{2}|v_0 - m_0|^2_{C_0} + \frac{1}{2}\sum_{j=0}^{J-1}|v_{j+1} - \Psi(v_j)|^2_{\Sigma} + \frac{1}{2}\sum_{j=0}^{J-1}|y_{j+1} - Hv_{j+1}|^2_{\Gamma}, \quad (9.5)$$

where $V = \{v_j\}_{j=0}^{J} \in \mathbb{R}^{d(J+1)}$, $Y = \{y_j\}_{j=1}^{J} \in \mathbb{R}^{kJ}$, $v_j \in \mathbb{R}^d$, $y_j \in \mathbb{R}^k$, $H$ is the observation function, $\Sigma$ is the random dynamical system covariance, $\Gamma$ is the data noise covariance, and $m_0$ and $C_0$ are the mean and covariance of the initial state. The three terms in the objective function enforce, in turn, information about the initial condition $v_0$, the dynamics model, and the data model. Note that, because $\Psi$ is nonlinear, the objective is not quadratic and cannot be optimized in closed form. Implementation of the 4DVAR smoothing algorithm involves therefore using a suitable numerical optimization algorithm; a brief discussion of some guiding principles for the construction of gradient-based optimization methods can be found in Chapter 3, but whole books are devoted to this subject. In contrast, each step of 3DVAR requires solution of a quadratic optimization problem, tractable in closed form.

**Theorem 9.3** (Minimizer Exists for w4DVAR)    *Assume that $\Psi$ is bounded and continuous. Then $J$ has a minimizer, which is a MAP estimator for the smoothing problem.*

*Proof*    Recall Theorem 3.5, which shows that the MAP estimator based on the smoothing distribution $\mathbb{P}(V \mid Y) \propto \exp(-J(V))$ is attained provided that $J$ is guaranteed to be non-negative, continuous, and satisfy $J(V) \to \infty$ as $|V| \to \infty$. Now, the objective $J$ defined by equation (9.5) is clearly non-negative, and it is continuous since $\Psi$ is assumed to be continuous. It remains to show that $J(V) \to \infty$ as $|V| \to \infty$. Let $R$ be a bound for $\Psi$, so that $|\Psi(v_j)|_\Sigma \le R$ for all $v_j \in \mathbb{R}^d$. Then, since

$$J(V) \ge \frac{1}{2}|v_0|^2_{C_0} - |v_0|_{C_0}|m_0|_{C_0} + \frac{1}{2}\sum_{j=0}^{J-1}\left(|v_{j+1}|^2_\Sigma - 2R|v_{j+1}|_\Sigma\right),$$

it follows that $J(V) \to \infty$ as $|V| \to \infty$ and the proof is complete.    $\square$

We now consider the vanishing dynamical noise limit of w4DVAR. This is to minimize

$$J_0(V) = \frac{1}{2}|v_0 - m_0|^2_{C_0} + \frac{1}{2}\sum_{j=0}^{J-1}|y_{j+1} - Hv_{j+1}|^2_{\Gamma}$$

subject to the hard constraint that

$$v_{j+1} = \Psi(v_j), \quad j = 0, \ldots, J-1.$$

This is 4DVAR. Note that by using the constraint, 4DVAR can be written as a minimization over $v_0$, rather than over the entire sequence $\{v_j\}_{j=0}^J$ as is required in w4DVAR.

We let $J_\sigma$ denote the objective function J from w4DVAR in the case where $\Sigma$ is replaced by $\sigma^2 \Sigma_0$. Roughly speaking, the following result shows that minimizers of $J_\sigma$ converge as $\sigma \to 0^+$ to points in $\mathbb{R}^{k(J+1)}$ which satisfy the hard constraint associated with 4DVAR.

**Theorem 9.4** (Small Signal Noise Limit of w4DVAR) *Suppose that $\Psi$ is bounded and continuous and let $V^\sigma$ be a minimizer of $J_\sigma$. Then as $\sigma \to 0^+$ there is a convergent subsequence of $V^\sigma$ with limit $V^*$ satisfying $v_{j+1}^* = \Psi(v_j^*)$.*

*Proof* Throughout this proof $c$ is a constant which may change from instance to instance, but is independent of $\sigma$. Consider $V \in \mathbb{R}^{d(J+1)}$ defined by $v_0 = m_0$ and $v_{j+1} = \Psi(v_j)$. Then $V$ is bounded, as $\Psi(\cdot)$ is bounded, and the bound is independent of $\sigma$. Furthermore,

$$J_\sigma(V) = \frac{1}{2} \sum_{j=0}^{J-1} |y_{j+1} - Hv_{j+1}|_\Gamma^2 \le c,$$

where $c$ is independent of $\sigma$. It follows that

$$J_\sigma(V^\sigma) \le J_\sigma(V) \le c.$$

Thus,

$$\frac{1}{2}|v_{j+1}^\sigma - \Psi(v_j^\sigma)|_{\Sigma_0}^2 = \frac{\sigma^2}{2}|v_{j+1}^\sigma - \Psi(v_j^\sigma)|_\Sigma^2 \le \sigma^2 J_\sigma(V^\sigma) \le \sigma^2 c,$$

$$\frac{1}{2}|v_0^\sigma - m_0|_{C_0}^2 \le J_\sigma(V^\sigma) \le c.$$

Since $\Psi$ is bounded, these bounds imply that $|V^\sigma|$ is bounded above independently of $\sigma$. Therefore, there is a limit $V^* \colon V^\sigma \to V^*$ along a subsequence. By continuity

$$0 \le \frac{1}{2}|v_{j+1}^* - \Psi(v_j^*)|_{\Sigma_0}^2 \leftarrow \frac{1}{2}|v_{j+1}^\sigma - \Psi(v_j^\sigma)|_{\Sigma_0}^2 \le \sigma^2 c.$$

Letting $\sigma \to 0^+$ we obtain that $v_{j+1}^* = \Psi(v_j^*)$.  □

## 9.4 Discussion and Bibliography

The 3DVAR and 4DVAR methodologies, in the context of weather forecasting, are discussed in Lorenc (1986) and Fisher et al. (2009), respectively. The implementation of these methodologies by the UK Meteorological Office is overviewed in Lorenc et al. (2000) and Rawlins et al. (2007). The accuracy analysis presented here is similar to that which first appeared in Brett et al. (2013) and Moodey et al. (2013) and was developed further in Law et al. (2014), Sanz-Alonso and Stuart (2015), and Law et al. (2016). It arises from considering stochastic perturbations of the seminal work of Titi and collaborators, exemplified in Hayden et al. (2011); this in turn is linked to earlier work on synchronization in dynamical systems (Pecora and Carroll, 1990). In all these works, particular emphasis is placed in estimating the state of deterministic chaotic dynamical systems from partial and noisy observations (Lalley, 1999; Paulin et al., 2019, 2018; Branicki et al., 2018; Oljaca et al., 2018). For an overview of variational data assimilation methods, and their links to problems in physics and mechanics, see Abarbanel (2013) and the references therein; see also Bröcker (2013).

# 10

# The Extended and Ensemble Kalman Filters

In this chapter we describe the Extended Kalman Filter (ExKF)[1] and the Ensemble Kalman Filter (EnKF). The ExKF approximates the predictive covariance by linearization, while the EnKF approximates it by the empirical covariance of a collection of particles. The ExKF is a provably accurate approximation of the filtering distribution if the dynamics are approximately linear and small noise is present in both signal and data, in which case the filtering distribution is well approximated by a Gaussian. In such settings, the EnKF can also provide a good approximation of the filtering distribution if a sufficiently large number of particles is used. For problems where the filtering distributions are not well approximated by Gaussians, ExKF and EnKF can still be successful on-line optimizers for state estimation; they may be thought of as generalizations of 3DVAR in which the model covariance, which weights the model contribution to the optimization problem solved at every step, is updated on the basis of linearized (ExKF) or ensemble (EnKF) information.

This chapter is organized as follows. We introduce the problem setting in Section 10.1. The ExKF and EnKF are described, in turn, in Sections 10.2 and 10.3. We close in Section 10.4 with extensions and bibliographical remarks.

## 10.1 The Setting

Throughout this chapter we consider the setting in which 3DVAR was introduced and may be applied: the dynamics model is nonlinear, but the observation

---

[1] The extended Kalman filter is often termed the EKF in the literature, a terminology introduced before the existence of the EnKF; we find it useful to write ExKF to unequivocally distinguish it from the EnKF.

133

function is linear. For purposes of exposition, we summarize it again here:

$$v_{j+1} = \Psi(v_j) + \xi_j, \qquad\qquad \xi_j \sim \mathcal{N}(0, \Sigma) \text{ i.i.d.,}$$
$$y_{j+1} = Hv_{j+1} + \eta_{j+1}, \qquad\qquad \eta_j \sim \mathcal{N}(0, \Gamma) \text{ i.i.d.,}$$

with, as in previous chapters, $v_0 \sim \mathcal{N}(m_0, C_0)$ independent of the independent i.i.d. sequences $\{\xi_j\}$ and $\{\eta_j\}$. Throughout this chapter we assume that $v_j \in \mathbb{R}^d$, $y_j \in \mathbb{R}^k$.

## 10.2  The Extended Kalman Filter

This method is derived by applying the Kalman methodology, using linearization to propagate the covariance $C_j$ to the predictive covariance $\widehat{C}_{j+1}$. Table 10.1 summarizes the idea, and in what follows we calculate the formulae required in full detail.

We first recall the Kalman filter update formulae and their derivation. We have

$$\widehat{v}_{j+1} = Mv_j + \xi_j, \quad v_j \sim \mathcal{N}(m_j, C_j), \quad \xi_j \sim \mathcal{N}(0, \Sigma). \tag{10.1}$$

From this we deduce, by taking expectations, that

$$\widehat{m}_{j+1} = \mathbb{E}[\widehat{v}_{j+1} \mid Y_j] = \mathbb{E}[Mv_j + \xi_j \mid Y_j] = \mathbb{E}[Mv_j \mid Y_j] + \mathbb{E}[\xi_j \mid Y_j] = Mm_j. \tag{10.2}$$

| Kalman Filter | ExKF |
|:---:|:---:|
| $m_{j+1} = \arg\min_v \mathsf{J}(v)$ | $m_{j+1} = \arg\min_v \mathsf{J}(v)$ |
| $\mathsf{J}(v) = \frac{1}{2}\lvert y_{j+1} - Hv\rvert_\Gamma^2 + \frac{1}{2}\lvert v - \widehat{m}_{j+1}\rvert_{\widehat{C}_{j+1}}^2$ | $\mathsf{J}(v) = \frac{1}{2}\lvert y_{j+1} - Hv\rvert_\Gamma^2 + \frac{1}{2}\lvert v - \widehat{m}_{j+1}\rvert_{\widehat{C}_{j+1}}^2$ |
| $\widehat{m}_{j+1} = Mm_j$ | $\widehat{m}_{j+1} = \Psi(m_j)$ |
| $\widehat{C}_{j+1}$ update exact | $\widehat{C}_{j+1}$ update by linearization |
| $m_{j+1} = (I - K_{j+1}H)\widehat{m}_{j+1} + K_{j+1}y_{j+1}$ | $m_{j+1} = (I - K_{j+1}H)\widehat{m}_{j+1} + K_{j+1}y_{j+1}$ |

Table 10.1 *Comparison of Kalman filter and ExKF update formulae.*

The covariance update is derived as follows:

$$\widehat{C}_{j+1} = \mathbb{E}\Big[(\widehat{v}_{j+1} - \widehat{m}_{j+1}) \otimes (\widehat{v}_{j+1} - \widehat{m}_{j+1}) \mid Y_j\Big]$$

$$= \mathbb{E}\Big[(M(v_j - m_j) + \xi_j) \otimes (M(v_j - m_j) + \xi_j) \mid Y_j\Big]$$

$$= \mathbb{E}\Big[(M(v_j - m_j)) \otimes (M(v_j - m_j)) \mid Y_j\Big] + \mathbb{E}\Big[\xi_j \otimes \xi_j \mid Y_j\Big] \quad (10.3)$$

$$+ \mathbb{E}\Big[(M(v_j - m_j)) \otimes \xi_j \mid Y_j\Big] + \mathbb{E}\Big[\xi_j \otimes (M(v_j - m_j)) \mid Y_j\Big]$$

$$= M\,\mathbb{E}\Big[(v_j - m_j) \otimes (v_j - m_j) \mid Y_j\Big]M^\top + \Sigma$$

$$= MC_j M^\top + \Sigma.$$

For the ExKF, the prediction map $\Psi$ is no longer linear. But since $\xi_j$ is independent of $Y_j$ and $v_j$, we obtain

$$\widehat{m}_{j+1} = \mathbb{E}\Big[\Psi(v_j) + \xi_j \mid Y_j\Big] = \mathbb{E}\Big[\Psi(v_j) \mid Y_j\Big] + \mathbb{E}\Big[\xi_j \mid Y_j\Big] = \mathbb{E}\Big[\Psi(v_j) \mid Y_j\Big].$$

If we assume that the fluctuations of $v_j$ around its mean $m_j$ (conditional on data) are small, then a reasonable approximation is to take $\Psi(v_j) \approx \Psi(m_j)$ so that

$$\widehat{m}_{j+1} = \Psi(m_j). \quad (10.4)$$

For the predictive covariance we use linearization; we have

$$\widehat{C}_{j+1} = \mathbb{E}\Big[(\widehat{v}_{j+1} - \widehat{m}_{j+1}) \otimes (\widehat{v}_{j+1} - \widehat{m}_{j+1}) \mid Y_j\Big]$$

$$= \mathbb{E}\Big[(\Psi(v_j) - \Psi(m_j) + \xi_j) \otimes (\Psi(v_j) - \Psi(m_j) + \xi_j) \mid Y_j\Big]$$

$$= \mathbb{E}\Big[(\Psi(v_j) - \Psi(m_j)) \otimes (\Psi(v_j) - \Psi(m_j)) \mid Y_j\Big] + \Sigma$$

$$\approx D\Psi(m_j)\,\mathbb{E}\Big[(v_j - m_j) \otimes (v_j - m_j) \mid Y_j\Big]D\Psi(m_j)^\top + \Sigma,$$

and so, again assuming that fluctuations of $v_j$ around its mean $m_j$ (conditional on data) are small, we invoke the approximation

$$\widehat{C}_{j+1} = D\Psi(m_j)C_j D\Psi(m_j)^\top + \Sigma. \quad (10.5)$$

To be self-consistent, $\Sigma$ itself should be small. We next summarize the steps of the ExKF.

---

**Algorithm 10.1** Extended Kalman Filter

---

1: **Input**: Initial mean $m_0 \in \mathbb{R}^d$ and covariance $C_0 \in \mathbb{R}^{d \times d}$.

2: For $j = 0, 1, \ldots, J - 1$ do the following prediction and analysis steps:

3: **Prediction**:

$$\widehat{m}_{j+1} = \Psi(m_j), \tag{10.6}$$

$$\widehat{C}_{j+1} = D\Psi(m_j)C_j D\Psi(m_j)^\top + \Sigma. \tag{10.7}$$

4: **Analysis**:

$$m_{j+1} = (I - K_{j+1}H)\widehat{m}_{j+1} + K_{j+1}y_{j+1},$$
$$C_{j+1} = (I - K_{j+1}H)\widehat{C}_{j+1}. \tag{10.8}$$

5: **Output**: Predictive means $\{\widehat{m}_j\}_{j=1}^J$ and covariances $\{\widehat{C}_j\}_{j=1}^J$, and analysis means $\{m_j\}_{j=1}^J$ and covariances $\{C_j\}_{j=1}^J$.

---

Note that the Kalman gain $K_{j+1}$ in equation (10.8) is defined in the same way as for the Kalman filter, namely

$$K_{j+1} = \widehat{C}_{j+1}H^\top S_{j+1}^{-1}, \qquad S_{j+1} = H\widehat{C}_{j+1}H^\top + \Gamma.$$

Thus, the analysis step is the same as for the Kalman filter. However, for the ExKF, the maps $C_j \mapsto \widehat{C}_{j+1} \mapsto C_{j+1}$ depend on the observed data through the dependence of the predictive covariance on the filter mean. To be self-consistent with the "small fluctuations around the mean" assumptions made in the derivation of the ExKF, $\Sigma$ and $\Gamma$ should both be small.

The analysis step can also be defined by

$$C_{j+1}^{-1} = \widehat{C}_{j+1}^{-1} + H^\top \Gamma^{-1} H,$$
$$m_{j+1} = \arg\min_v J(v),$$

where

$$J(v) = \frac{1}{2}|y_{j+1} - Hv|_\Gamma^2 + \frac{1}{2}|v - \widehat{m}_{j+1}|_{\widehat{C}_{j+1}}^2 \tag{10.9}$$

and $\widehat{m}_{j+1}, \widehat{C}_{j+1}$ are calculated as above in the prediction step (10.6). The constraint formulation of the minimization problem, derived for the Kalman filter in Section 8.1.2, may also be used to derive the update formulae above.

## 10.3 The Ensemble Kalman Filter

When the dynamical system is in high dimension, evaluation and storage of the predictive covariance, and in particular the Jacobian required for the update formula (10.5), becomes computationally inefficient and expensive for the ExKF. The EnKF was developed to overcome this issue. The basic idea is to maintain an ensemble of particles, and to use their empirical covariance within a Kalman-type update. The method is summarized in Table 10.2. It may be thought of as an ensemble 3DVAR technique in which a collection of particles are generated similarly to 3DVAR, but interact through an ensemble estimate of their covariance.

In the basic form which we present here, the EnKF is applied when $\Psi$ is nonlinear, while the observation function $H$ is linear. The $N$ particles used at step $j$ are denoted $\{v_j^{(n)}\}_{n=1}^N$. They are all given equal weight, so it is possible, in principle, to make an approximation to the filtering distribution of the form

$$\pi_j^N(v_j) \approx \frac{1}{N} \sum_{n=1}^N \delta\big(v_j - v_j^{(n)}\big).$$

This approximation can in principle be accurate if $N$ is sufficiently large and the filtering distributions are approximately Gaussian. In problems where approximate Gaussianity of the filtering distribution fails – for instance due to strong nonlinearity of $\Psi$ and large observation noise – EnKF is better understood as a sequential optimization method, similar in spirit to 3DVAR, as described in the introduction to the chapter.

The states of all the particles at time $j + 1$ are predicted to give $\{\widehat{v}_{j+1}^{(n)}\}_{n=1}^N$ using the dynamical model. The resulting empirical covariance is then used to define an objective function which is minimized in order to perform the analysis step and obtain $\{v_{j+1}^{(n)}\}_{n=1}^N$. The updates are denoted schematically by

$$\{v_j^{(n)}\}_{n=1}^N \mapsto \{\widehat{v}_{j+1}^{(n)}\}_{n=1}^N \mapsto \{v_{j+1}^{(n)}\}_{n=1}^N.$$

The idea of the EnKF is summarized in Table 10.2. A full description of the algorithm is given below.

| Kalman Filter | EnKF |
|---|---|
| $m_{j+1} = \arg\min_v J(v)$ | $v_{j+1}^{(n)} = \arg\min_v J_n(v)$ |
| $J(v) = \frac{1}{2}\lvert y_{j+1} - Hv \rvert_\Gamma^2 + \frac{1}{2}\lvert v - \widehat{m}_{j+1} \rvert_{\widehat{C}_{j+1}}^2$ | $J_n(v) = \frac{1}{2}\lvert y_{j+1}^{(n)} - Hv \rvert_\Gamma^2 + \frac{1}{2}\lvert v - \widehat{v}_{j+1}^{(n)} \rvert_{\widehat{C}_{j+1}}^2$ |
| $\widehat{m}_{j+1} = Mm_j$ | $\widehat{v}_{j+1}^{(n)} = \Psi(v_j^{(n)}) + \xi_j^{(n)}$ |
| $\widehat{C}_{j+1}$ update exact | $\widehat{C}_{j+1}$ update by ensemble estimate |
| $m_{j+1} = (I - K_{j+1}H)\widehat{m}_{j+1} + K_{j+1}y_{j+1}$ | $v_{j+1}^{(n)} = (I - K_{j+1}H)\widehat{v}_{j+1}^{(n)} + K_{j+1}y_{j+1}^{(n)}$ |

Table 10.2 *Comparison of Kalman filter and EnKF update formulae.*

## 10.3.1 Algorithmic Implementation of EnKF

We next summarize the steps of the EnKF:

---

**Algorithm 10.2** Ensemble Kalman Filter

1: **Input**: Ensemble size $N$. Initial ensemble $\{v_0^{(n)}\}_{n=1}^N$. Parameter $s \in \{0, 1\}$.
2: For $j = 0, 1, \ldots, J - 1$ do the following prediction and analysis steps:
3: **Prediction**:

$$\xi_j^{(n)} \sim \mathcal{N}(0, \Sigma), \quad \text{i.i.d.}, \quad n = 1, \ldots, N,$$
$$\widehat{v}_{j+1}^{(n)} = \Psi(v_j^{(n)}) + \xi_j^{(n)}, \quad n = 1, \ldots, N,$$
$$\widehat{m}_{j+1} = \frac{1}{N} \sum_{n=1}^N \widehat{v}_{j+1}^{(n)}, \tag{10.10}$$
$$\widehat{C}_{j+1} = \frac{1}{N} \sum_{n=1}^N \left(\widehat{v}_{j+1}^{(n)} - \widehat{m}_{j+1}\right) \otimes \left(\widehat{v}_{j+1}^{(n)} - \widehat{m}_{j+1}\right).$$

4: **Analysis**:

$$\eta_{j+1}^{(n)} \sim \mathcal{N}(0, \Gamma), \quad n = 1, \ldots, N,$$
$$y_{j+1}^{(n)} = y_{j+1} + s\eta_{j+1}^{(n)}, \quad n = 1, \ldots, N, \tag{10.11}$$
$$v_{j+1}^{(n)} = (I - K_{j+1}H)\widehat{v}_{j+1}^{(n)} + K_{j+1}y_{j+1}^{(n)}, \quad n = 1, \ldots, N.$$

5: **Output**: Ensembles $\{v_j^{(n)}\}_{n=1}^N, \quad j = 0, 1, \ldots, J.$

---

Once again the Kalman gain $K_{j+1}$ in equation (10.11) is defined in the same way as for the Kalman filter, namely

$$K_{j+1} = \widehat{C}_{j+1} H^\top S_{j+1}^{-1}, \qquad S_{j+1} = H\widehat{C}_{j+1} H^\top + \Gamma.$$

However $\widehat{C}_{j+1}$ is estimated in a novel fashion, using an ensemble of particles; this is the key innovation behind the EnKF. The parameter $s$ may be chosen to be 0 or 1. The choice $s = 1$ is natural when aiming at approximating the Kalman filter in linear-Gaussian settings; in such case the $y_{j+1}^{(n)}$ are referred to as *perturbed observations*. The choice $s = 0$ is natural if viewing the algorithm as a sequential optimizer in problems where the filtering distributions are not well approximated by Gaussians.

The analysis step may be written as

$$v_{j+1}^{(n)} = \arg\min_v \mathsf{J}_n(v), \tag{10.12}$$

where

$$\mathsf{J}_n(v) := \frac{1}{2}|y_{j+1}^{(n)} - Hv|_\Gamma^2 + \frac{1}{2}|v - \widehat{v}_{j+1}^{(n)}|_{\widehat{C}_{j+1}}^2 \tag{10.13}$$

and the predictive mean and covariance are given by (10.10). Note that $\widehat{C}_{j+1}$ is typically not invertible as it is a rank $N$ matrix and $N$ is usually less than the dimension $d$ of the space on which $\widehat{C}_{j+1}$ acts; this is since the typical use of ensemble methods is for high-dimensional state-space estimation, with a small ensemble size. The minimizing solution can be found by regularizing $\widehat{C}_{j+1}$ by adding $\epsilon I$ for $\epsilon > 0$, deriving the update equations as above, and then letting $\epsilon \to 0^+$. Alternatively, the constraint formulation of the minimization problem, derived for the Kalman filter in Subsection 8.1.2, may also be used to derive the update formulae above.

The following theorem explains why perturbing the observations with $s = 1$ may be favored when aiming at approximating the Kalman filter in (close to) linear-Gaussian settings. Setting $s = 1$ ensures that if each prediction particle $\widehat{v}_{j+1}^{(n)}$ is distributed according to a non-degenerate Gaussian predictive distribution $\mathcal{N}(\widehat{m}_{j+1}, \widehat{C}_{j+1})$, then, in the linear-Gaussian setting, each analysis particle $\widehat{v}_{j+1}^{(n)}$ will be Gaussian distributed with mean and covariance given by the filtering distribution found by the Kalman filter formulae. This is achieved by updating each particle minimizing an objective defined using a randomization of the likelihood function.

**Theorem 10.1** (Perturbed Observation EnKF – Randomized Likelihood Viewpoint) *Suppose that $\widehat{v}_{j+1}^{(n)} \sim \mathcal{N}(\widehat{m}_{j+1}, \widehat{C}_{j+1})$ with $\widehat{C}_{j+1}$ positive definite. Let $v_{j+1}^{(n)}$ be the minimizer of*

$$J_n(v) := \frac{1}{2}|y_{j+1} + \eta_{j+1}^{(n)} - Hv|_\Gamma^2 + \frac{1}{2}|v - \widehat{v}_{j+1}^{(n)}|_{\widehat{C}_{j+1}}^2, \qquad \eta_{j+1}^{(n)} \sim \mathcal{N}(0,\Gamma), \quad (10.14)$$

*where $\widehat{v}_{j+1}^{(n)}$ and $\eta_{j+1}^{(n)}$ are independent. Then $v_{j+1}^{(n)} \sim \mathcal{N}(m_{j+1}, C_{j+1})$, where $m_{j+1}$ and $C_{j+1}$ are defined by*

$$m_{j+1} = \widehat{m}_{j+1} + K_{j+1}(y_{j+1} - H\widehat{m}_{j+1}), \tag{10.15}$$

$$C_{j+1} = (I - K_{j+1}H)\widehat{C}_{j+1}, \tag{10.16}$$

*and*

$$K_{j+1} := \widehat{C}_{j+1}H^\top (H\widehat{C}_{j+1}H^\top + \Gamma)^{-1}.$$

*Proof*   The minimizer of (10.14) is given by

$$v_{j+1}^{(n)} = \widehat{v}_{j+1}^{(n)} + K_{j+1}(y_{j+1} + \eta_{j+1}^{(n)} - H\widehat{v}_{j+1}^{(n)}) \tag{10.17}$$

$$= C_{j+1}\left\{ \widehat{C}_{j+1}^{-1}\widehat{v}_{j+1}^{(n)} + H^\top \Gamma^{-1}(y_{j+1} + \eta_{j+1}^{(n)}) \right\}, \tag{10.18}$$

where $C_{j+1}$ is defined in (10.16) and the equivalence between (10.17) and (10.18) follows from the equivalence of precision and covariance characterizations of the Kalman filter in Theorem 8.3 and equations (8.6) and (8.7). Notice that (10.17) and (10.18) show that $v_{j+1}^{(n)}$ can be written as a linear combination of Gaussian random variables, so $v_{j+1}^{(n)}$ is Gaussian. We next show that its mean and covariance are given by (10.15) and (10.16).
    First, from (10.17) we deduce that

$$\mathbb{E}[v_{j+1}^{(n)}] = \mathbb{E}\left[ \widehat{v}_{j+1}^{(n)} + K_{j+1}(y_{j+1} + \eta_{j+1}^{(n)} - H\widehat{v}_{j+1}^{(n)}) \right]$$
$$= \widehat{m}_{j+1} + K_{j+1}(y_{j+1} - H\widehat{m}_{j+1}),$$

where we used that by assumption $\mathbb{E}[\widehat{v}_{j+1}^{(n)}] = \widehat{m}_{j+1}$ and that $\mathbb{E}[\eta_{j+1}^{(n)}] = 0$.
    Second, from (10.18) we deduce that

$$\mathbb{E}[(v_{j+1}^{(n)} - m_{j+1}) \otimes (v_{j+1}^{(n)} - m_{j+1})] = C_{j+1}\widehat{C}_{j+1}^{-1}C_{j+1} + C_{j+1}H^\top \Gamma^{-1}HC_{j+1}$$
$$= C_{j+1}(\widehat{C}_{j+1}^{-1} + H^\top \Gamma^{-1}H)C_{j+1}$$
$$= C_{j+1},$$

where we used that $C_{j+1}^{-1} = \widehat{C}_{j+1}^{-1} + H^\top \Gamma^{-1}H$ by the equivalent characterization of the Kalman filter covariance in Theorem 8.3 and equations (8.6) and (8.7).   □

## 10.3.2 Subspace Property of EnKF

We now give another way to think of, and exploit in algorithms, the low rank property of $\widehat{C}_{j+1}$. Note that $\mathsf{J}_n(v)$ is undefined unless

$$v - \widehat{v}_{j+1}^{(n)} = \widehat{C}_{j+1} a$$

for some $a \in \mathbb{R}^d$. From the structure of $\widehat{C}_{j+1}$ it follows that

$$v = \widehat{v}_{j+1}^{(n)} + \frac{1}{N} \sum_{m=1}^{N} b_m \big( \widehat{v}_{j+1}^{(m)} - \widehat{m}_{j+1} \big) \tag{10.19}$$

for some unknown vector $b = \{b_m\}_{m=1}^{N} \in \mathbb{R}^N$ to be determined. Note that both $a$ and $b$ depend on the ensemble member $n$, but we suppress that dependence from the notation. This form for $v$ can be substituted into (10.13) to obtain a functional $\mathsf{I}_n(b)$ to be minimized over $b \in \mathbb{R}^N$. We re-emphasize that $N$ will typically be much smaller than $d$, the state-space dimension. Once $b$ is determined, it may be substituted back into (10.19) to obtain the solution to the minimization problem.

To dig a little deeper into this calculation, we define

$$e^{(m)} = \widehat{v}_{j+1}^{(m)} - \widehat{m}_{j+1}$$

and note that then

$$\widehat{C}_{j+1} = \frac{1}{N} \sum_{m=1}^{N} e^{(m)} \otimes e^{(m)}.$$

Since

$$\widehat{C}_{j+1} a = \frac{1}{N} \sum_{m=1}^{N} b_m e^{(m)}$$

we deduce that

$$b_m = \langle e^{(m)}, a \rangle.$$

Now note that

$$\frac{1}{2} |v - \widehat{v}_{j+1}^{(n)}|_{\widehat{C}_{j+1}}^2 = \frac{1}{2} \langle a, \widehat{C}_{j+1} a \rangle = \frac{1}{2N} \sum_{m=1}^{N} b_m^2.$$

Therefore, defining

$$\mathsf{F}_n(b) := \frac{1}{2} \Big| y_{j+1}^{(n)} - H\widehat{v}_{j+1}^{(n)} - \frac{1}{N} \sum_{m=1}^{N} b_m H(\widehat{v}_{j+1}^{(n)} - \widehat{m}_{j+1}) \Big|_\Gamma^2 + \frac{1}{2N} \sum_{m=1}^{N} b_m^2 \tag{10.20}$$

we have proved the following:

**Theorem 10.2** (Implementation of EnKF in $N$-Dimensional Subspace)    *Given the prediction defined by* (10.10), *the Kalman update formulae* (10.11) *may be found by minimizing* $\mathsf{F}_n(b)$ *with respect to $b$ and substituting into* (10.19).

## 10.4  Discussion and Bibliography

In this chapter we have considered a derivative-based filtering algorithm (ExKF) and an ensemble-based filtering algorithm (EnKF). Extended and ensemble Kalman algorithms for the smoothing problem are also available, see e.g. Evensen and Van Leeuwen (2000) or Bell (1994). The development and theory of the ExKF is documented in Jazwinski (2007). A methodology for analyzing evolving probability distributions with small variance, and establishing the validity of the Gaussian approximation, is described in Sanz-Alonso and Stuart (2017). The use of the ExKF for weather forecasting was proposed in Ghil et al. (1981). However, the dimension of the state-space in most geophysical applications renders the ExKF impractical. The EnKF provided an innovation with far reaching consequences in geophysical applications, because it allowed for the use of partial, low-rank, empirical correlation information, without the computation of the full covariance. An overview of ensemble Kalman methods may be found in Evensen (2009), which includes a historical perspective on the subject, originating from the work of Evensen (1995) and Evensen and Leeuwen (1996); a similar idea was also developed by Houtekamer within the Canadian meteorological service, around the same time (Houtekamer and Derome, 1995; Houtekamer and Mitchell, 1998).

The presentation of the EnKF as a smart sequential optimization tool, adopted here, is developed in Law et al. (2015). The derivation of the update equations in a space whose dimension is that of the ensemble is well known to practitioners in the field (Asch et al., 2016) and is also described in Albers et al. (2019). The form of EnKF with perturbed observations ($s = 1$) presented in these notes is closely related to randomized maximum likelihood (Chen and Oliver, 2002), but other implementations of the algorithm are available, see e.g. Tippett et al. (2003), Anderson (2001), Bishop et al. (2001), and Majda and Harlim (2012). See also Kelly et al. (2014) for a proof of Theorem 10.1 and for further details on the connection between randomized maximum likelihood and perturbed observation EnKF.

The analysis of ensemble methods is difficult and theory is only just starting to emerge. In the linear case the method converges in the large ensemble limit to the Kalman filter (Gland et al., 2009; Mandel et al., 2011; Kwiatkowski and Mandel, 2015), but in the nonlinear case the limit does not reproduce the filtering distribution (Ernst et al., 2015). An overview of ensemble Kalman methods, adopting a unifying mean-field perspective in which $N \to \infty$, may be found in Calvello et al. (2022). That framework provides the basis for an analysis of the accuracy of the EnKF (Carrillo et al., 2022), in terms of its ability to approximate the true filtering distribution. However it is arguable that a major advantage of ensemble methods is that they can provide good state estimation when the number of particles is *not* large; this subject is discussed in Gottwald and Majda (2013), Kelly et al. (2014), Tong et al. (2015, 2016), and Al Ghattas and Sanz-Alonso (2022). In particular the paper Al Ghattas and Sanz-Alonso develops a unified non-asymptotic analysis of ensemble Kalman methods from the perspective of high-dimensional statistics, which explains why a small sample size $N$ suffices in applications where the covariance models have moderate effective dimension.

# 11

# Particle Filter

This chapter is devoted to the particle filter, a method that approximates the filtering distribution by a sum of Dirac masses. Particle filters provably converge to the filtering distribution as the number of particles, and hence the number of Dirac masses, approaches infinity. We focus on the bootstrap particle filter (BPF), also known as sequential importance resampling; it is linked to the material on Monte Carlo and importance sampling described in Chapter 5. We note that the Kalman filter completely characterizes the filtering distribution in the linear-Gaussian setting. The Kalman-based methods introduced in the two previous chapters apply outside the linear-Gaussian setting and are built by approximating the predictive distribution using a Gaussian ansatz, and then applying the Kalman formulae for the analysis step. The bootstrap particle filter approximates the predictive distribution by a sum of Dirac masses and, using this structure, exactly solves the analysis step. Thus, both Kalman-based methods (with linear observations) and the bootstrap particle filter use exact application of Bayes' formula, but with approximate priors found by approximating the outcome of the prediction step. However, whilst Kalman-based methods use an approximation that is only valid for problems which are close to Gaussian, particle filters have the potential of recovering an accurate approximation to the filtering distribution in nonlinear, non-Gaussian settings provided that the number of particles is large enough. However, an important disadvantage of particle filters is that they tend to struggle in high-dimensional problems for practically implementable particle numbers. In contrast, Kalman-based methods are robust, but harder to interpret in a rigorous fashion except for linear-Gaussian problems.

This chapter is organized as follows. We describe the problem setting in Section 11.1. We then introduce the bootstrap particle filter in Section 11.2 and analyze its convergence in Section 11.3. Section 11.4 describes how the bootstrap particle filter can be interpreted as a random dynamical system. We close in Section 11.5 with extensions and bibliographical remarks.

## 11.1 The Setting

Let us return to the setting in which we introduced filtering and smoothing in Chapter 7, with nonlinear stochastic dynamics and nonlinear observation function, namely the model

$$v_{j+1} = \Psi(v_j) + \xi_j, \qquad \xi_j \sim \mathcal{N}(0, \Sigma) \text{ i.i.d.,}$$
$$y_{j+1} = h(v_{j+1}) + \eta_{j+1}, \qquad \eta_j \sim \mathcal{N}(0, \Gamma) \text{ i.i.d.,}$$

with $v_0 \sim \pi_0 := \mathcal{N}(m_0, C_0)$ independent of the i.i.d. sequences $\{\xi_j\}$ and $\{\eta_j\}$. Here $\Psi(\cdot)$ drives the dynamics and $h(\cdot)$ is the observation function. Recall that we denote by $Y_j = \{y_1, \ldots, y_j\}$ all the data up to time $j$ and by $\pi_j$ the pdf of $v_j \mid Y_j$; that is, $\pi_j = \mathbb{P}(v_j \mid Y_j)$. The filtering problem is to determine $\pi_{j+1}$ from $\pi_j$. We may do so in two steps: first, we run forward the Markov chain generated by the stochastic dynamical system (prediction), and second, we incorporate the data by an application of Bayes' theorem (analysis).

For the prediction step, we define the operator $\mathcal{P}$ acting on a pdf $\pi$ as an application of a Markov kernel defined by

$$(\mathcal{P}\pi)(v) = \int_{\mathbb{R}^d} p(u, v)\pi(u)\, du, \tag{11.1}$$

where $p(u, v)$ is the associated pdf of the stochastic dynamics, so that

$$p(u, v) = \frac{1}{\sqrt{(2\pi)^d \det \Sigma}} \exp\left(-\frac{1}{2}|v - \Psi(u)|_\Sigma^2\right).$$

Thus, we obtain

$$\mathbb{P}(v_{j+1} \mid Y_j) = \widehat{\pi}_{j+1} = \mathcal{P}\pi_j.$$

We then define the analysis operator $\mathcal{A}_j$ acting on a pdf $\pi$ to correspond to an application of Bayes' theorem, namely

$$(\mathcal{A}_j\pi)(v) = \frac{l_j(v)\pi(v)}{\int_{\mathbb{R}^d} l_j(v)\pi(v)\, dv}, \qquad l_j(v) = \exp\left(-\frac{1}{2}|y_{j+1} - h(v)|_\Gamma^2\right).$$

Finally, combining the prediction and analysis steps, we obtain

$$\pi_{j+1} = \mathcal{A}_j\widehat{\pi}_{j+1} = \mathcal{A}_j\mathcal{P}\pi_j.$$

We now describe a way to numerically approximate, and update, the pdfs $\pi_j$.

## 11.2 The Bootstrap Particle Filter

The bootstrap particle filter can be thought of as performing sequential importance resampling. Let $S^N$ be an operator acting on a pdf $\pi$ by producing an $N$-samples Dirac approximation of $\pi$; that is,

$$(S^N \pi)(u) = \sum_{n=1}^{N} w_n \delta(u - u^{(n)}),$$

where $u^{(1)}, \ldots, u^{(N)}$ are i.i.d. samples from $\pi$ that are weighted uniformly, i.e. $w_n = \frac{1}{N}$. Note that $S^N \pi = \pi_{MC}^N$, as introduced in Chapter 5, equation (5.6). We will use the operator $S^N$ to approximate the measure produced by the Markov kernel step $\mathcal{P}$ within the overall filtering map $\mathcal{A}_j \mathcal{P}$. Note that $S^N$ is a *random* map taking pdfs into pdfs if we interpret weighted sums of Dirac masses as a pdf.

Let $\pi_0^N = \pi_0 = \mathcal{N}(m_0, C_0)$ and let $\pi_j^N$ denote a particle approximation of the pdf $\pi_j$ that we will determine in what follows. We define

$$\widehat{\pi}_{j+1}^N = S^N \mathcal{P} \pi_j^N;$$

this is an approximation of $\widehat{\pi}_{j+1}$ from the previous section. We then apply the operator $\mathcal{A}_j$ to act on $\widehat{\pi}_{j+1}^N$ by appropriately reconfiguring the weights $w_j$ according to the data.

To understand this reconfiguration of the weights we use the fact that, if

$$\pi(v) = \frac{1}{N} \sum_{n=1}^{N} \delta(v - v^{(n)}),$$

then

$$(\mathcal{A}_j \pi)(v) = \sum_{n=1}^{N} w^{(n)} \delta(v - v^{(n)}),$$

where

$$\overline{w}^{(n)} = l_j(v^{(n)})$$

and the $w^{(n)}$ are found from the $\overline{w}^{(n)}$ by renormalizing them to sum to one. We use this calculation concerning the application of Bayes' formula to sums of Dirac masses within the following desired approximation of the filtering update formula:

$$\pi_{j+1} \approx \pi_{j+1}^N = \mathcal{A}_j \widehat{\pi}_{j+1}^N = \mathcal{A}_j S^N \mathcal{P} \pi_j^N.$$

The steps for the method are summarized in Algorithm 11.1.

---

**Algorithm 11.1** Bootstrap Particle Filter

1: **Input**: Initial distribution $\pi_0^N = \pi_0$, number of particles $N$.

2: **Particle Generation**: For $j = 0, 1, \ldots, J - 1$, perform

1  Draw $v_j^{(n)} \sim \pi_j^N$ for $n = 1, \ldots, N$ i.i.d.

2  Set $\widehat{v}_{j+1}^{(n)} = \Psi(v_j^{(n)}) + \xi_j^{(n)}$ with $\xi_j^{(n)}$ i.i.d. $\mathcal{N}(0, \Sigma)$.

3  Set $\overline{w}_{j+1}^{(n)} = \exp\left(-\frac{1}{2}|y_{j+1} - h(\widehat{v}_{j+1}^{(n)})|_\Gamma^2\right)$.

4  Set $w_{j+1}^{(n)} = \overline{w}_{j+1}^{(n)} / \sum_{n=1}^N \overline{w}_{j+1}^{(n)}$.

5  Set $\pi_{j+1}^N(u) = \sum_{n=1}^N w_{j+1}^{(n)} \delta(u - \widehat{v}_{j+1}^{(n)})$.

3: **Output**: Particle approximations $\pi_j^{lN} \approx \pi_j$, $j = 1, \ldots, J$.

---

## 11.3  Bootstrap Particle Filter Convergence

We will now show that, under certain conditions, the BPF converges to the true filtering distribution in the limit $N \to \infty$. The proof is similar to that of the Lax Equivalence Theorem from the numerical approximation of evolution equations, part of which is the statement that consistency and stability together imply convergence. For the BPF, consistency refers to a Monte Carlo error estimate, similar to that derived in the chapter on importance sampling, and stability manifests in bounds on the Lipschitz constants for the operators $\mathcal{P}$ and $\mathcal{A}_j$.

Our first step is to define what we mean by convergence, that is, we need a metric on probability measures. Notice that the operators $\mathcal{P}$ and $\mathcal{A}_j$ are deterministic, but the operator $S^N$ is random since it requires sampling. As a consequence, the approximate pdfs $\pi_j^N$ are also random. Thus, in fact, we need a distance between random probability measures. To this end, for random pdfs $\pi$ and $\pi'$, we define

$$d(\pi, \pi') = \sup_{|f|_\infty \le 1} \left( \mathbb{E}\left[ \left( \pi(f) - \pi'(f) \right)^2 \right] \right)^{1/2},$$

where the expectation is taken over the random variable, in our case, the randomness from sampling with $S^N$. This distance between random probability measures was introduced in Chapter 5 to study Monte Carlo integration: see equation (5.7).

We now prove three lemmas, which together will enable us to prove convergence of the BPF. The first shows consistency; the second and third show stability estimates for $\mathcal{P}$ and $\mathcal{A}_j$, respectively.

**Lemma 11.1**  *For any pdf $\pi$, it holds that*

$$d(\pi, S^N \pi) \le \frac{1}{\sqrt{N}}.$$

*Proof*  This is a consequence of Theorem 5.1, since $S^N \pi$ agrees with $\pi_{\text{MC}}^N$ as defined in Chapter 5.  □

Now we prove a stability bound for the operator $\mathcal{P}$ defined in equation (11.1).

**Lemma 11.2**  *For any pdfs $\pi, \pi'$, it holds that*

$$d(\mathcal{P}\pi, \mathcal{P}\pi') \le d(\pi, \pi').$$

*Proof*  For $|f|_\infty \le 1$ define a function $q$ on $\mathbb{R}^d$ by

$$q(v') = \int_{\mathbb{R}^d} p(v', v) f(v) \, dv,$$

where, recall, $p$ denotes the transition pdf associated to the stochastic dynamics model. Note that

$$|q(v')| \le \int_{\mathbb{R}^d} p(v', v) \, dv = 1,$$

and so $|q|_\infty \le 1$. Moreover, it holds that

$$\pi(q) = (\mathcal{P}\pi)(f).$$

To see this, note that by exchanging the order of integration, we have

$$\pi(q) = \int_{\mathbb{R}^d} q(v') \pi(v') \, dv' = \int_{\mathbb{R}^d} \left[ \int_{\mathbb{R}^d} p(v', v) f(v) \, dv \right] \pi(v') \, dv'$$

$$= \int_{\mathbb{R}^d} \left[ \int_{\mathbb{R}^d} p(v', v) \pi(v') \, dv' \right] f(v) \, dv$$

$$= \int_{\mathbb{R}^d} (\mathcal{P}\pi)(v) f(v) \, dv.$$

Finally, using that $|q|_\infty \le 1$ and $\pi(q) = (\mathcal{P}\pi)(f)$, we deduce that

$$d(\mathcal{P}\pi, \mathcal{P}\pi') = \sup_{|f|_\infty \le 1} \left( \mathbb{E}\left[ ((\mathcal{P}\pi)(f) - (\mathcal{P}\pi')(f))^2 \right] \right)^{1/2}$$

$$\le \sup_{|q|_\infty \le 1} \left( \mathbb{E}\left[ (\pi(q) - \pi'(q))^2 \right] \right)^{1/2}$$

$$= d(\pi, \pi').$$

□

To prove the next lemma and the main convergence theorem of the BPF below, we will make the following assumption, which encodes the idea of a bound on the observation function.

**Assumption 11.3** *There exists $\kappa \in (0,1)$ such that, for all $v \in \mathbb{R}^d$ and $j \in \{0, \ldots, J-1\}$,*

$$\kappa \leq \mathsf{l}_j(v) \leq \kappa^{-1}.$$

It may initially appear strange to use the same constant $\kappa$ in the upper and lower bounds, but recall that $\mathsf{l}_j$ is undefined up to a multiplicative constant. Consequently, given any upper and lower bounds, $\mathsf{l}_j$ can be scaled to achieve the bound as stated. Relatedly, it is $\kappa^{-2}$ which appears in the stability constant in the next lemma; if $\mathsf{l}_j$ is not scaled to produce the same constant $\kappa$ in the upper and lower bounds in Assumption 11.3, then it is the ratio of the upper and lower bounds which would appear in the stability bound.

**Lemma 11.4** *Let Assumption 11.3 hold. Then, for all pdfs $\pi, \pi'$ and $j \in \{0, \ldots, J-1\}$, it holds that*

$$d(\mathcal{A}_j\pi, \mathcal{A}_j\pi') \leq \frac{2}{\kappa^2} d(\pi, \pi').$$

*Proof* To ease the notation, we drop the $j$ subscripts in $\mathsf{l}_j$ and $\mathcal{A}_j$. Let $|f|_\infty \leq 1$. Following the proof of Theorem 5.6 in Chapter 5, we use the following identity:

$$
\begin{aligned}
(\mathcal{A}\pi)(f) - (\mathcal{A}\pi')(f) &= \frac{\pi(f\mathsf{l})}{\pi(\mathsf{l})} - \frac{\pi'(f\mathsf{l})}{\pi'(\mathsf{l})} \\
&= \frac{\pi(f\mathsf{l})}{\pi(\mathsf{l})} - \frac{\pi'(f\mathsf{l})}{\pi(\mathsf{l})} + \frac{\pi'(f\mathsf{l})}{\pi(\mathsf{l})} - \frac{\pi'(f\mathsf{l})}{\pi'(\mathsf{l})} \\
&= \frac{1}{\kappa}\left(\frac{\pi(\kappa f\mathsf{l}) - \pi'(\kappa f\mathsf{l})}{\pi(\mathsf{l})} + \frac{\pi'(f\mathsf{l})}{\pi'(\mathsf{l})}\frac{\pi'(\kappa\mathsf{l}) - \pi(\kappa\mathsf{l})}{\pi(\mathsf{l})}\right).
\end{aligned}
$$

Applying Bayes' Theorem 1.2 and using that $|f|_\infty \leq 1$ gives

$$\left|\frac{\pi'(f\mathsf{l})}{\pi'(\mathsf{l})}\right| = |(\mathcal{A}\pi')(f)| \leq 1.$$

Therefore,

$$\left|(\mathcal{A}\pi)(f) - (\mathcal{A}\pi')(f)\right| \leq \frac{1}{\kappa^2}\left(\left|\pi(\kappa f\mathsf{l}) - \pi'(\kappa f\mathsf{l})\right| + \left|\pi'(\kappa\mathsf{l}) - \pi(\kappa\mathsf{l})\right|\right).$$

It follows that

$$\mathbb{E}\left[\left((\mathcal{A}\pi)(f) - (\mathcal{A}\pi')(f)\right)^2\right] \leq \frac{2}{\kappa^4}\left(\mathbb{E}\left[\left(\pi(\kappa f\mathsf{l}) - \pi'(\kappa f\mathsf{l})\right)^2\right] + \mathbb{E}\left[\left(\pi'(\kappa\mathsf{l}) - \pi(\kappa\mathsf{l})\right)^2\right]\right).$$

Since $|\kappa| \le 1$, we find that

$$\sup_{|f|_\infty \le 1} \mathbb{E}\Big[\big((\mathscr{A}\pi)(f) - (\mathscr{A}\pi')(f)\big)^2\Big] \le \frac{4}{\kappa^4} \sup_{|f|_\infty \le 1} \mathbb{E}\Big[\big(\pi(f) - \pi'(f)\big)^2\Big],$$

and hence

$$d(\mathscr{A}\pi, \mathscr{A}\pi') \le \frac{2}{\kappa^2} d(\pi, \pi').$$

$\square$

**Theorem 11.5** (Convergence of the BPF)   *Let Assumption 11.3 hold. Then there exists a $c = c(J, \kappa)$ independent of $N$ such that, for all $j = 1, \ldots, J$,*

$$d(\pi_j, \pi_j^N) \le \frac{c}{\sqrt{N}}.$$

*Proof*   Let $e_j = d(\pi_j, \pi_j^N)$. Using the triangle inequality,

$$\begin{aligned}
e_{j+1} = d(\pi_{j+1}, \pi_{j+1}^N) &= d(\mathscr{A}_j\mathscr{P}\pi_j, \mathscr{A}_j S^N \mathscr{P}\pi_j^N) \\
&\le d(\mathscr{A}_j\mathscr{P}\pi_j, \mathscr{A}_j\mathscr{P}\pi_j^N) + d(\mathscr{A}_j\mathscr{P}\pi_j^N, \mathscr{A}_j S^N \mathscr{P}\pi_j^N).
\end{aligned}$$

Applying the stability bound for $\mathscr{A}_j$, we have

$$e_{j+1} \le \frac{2}{\kappa^2}\Big[d(\mathscr{P}\pi_j, \mathscr{P}\pi_j^N) + d(\widehat{\pi}_j^N, S^N \widehat{\pi}_j^N)\Big],$$

where $\widehat{\pi}_j^N = \mathscr{P}\pi_j^N$. By the stability bound for $\mathscr{P}$,

$$d(\mathscr{P}\pi_j, \mathscr{P}\pi_j^N) \le d(\pi_j, \pi_j^N)$$

and by the consistency bound for $S^N$,

$$d(\widehat{\pi}_j^N, S^N \widehat{\pi}_j^N) \le \frac{1}{\sqrt{N}}.$$

Therefore,

$$\begin{aligned}
e_{j+1} &\le \frac{2}{\kappa^2}\Big(d(\pi_j, \pi_j^N) + \frac{1}{\sqrt{N}}\Big) \\
&\le \frac{2}{\kappa^2}\Big(e_j + \frac{1}{\sqrt{N}}\Big).
\end{aligned}$$

We let $\lambda = 2/\kappa^2$ and note that $\lambda \ge 2$ since $\kappa \in (0, 1]$. Then the discrete Gronwall inequality of Theorem 1.19 gives

$$e_j \le \lambda^j e_0 + \frac{\lambda}{\sqrt{N}} \frac{1 - \lambda^j}{1 - \lambda}.$$

Recall that $\pi_0^N = \pi_0$ hence $e_0 = 0$. Thus, letting

$$c = \frac{\lambda(1 - \lambda^J)}{1 - \lambda}$$

completes the proof since $\lambda(1 - \lambda^j)/(1 - \lambda)$ is increasing in $j$. $\qquad\square$

## 11.4 Random Dynamical System Formulation

A nice interpretation of the BPF is to view it as a random dynamical system for a set of interacting particles $\{v_j^{(n)}\}_{n=1}^N$. To this end, a measure

$$\bar{\pi}_j^N(u) = \frac{1}{N}\sum_{n=1}^N \delta(u - v_j^{(n)}) \approx \pi_j^N(u) \approx \pi_j(u)$$

with equally weighted particles may be naturally defined after the resampling step from $\pi_j^N$. It can then be seen that the BPF updates the particle positions

$$\{v_j^{(n)}\}_{n=1}^N \mapsto \{v_{j+1}^{(n)}\}_{n=1}^N$$

via the random map

$$\hat{v}_{j+1}^{(n)} = \Psi(v_j^{(n)}) + \xi_j^{(n)}, \qquad\qquad \xi_j^{(n)} \sim \mathcal{N}(0, \Sigma) \text{ i.i.d.,}$$

$$v_{j+1}^{(n)} = \sum_{m=1}^N \mathbb{1}_{I_{j+1}^{(m)}}\left(r_{j+1}^{(n)}\right)\hat{v}_{j+1}^{(m)}, \qquad r_{j+1}^{(n)} \sim \text{Uniform}(0, 1) \text{ i.i.d.}$$

Here the supports $I_j^{(m)}$ of the indicator functions have widths given by the weights appearing in $\pi_j^N(u)$. Specifically, we have

$$I_{j+1}^{(m)} = \left[\alpha_{j+1}^{(m-1)}, \alpha_{j+1}^{(m)}\right), \qquad \alpha_{j+1}^{(m+1)} = \alpha_{j+1}^{(m)} + w_{j+1}^{(m)}, \quad \alpha_{j+1}^{(0)} = 0.$$

Note that, by construction, $\alpha_j^{(N)} = 1$.

Thus, the underlying dynamical system on particles comprises $N$ particles governed by two steps: (i) the underlying stochastic dynamics model, in which the particles do not interact; (ii) a resampling of the resulting collection of particles, to reflect the different weights associated with them, in which the particles do then interact. The interaction is driven by the weights, which see all the particle positions and measure their goodness of fit to the data. Note that the same particle may be replicated more than once through the resampling in (ii) and, relatedly, a particle may disappear through the resampling.

## 11.5  Discussion and Bibliography

Particle filters are overviewed from an algorithmic viewpoint in Doucet et al. (2001, 2000), and from a more mathematical perspective in Del Moral (2004) and Chopin and Papaspiliopoulos (2020). The latter also reviews and compares a variety of ways of resampling the weights. The convergence of particle filters is addressed in Crisan et al. (1998); the clean proof presented here originates in Rebeschini and Handel (2015) and may also be found in Law et al. (2015). We refer to Crisan and Doucet (2002) for a review of convergence results for particle filters. They have been enormously successful for problems in which the dynamics evolve in relatively low-dimensional spaces. However, particle filters often perform poorly in high-dimensional systems due to the fact that the particle weight typically concentrates on one, or a small number, of particles – the phenomenon of weight collapse; see Bickel et al. (2008), Snyder et al. (2016), and Snyder (2011). Generalizing them so that they work for the high-dimensional problems that arise, for example, in geophysical applications, provides a major challenge (Leeuwen et al., 2015). This fact also motivates the widespread adoption of the EnKF in the geophysical sciences – despite the relative paucity of theoretical justification; in comparison with the particle filter, the EnKF automatically avoids weight collapse since all particles are equally weighted.

# 12

# Optimal Particle Filter

This chapter is devoted to the optimal particle filter (OPF). Like the bootstrap particle filter (BPF) from the previous chapter, the OPF approximates the filtering distribution by a sum of Dirac masses. But while the BPF is conceptually derived by factorizing the update of the filtering distribution into a prediction and an analysis step, the OPF uses a different factorization which can result in improved performance.

We introduce the decomposition of the filtering update used by the OPF in Section 12.1. The setting will initially be the same as for the BPF (nonlinear stochastic dynamics and nonlinear observations), and in this general setting we will prove a convergence result, similar to that for the BPF from the previous chapter. However, we will see that the OPF cannot be implemented in the fully nonlinear case without additional approximate sampling. For this reason, we will specify in Section 12.2 to the case of linear observations, where the OPF can be implemented in a straightforward fashion, without additional approximate sampling; indeed we will see that in this setting the method may be characterized as a set of interacting 3DVAR filters. Section 12.3 discusses the sense in which the OPF has desirable properties in comparison with the BPF. We close in Section 12.4 with bibliographical remarks.

## 12.1 The Bootstrap and Optimal Particle Filters Compared

We initially work in the setting in which we introduced filtering and smoothing in Chapter 7, with nonlinear stochastic dynamics and nonlinear observation function, namely the model

$$v_{j+1} = \Psi(v_j) + \xi_j, \qquad \xi_j \sim \mathcal{N}(0, \Sigma) \text{ i.i.d.,}$$
$$y_{j+1} = h(v_{j+1}) + \eta_{j+1}, \qquad \eta_j \sim \mathcal{N}(0, \Gamma) \text{ i.i.d.,}$$

with $v_0 \sim \pi_0 := \mathcal{N}(m_0, C_0)$ independent of the i.i.d. sequences $\{\xi_j\}$ and $\{\eta_j\}$. Here $\Psi(\cdot)$ drives the dynamics and $h(\cdot)$ is the observation function. Recall that we denote by $Y_j = \{y_1, \ldots, y_j\}$ all the data up to time $j$ and by $\pi_j$ the pdf of $v_j \mid Y_j$; that is, $\pi_j = \mathbb{P}(v_j \mid Y_j)$. The filtering problem is to determine $\pi_{j+1}$ from $\pi_j$.

The fundamental filtering problem that we are interested in is thus determination of $\mathbb{P}(v_{j+1} \mid Y_{j+1})$ from $\mathbb{P}(v_j \mid Y_j)$. The BPF is based on applying sampling to the outcome of the following manipulation:

$$
\begin{aligned}
\mathbb{P}(v_{j+1} \mid Y_{j+1}) &= \mathbb{P}(v_{j+1} \mid y_{j+1}, Y_j) \\
&= \frac{\mathbb{P}(y_{j+1} \mid v_{j+1}, Y_j)\, \mathbb{P}(v_{j+1} \mid Y_j)}{\mathbb{P}(y_{j+1} \mid Y_j)} \\
&= \frac{\mathbb{P}(y_{j+1} \mid v_{j+1}, Y_j)}{\mathbb{P}(y_{j+1} \mid Y_j)} \int_{\mathbb{R}^d} \mathbb{P}(v_{j+1} \mid v_j, Y_j)\, \mathbb{P}(v_j \mid Y_j)\, dv_j \\
&= \frac{\mathbb{P}(y_{j+1} \mid v_{j+1})}{\mathbb{P}(y_{j+1} \mid Y_j)} \int_{\mathbb{R}^d} \mathbb{P}(v_{j+1} \mid v_j)\, \mathbb{P}(v_j \mid Y_j)\, dv_j \\
&= \mathcal{A}_j \mathcal{P}\, \mathbb{P}(v_j \mid Y_j).
\end{aligned}
$$

The Markov kernel $\mathcal{P}$ acts on arbitrary density $\pi$ by

$$
\mathcal{P}\pi(v_{j+1}) = \int_{\mathbb{R}^d} \mathbb{P}(v_{j+1} \mid v_j)\pi(v_j)\, dv_j,
$$

and $\mathcal{A}_j$ acts on an arbitrary density $\pi$ by application of Bayes' theorem, taking into account the likelihood of the data

$$
\mathcal{A}_j \pi(v_{j+1}) = \frac{1}{Z} \mathbb{P}(y_{j+1} \mid v_{j+1})\pi(v_{j+1}),
$$

with $Z$ normalization to a probability density. The above manipulations are summarized by the relationship

$$
\pi_{j+1} = \mathcal{A}_j \mathcal{P} \pi_j. \tag{12.1}
$$

Note that in this factorization we apply a Markov kernel and then Bayes' theorem.

In contrast, to derive the OPF we perform the following manipulation:

$$
\begin{aligned}
\mathbb{P}(v_{j+1} \mid Y_{j+1}) &= \int_{\mathbb{R}^d} \mathbb{P}(v_{j+1}, v_j \mid Y_{j+1}) \, dv_j \\
&= \int_{\mathbb{R}^d} \mathbb{P}(v_{j+1} \mid v_j, Y_{j+1}) \, \mathbb{P}(v_j \mid Y_{j+1}) \, dv_j \\
&= \int_{\mathbb{R}^d} \mathbb{P}(v_{j+1} \mid v_j, y_{j+1}, Y_j) \, \mathbb{P}(v_j \mid y_{j+1}, Y_j) \, dv_j \\
&= \int_{\mathbb{R}^d} \mathbb{P}(v_{j+1} \mid v_j, y_{j+1}) \, \mathbb{P}(v_j \mid y_{j+1}, Y_j) \, dv_j \\
&= \int_{\mathbb{R}^d} \mathbb{P}(v_{j+1} \mid v_j, y_{j+1}) \frac{\mathbb{P}(y_{j+1} \mid v_j, Y_j)}{\mathbb{P}(y_{j+1} \mid Y_j)} \mathbb{P}(v_j \mid Y_j) \, dv_j \\
&= \int_{\mathbb{R}^d} \mathbb{P}(v_{j+1} \mid v_j, y_{j+1}) \frac{\mathbb{P}(y_{j+1} \mid v_j)}{\mathbb{P}(y_{j+1} \mid Y_j)} \mathbb{P}(v_j \mid Y_j) \, dv_j \\
&= \mathcal{P}_j^{\mathrm{OPF}} \mathcal{A}_j^{\mathrm{OPF}} \, \mathbb{P}(v_j \mid Y_j),
\end{aligned}
$$

with Markov kernel for particle update

$$
\mathcal{P}_j^{\mathrm{OPF}} \pi(v_{j+1}) = \int_{\mathbb{R}^d} \mathbb{P}(v_{j+1} \mid v_j, y_{j+1}) \pi(v_j) \, dv_j
$$

and application of Bayes' theorem to include the likelihood

$$
\mathcal{A}_j^{\mathrm{OPF}} \pi(v_j) = \frac{1}{Z} \mathbb{P}(y_{j+1} \mid v_j) \pi(v_j).
$$

Thus, we have

$$
\pi_{j+1} = \mathcal{P}_j^{\mathrm{OPF}} \mathcal{A}_j^{\mathrm{OPF}} \pi_j. \tag{12.2}
$$

Note that in the factorization given by OPF we apply Bayes' theorem and then a Markov kernel, the opposite order to the BPF. Moreover, the propagation mechanism is different – it sees the data through the Markov kernel $\mathcal{P}_j^{\mathrm{OPF}}$ – and hence the weighting of the particles is also different: the BPF weights are proportional to the likelihood $\mathbb{P}(y_{j+1} \mid v_{j+1})$ and the OPF weights are proportional to $\mathbb{P}(y_{j+1} \mid v_j)$ which may be, in general, not available in closed form. In the BPF, the evolution of the particles and the observation of the data are kept separate from each other – the Markov kernel $\mathcal{P}$ depends only on the dynamics and not the observed data and is thus independent of $j$. Furthermore, sampling from the Markov kernel $\mathcal{P}_j^{\mathrm{OPF}}$ may not be possible and may require further approximation. In the next subsection we will see that these two issues may be overcome when the observation function is linear, and particle updates use a 3DVAR procedure. However, in the remainder of this subsection we study particle approximations of (12.2), simply assuming that the OPF weights are computed exactly and that $\mathcal{P}_j^{\mathrm{OPF}}$ can be sampled from without approximation.

The natural particle approximation of (12.2), generalizing the BPF from the preceding chapter, is to consider the iteration

$$\pi_{j+1}^N = \mathcal{P}_j^{\text{OPF}} S^N \mathcal{A}_j^{\text{OPF}} \pi_j^N, \quad \pi_0^N = S^N \pi_0.$$

We refer to this as the OPF. It is possible to show that, under suitable assumptions, the OPF satisfies a convergence result analogous to Theorem 11.5 for the BPF. Here we will analyze a slight modification of the OPF, called the Gaussianized optimal particle filter (GOPF), which reorders the resampling and propagation steps. We first write the resulting algorithm and then establish a convergence result.

The GOPF satisfies the recursion

$$\pi_{j+1}^N = S^N \mathcal{P}_j^{\text{OPF}} \mathcal{A}_j^{\text{OPF}} \pi_j^N, \quad \pi_0^N = S^N \pi_0.$$

This recursion is similar in spirit to the one we derived for the BPF, but note that the order of the analysis, sampling, and prediction steps is different. Our goal now is to show a convergence result for the GOPF. We will make the following assumption, which is analogous to Assumption 11.3 in Chapter 11 for the bootstrap filter.

**Assumption 12.1** *There exists $\kappa \in (0, 1)$ such that, for all $v_j \in \mathbb{R}^d$, and for all $j \in \{0, \ldots, J-1\}$,*

$$\kappa \le \mathbb{P}(y_{j+1} \mid v_j) \le \kappa^{-1}.$$

We are ready to establish a convergence result for the GOPF. The proof employs the same distance (5.7) between random probability measures used in Theorem 11.5 to establish convergence for the BPF and in Chapter 5 to study Monte Carlo and importance sampling.

**Theorem 12.2** (Convergence of GOPF) *Let Assumption 12.1 hold. Then there is a $c = c(J, \kappa)$ independent of $N$ such that, for all $j = 1, \ldots, J$,*

$$d(\pi_j, \pi_j^N) \le \frac{c}{\sqrt{N}}.$$

*Proof* Let $e_j = d(\pi_j, \pi_j^N)$. Then,

$$
\begin{aligned}
e_{j+1} &= d(\pi_{j+1}, \pi_{j+1}^N) \\
&= d(\mathcal{P}_j^{\text{OPF}} \mathcal{A}_j^{\text{OPF}} \pi_j, S^N \mathcal{P}_j^{\text{OPF}} \mathcal{A}_j^{\text{OPF}} \pi_j^N) \\
&\le d(\mathcal{P}_j^{\text{OPF}} \mathcal{A}_j^{\text{OPF}} \pi_j, \mathcal{P}_j^{\text{OPF}} \mathcal{A}_j^{\text{OPF}} \pi_j^N) \\
&\quad + d(\mathcal{P}_j^{\text{OPF}} \mathcal{A}_j^{\text{OPF}} \pi_j^N, S^N \mathcal{P}_j^{\text{OPF}} \mathcal{A}_j^{\text{OPF}} \pi_j^N) \\
&\le \frac{2}{\kappa^2} e_j + \frac{1}{\sqrt{N}},
\end{aligned}
$$

where we have used Lemmas 11.1, 11.2 and Lemma 11.4, replacing Assumption 11.3 by Assumption 12.1 in order to guarantee the stability of $\mathcal{A}^{\text{OPF}}$. The rest of the proof is identical to that of Theorem 11.5. $\qquad\square$

## 12.2 Implementation: Linear Observation Setting

In general it is not possible to implement the OPF in the fully nonlinear setting because of two computational bottlenecks:

- There may not be a closed formula for evaluating the likelihood $\mathbb{P}(y_{j+1} \mid v_j)$, making unfeasible the computation of the particle weights.
- It may not be possible to sample from the Markov kernel $\mathbb{P}(v_{j+1} \mid v_j, y_{j+1})$, making unfeasible the propagation of particles.

However, when the observation function $h(\cdot)$ is linear, i.e. $h(\cdot) = H\cdot$ for some $H \in \mathbb{R}^{k \times d}$, both bottlenecks are overcome. We thus consider the following setting, which arises in many applications:

$$v_{j+1} = \Psi(v_j) + \xi_j, \qquad\qquad \xi_j \sim \mathcal{N}(0, \Sigma) \text{ i.i.d.,}$$
$$y_{j+1} = Hv_{j+1} + \eta_{j+1}, \qquad\qquad \eta_j \sim \mathcal{N}(0, \Gamma) \text{ i.i.d.,}$$

with $v_0 \sim \mathcal{N}(m_0, C_0)$ and $v_0, \{\xi_j\}, \{\eta_j\}$ independent. First, note that combining the stochastic dynamics and data models we may write

$$y_{j+1} = H\Psi(v_j) + H\xi_j + \eta_{j+1},$$

which shows that the conditional distribution for $y_{j+1}$ given $v_j$ is

$$\mathbb{P}(y_{j+1} \mid v_j) = \mathcal{N}(H\Psi(v_j), S),$$

where $S = H\Sigma H^\top + \Gamma$. We will use this formula to compute the weights, thus overcoming the first computational bottleneck.

We now show that, under the linear observation assumption, $\mathcal{P}_j^{\text{OPF}}$ is a Gaussian kernel, and hence the second computational bottleneck is overcome too. We have

$$\mathbb{P}(v_{j+1} \mid v_j, y_{j+1}) \propto \mathbb{P}(y_{j+1} \mid v_{j+1}, v_j) \, \mathbb{P}(v_{j+1} \mid v_j)$$
$$= \mathbb{P}(y_{j+1} \mid v_{j+1}) \, \mathbb{P}(v_{j+1} \mid v_j)$$
$$\propto \exp\left(-\frac{1}{2}|y_{j+1} - Hv_{j+1}|_\Gamma^2 - \frac{1}{2}|v_{j+1} - \Psi(v_j)|_\Sigma^2\right)$$
$$= \exp\left(-\mathsf{J}_{\text{OPT}}(v_{j+1})\right).$$

This is a Gaussian distribution for $v_{j+1}$ as

$$J_{\text{OPT}}(v_{j+1}) := \frac{1}{2}|y_{j+1} - Hv_{j+1}|_{\Gamma}^2 + \frac{1}{2}|v_{j+1} - \Psi(v_j)|_{\Sigma}^2$$

is quadratic with respect to $v_{j+1}$.[1] Consequently, we can compute the mean $m_{j+1}$ and covariance $C$ (which, note, is independent of $j$) of this Gaussian by matching the mean and quadratic terms in the relevant quadratic forms:

$$C^{-1} = H^{\top}\Gamma^{-1}H + \Sigma^{-1},$$
$$C^{-1}m_{j+1} = \Sigma^{-1}\Psi(v_j) + H^{\top}\Gamma^{-1}y_{j+1}.$$

Then $\mathbb{P}(v_{j+1} \mid y_{j+1}, v_j) = \mathcal{N}(m_{j+1}, C)$. This is hence a special case of 3DVAR in which the analysis covariance is fixed at $C$; note that when we derived 3DVAR we fixed the predictive covariance $\widehat{C}$ which, here, is fixed at $\Sigma$. As with the Kalman filter, and with 3DVAR, it is possible to implement the prediction step through the following mean and covariance formulae which avoid inversion in state-space, and require inversion only in data space:

$$m_{j+1} = (I - KH)\Psi(v_j) + Ky_{j+1},$$
$$C = (I - KH)\Sigma,$$
$$K = \Sigma H^{\top}S^{-1},$$
$$S = H\Sigma H^{\top} + \Gamma.$$

Furthermore, as for 3DVAR, the inversion of $S$ need only be performed once in a pre-processing step before the algorithm is run. Since the expression for $\mathbb{P}(v_{j+1} \mid v_j, y_{j+1})$ is Gaussian we now have the ability to sample directly from $\mathcal{P}_j^{\text{OPF}}$. The OPF is thus given by the following update algorithm for approximations $\pi_j^N \approx \pi_j$ in which we generalize the notational conventions used in the previous chapter to formulate particle filters as random dynamical systems:[2]

---

[1] $J_{\text{OPT}}$ is identical to $J$ on the right-hand side of Table 9.1, with $\widehat{C}$ replaced by $\Sigma$.
[2] The notation used in step 4 for the resampling step was introduced in Subsection 11.4.

---

**Algorithm 12.1** Optimal Particle Filter

---

1: **Input**: Initial distribution $\mathbb{P}(v_0) = \pi_0$, number of particles $N$.
2: **Initial Sampling**: Draw $N$ particles $v_0^{(n)} \sim \pi_0$ so that $\pi_0^N = S^N \pi_0$.
3: **Subsequent Sampling** For $j = 0, 1, \ldots, J - 1$, perform:

  1 Set $\widehat{v}_{j+1}^{(n)} = (I - KH)\Psi(v_j^{(n)}) + Ky_{j+1} + \zeta_{j+1}^{(n)}$ with $\zeta_{j+1}^{(n)}$ i.i.d. $\mathcal{N}(0, C)$.

  2 Set $\overline{w}_{j+1}^{(n)} = \exp\left(-\frac{1}{2}|y_{j+1} - H\Psi(v_j^{(n)})|_S^2\right)$.

  3 Set $w_{j+1}^{(n)} = \overline{w}_{j+1}^{(n)} / \sum_{n=1}^{N} \overline{w}_{j+1}^{(n)}$.

  4 Set $v_{j+1}^{(n)} = \sum_{m=1}^{N} \mathbb{1}_{I_{j+1}^{(m)}}(r_{j+1}^{(n)})\widehat{v}_{j+1}^{(m)}$.

  5 Set $\pi_{j+1}^N(v_{j+1}) = \frac{1}{N}\sum_{n=1}^{N}\delta\left(v_{j+1} - v_{j+1}^{(n)}\right)$.

4: **Output**: Particle approximations $\pi_j^N \approx \pi_j$, $j = 1, \ldots, J$.

---

The GOPF has a similar form, after a reordering of the sampling and propagation steps: [3]

---

**Algorithm 12.2** Gaussianized Optimal Particle Filter

---

1: **Input**: Initial distribution $\mathbb{P}(v_0) = \pi_0$, number of particles $N$.
2: **Initial Sampling**: Draw $N$ particles $v_0^{(n)} \sim \pi_0$ so that $\pi_0^N = S^N \pi_0$.
3: **Subsequent Sampling** For $j = 0, 1, \ldots, J - 1$, perform:

  1 Set $\overline{w}_{j+1}^{(n)} = \exp\left(-\frac{1}{2}|y_{j+1} - H\Psi(v_j^{(n)})|_S^2\right)$.

  2 Set $w_{j+1}^{(n)} = \overline{w}_{j+1}^{(n)} / \sum_{n=1}^{N} \overline{w}_{j+1}^{(n)}$.

  3 Set $\widehat{v}_j^{(n)} = \sum_{m=1}^{N} \mathbb{1}_{I_{j+1}^{(m)}}(r_{j+1}^{(n)})v_j^{(m)}$.

  4 Set $v_{j+1}^{(n)} = (I - KH)\Psi(\widehat{v}_j^{(n)}) + Ky_{j+1} + \zeta_{j+1}^{(n)}$ with $\zeta_{j+1}^{(n)}$ i.i.d. $\mathcal{N}(0, C)$.

  5 Set $\pi_{j+1}^N(v_{j+1}) = \frac{1}{N}\sum_{n=1}^{N}\delta\left(v_{j+1} - v_{j+1}^{(n)}\right)$.

4: **Output**: Particle approximations $\pi_j^N \approx \pi_j$, $j = 1, \ldots, J$.

---

[3] Here again, the resampling step 3 follows the notation introduced in Subsection 11.4.

## 12.3 "Optimality" of the Optimal Particle Filter

Particle filter methods rely on approximating the target distribution by a swarm of Dirac masses; it is clear that the distribution will not be well approximated by only a small number of particles in most cases. Consequently, a performance requirement for particle filter methods is that they do not lead to degeneracy of the particles. Resampling leads to degeneracy if a few particles have all the weights. Conversely, non-degeneracy may be promoted by ensuring that the weights $w_j^{(n)}$ are similar in magnitude, so that a small number of particles are not overly favored during the resampling step. This condition can be formulated as a requirement that the variance of the weights be minimized; doing this results in the OPF.

To understand this perspective, we consider an arbitrary particle update kernel of the form $\pi(v_{j+1} \mid v_j^{(n)}, Y_{j+1})$ and we study the resulting particle filter without resampling. It is then the case that the unnormalized particle weights are updated according to the formula

$$\overline{w}_{j+1}^{(n)} = \overline{w}_j^{(n)} \frac{\mathbb{P}(y_{j+1} \mid v_{j+1}) \, \mathbb{P}(v_{j+1} \mid v_j^{(n)})}{\pi(v_{j+1} \mid v_j^{(n)}, Y_{j+1})}. \tag{12.3}$$

**Theorem 12.3** (Meaning of Optimality) *The choice of* $\mathbb{P}(v_{j+1} \mid v_j^{(n)}, y_{j+1})$ *as the particle update kernel* $\pi(v_{j+1} \mid v_j^{(n)}, Y_{j+1})$ *results in the minimal variance of the weight* $w_{j+1}^{(n)}$ *with respect to all possible choices of the particle update kernel* $\pi(v_{j+1} \mid v_j^{(n)}, Y_{j+1})$.

*Proof* We calculate the variance of the unnormalized weights (treated as random variables) $\overline{w}_{j+1}^{(n)}$ with respect to the transition density $\pi(v_{j+1} \mid v_j^{(n)}, Y_{j+1})$ and obtain

$$\mathrm{Var}_{\pi(v_{j+1} \mid v_j^{(n)}, Y_{j+1})}[\overline{w}_{j+1}^{(n)}] = \int_{\mathbb{R}^d} \left(\overline{w}_{j+1}^{(n)}\right)^2 \pi(v_{j+1} \mid v_j^{(n)}, Y_{j+1}) \, dv_{j+1}$$

$$- \left[\int_{\mathbb{R}^d} \overline{w}_{j+1}^{(n)} \pi(v_{j+1} \mid v_j^{(n)}, Y_{j+1}) \, dv_{j+1}\right]^2$$

$$= \left(\overline{w}_j^{(n)}\right)^2 \int_{\mathbb{R}^d} \frac{\left(\mathbb{P}(y_{j+1} \mid v_{j+1}) \, \mathbb{P}(v_{j+1} \mid v_j^{(n)})\right)^2}{\pi(v_{j+1} \mid v_j^{(n)}, Y_{j+1})} \, dv_{j+1}$$

$$- \left(\overline{w}_j^{(n)}\right)^2 \left[ \int_{\mathbb{R}^d} \mathbb{P}(y_{j+1} \mid v_{j+1}) \, \mathbb{P}(v_{j+1} \mid v_j^{(n)}) \, dv_{j+1} \right]^2$$

$$= \left(\overline{w}_j^{(n)}\right)^2 \left[ \int_{\mathbb{R}^d} \frac{\left(\mathbb{P}(y_{j+1} \mid v_{j+1}) \, \mathbb{P}(v_{j+1} \mid v_j^{(n)})\right)^2}{\pi(v_{j+1} \mid v_j^{(n)}, Y_{j+1})} \, dv_{j+1} \right.$$

$$\left. - \mathbb{P}(y_{j+1} \mid v_j^{(n)})^2 \right] \qquad \square$$

Choosing $\pi(v_{j+1} \mid v_j^{(n)}, Y_{j+1}) = \mathbb{P}(v_{j+1} \mid v_j^{(n)}, y_{j+1})$, as in the OPF, we obtain

$$\mathrm{Var}_{\mathbb{P}(v_{j+1} \mid v_j^{(n)}, Y_{j+1})} \left[\overline{w}_{j+1}^{(n)}\right]$$

$$= \left(\overline{w}_j^{(n)}\right)^2 \left[ \int_{\mathbb{R}^d} \frac{\left(\mathbb{P}(y_{j+1} \mid v_{j+1}) \, \mathbb{P}(v_{j+1} \mid v_j^{(n)})\right)^2}{\mathbb{P}(v_{j+1} \mid v_j^{(n)}, y_{j+1})} \, dv_{j+1} - \mathbb{P}(y_{j+1} \mid v_j^{(n)})^2 \right]$$

$$= \left(\overline{w}_j^{(n)}\right)^2 \left[ \mathbb{P}(y_{j+1} \mid v_j^{(n)})^2 - \mathbb{P}(y_{j+1} \mid v_j^{(n)})^2 \right]$$

$$= 0.$$

**Remark 12.4** Directly from (12.3) we see that choosing $\pi(v_{j+1} \mid v_j^{(n)}, Y_{j+1}) = \mathbb{P}(v_{j+1} \mid v_j^{(n)}, y_{j+1})$ gives the weight update

$$\overline{w}_{j+1}^{(n)} = \overline{w}_j^{(n)} \, \mathbb{P}(y_{j+1} \mid v_j^{(n)}),$$

which does not depend on the draw $v_{j+1} \sim \mathbb{P}(v_{j+1} \mid v_j^{(n)}, y_{j+1})$, and is deterministic given $y_{j+1}$ and $v_j^{(n)}$. ◇

**Remark 12.5** The OPF is optimal in the very precise sense of the theorem. Note that no optimality criterion is asserted by this theorem with respect to iterating the particle updates, and in particular when resampling is included. The nomenclature "optimal" should thus be treated with caution. ◇

**Example 12.6** (Linear-Gaussian One-Step Filter)   Recall Example 5.8 from Chapter 5. We considered a linear-Gaussian one-dimensional inverse problem with prior $\rho(u) = \mathcal{N}(0, \widehat{c}^2)$ and likelihood $\mathbb{P}(y \mid u) = \mathcal{N}(au, \gamma^2)$, and we showed that the $\chi^2$ divergence between the posterior $\pi$ and the prior $\rho$ is given by

$$\zeta = d_{\chi^2}(\pi \| \rho) + 1 = \frac{\delta^2 + 1}{\sqrt{2\delta^2 + 1}} \exp\left(\frac{\delta^2}{2\delta^2 + 1} z^2\right), \qquad z \sim \mathcal{N}(0, 1),$$

where $\delta^2 := a^2 \widehat{c}^2 / \gamma^2$. It is easy to see that $\zeta$ is monotonically increasing as a function of $\delta$. We saw in Chapter 5 that a large $\chi^2$ divergence between target (posterior) and proposal (prior) leads to a poor approximation of the target by reweighing prior samples.

Now we consider a scalar, linear-Gaussian filtering step

$$v_1 = \alpha v_0 + \xi, \qquad v_0 \sim \mathcal{N}(0, c_0^2), \quad \xi \sim \mathcal{N}(0, \sigma^2),$$
$$y_1 = h v_1 + \eta, \qquad \eta \sim \mathcal{N}(0, \gamma^2).$$

In the analysis step, the BPF updates the prior $\mathbb{P}(v_1) = \mathcal{N}(0, \alpha^2 c_0^2 + \sigma^2)$ with likelihood $\mathbb{P}(y_1 \mid v_1) = \mathcal{N}(hv_1, \gamma^2)$, while the OPF updates the prior $\mathbb{P}(v_0) = \mathcal{N}(0, c_0^2)$ with likelihood $\mathbb{P}(y_1 \mid v_0) = \mathcal{N}(h\alpha v_0, h^2 \sigma^2 + \gamma^2)$. Both bootstrap and optimal analysis steps reweigh samples from their respective priors using their given likelihoods; since in both cases the prior is Gaussian and the observation model is linear, we are in the setting of Example 5.8. Here, the $\chi^2$ divergences between the target and proposal for the bootstrap and optimal filters are determined by

$$\delta_{\mathrm{BPF}} = \frac{h^2 \alpha^2 c_0^2 + h^2 \sigma^2}{\gamma^2},$$

$$\delta_{\mathrm{OPF}} = \frac{h^2 \alpha^2 c_0^2}{h^2 \sigma^2 + \gamma^2}.$$

Clearly, $\delta_{\mathrm{OPF}} \leq \delta_{\mathrm{BPF}}$, which indicates that the $\chi^2$ divergence between target and proposal is smaller for the optimal than for the bootstrap filter. In particular, note that in the small observation noise limit $\gamma \to 0^+$, the $\chi^2$ divergence for the bootstrap filter diverges, while for the optimal filter it remains bounded provided that $h^2 \sigma^2 > 0$. In such a small observation noise regime, the OPF is clearly advantageous over the BPF. Finally, it is illustrative to see that the bootstrap and optimal filter agree and $\delta_{\mathrm{BPF}} = \delta_{\mathrm{OPF}}$ if there is no noise in the stochastic dynamics model, i.e. if $\sigma^2 = 0$.                                    ◇

## 12.4 Discussion and Bibliography

The OPF is discussed, and further references given, in Doucet et al. (2000); see section IID. Throughout much of this chapter we assumed Gaussian additive noise and linear observation function, in which case the prediction step is tractable; the order in which the prediction and resampling is performed can be commuted, leading to the distinction between what we term the GOPF and the OPF. Doucet et al. (2000) discusses the general setting, beyond that in which Gaussian additive noise and linear observation function are assumed; the idea that the order of prediction and resampling can be commuted was observed in the general setting in Pitt and Shephard (1999). The convergence of the OPF is studied in Johansen and Doucet (2008). The formulation of the bootstrap and optimal particle filters as random dynamical systems may be found in Kelly and Stuart (2019).

The performance of the BPF is poor when the filtering distributions are far from the predictive distributions, a situation that arises in high-dimensional or small observation noise filtering settings.s In such cases, the update of the weights in the analysis step of the BPF results in a degenerate distribution of weights, with the largest weight being close to 1 (Bickel et al., 2008; Snyder et al., 2016; Snyder, 2011). This is the issue that the OPF tries to ameliorate; Snyder et al. (2015), Agapiou et al. (2017a), and Sanz-Alonso and Wang (2021) provide calculations which demonstrate the extent to which this amelioration is manifest in theory. In practice, further exploiting decay of correlations through *localization* is often needed. A review of local particle filters can be found in Farchi and Bocquet (2018); and Rebeschini and Handel (2015) investigates, from a theoretical viewpoint, whether localization can help to beat the curse of dimensionality. Attempts to bridge particle filters with ensemble Kalman filters to alleviate this curse include Frei and Künsch (2013) and Stordal et al. (2011), and the relation between the collapse of ensemble and particle methods is investigated by Morzfeld et al. (2017), who also emphasizes the importance of localization.

# Exercises for Part II

**Exercise 1** (Scalar Linear-Gaussian Dynamics)   Consider the scalar stochastic dynamics model

$$v_{j+1} = av_j + \xi_j, \qquad \xi_j \sim N(0, \sigma^2) \text{ i.i.d.,}$$
$$v_0 \sim N(m_0, c_0^2), \qquad v_0 \perp \{\xi_j\}.$$

(i) Show that

$$v_j = a^j v_0 + \sum_{i=0}^{j-1} a^{j-i-1} \xi_i.$$

Why does it follow that $v_j$ is Gaussian?

(ii) Show that the mean and variance of $v_j$ are given by

$$m_j = a^j m_0,$$

$$c_j^2 = a^{2j} c_0^2 + \sigma^2 \sum_{i=0}^{j-1} a^{2i}.$$

(iii) Find explicit formulae for the maps $m_j \mapsto m_{j+1}$ and $c_j^2 \mapsto c_{j+1}^2$.

(iv) If $|a| < 1$ find the limit of $m_j$ and $c_j^2$ as $j \to \infty$. What happens if $a = -1, 1$ or if $|a| > 1$?

**Exercise 2** (Filtering and Smoothing: Scalar Linear-Gaussian Setting)   Consider the scalar stochastic dynamics and observation models given by

$$v_{j+1} = av_j + \xi_j, \qquad \xi_j \sim N(0, \sigma^2), \qquad v_0 \sim N(m_0, c_0^2),$$
$$y_{j+1} = v_{j+1} + \eta_{j+1}, \qquad \eta_{j+1} \sim N(0, \gamma^2),$$

where $\{\xi_j\}$ and $\{\eta_j\}$ are i.i.d. sequences and $v_0 \perp \{\xi_j\} \perp \{\eta_j\}$.

(i) Set $a = 1.25$, $\sigma^2 = 0.5$, $m_0 = 1$, $c_0^2 = 1$, and $\gamma^2 = 0.1$. Generate synthetic data $\{y_j\}_{j=1}^{J}$ with $J = 10$ from this model following these steps:

(a) Sample $v_0^\dagger \sim \mathcal{N}(1, 1)$.

(b) For $j = 0, \ldots, 9$, sample $v_{j+1}^\dagger \sim \mathcal{N}(1.25v_j^\dagger, 0.5)$.

(c) For $j = 0, \ldots, 9$, sample $y_{j+1} \sim \mathcal{N}(v_{j+1}^\dagger, 0.1)$.

We interpret $\{v_j^\dagger\}_{j=0}^{10}$ as the true signal underlying the synthetic data $\{y_j\}_{j=1}^{10}$.

(ii) For the synthetic data generated above, find, using the Kalman filter, the filtering distributions $\pi_j(v_j) = \mathbb{P}(v_j \mid y_1, \ldots, y_j)$ for $j = 0, 1, \ldots, 10$. Using the Kalman smoother, find the smoothing distribution $\mathbb{P}(\{v_j\}_{j=0}^{10} \mid \{y_j\}_{j=1}^{10})$.

(iii) Plot, for discrete time $1 \le j \le 10$, the mean of the filtering and smoothing distributions, together with the true signal and the observations.

**Exercise 3** (The Pendulum Problem)    The dynamics of a pendulum are characterized by the following linear system:

$$\ddot{u} + \delta\dot{u} + \sin(u) = 0,$$

where $u(t)$ denotes the location of the pendulum, $\dot{u}(t)$ denotes the velocity and $\delta$ is a scalar parameter.

(i) Show that this dynamical system implies the identity:

$$\frac{d}{dt}\left[\frac{1}{2}\dot{u}^2 - \cos(u)\right] = -\delta\dot{u}^2.$$

Use this identity to prove that for $\delta \ge 0$ the solution will not blow up in finite time. What happens when $\delta = 0$?

(ii) Show that the dynamical system can be equivalently expressed using the following first-order differential equation:

$$\begin{cases} \dot{u} = w, \\ \dot{w} = -\delta w - \sin(u); \end{cases} \tag{12.4}$$

let $v = (u, w)^\top$ and consider this as an equation for $v$. Let $\Psi(v)$ denote the solution of (12.4) at time $t = 0.2$ with initial condition $v(0) = \mathsf{v}$. Set $v_0 = (u_0, w_0)^\top = (\pi/4, 0)^\top$ and consider the deterministic dynamics model and observation model given by

$$\begin{aligned} v_{j+1} &= \Psi(v_j), \\ y_{j+1} &= u_{j+1} + \eta_{j+1}, \quad \eta_j \sim \mathcal{N}(0, \gamma^2) \text{ i.i.d.} \end{aligned} \tag{12.5}$$

Set $\gamma^2 = 0.01$ and $\delta = 0.1$. Solve numerically the differential equation (12.4) to generate solutions of (12.5) and thereby obtain 20 observations $\{y_j\}_{j=1}^{20}$. Plot these values.

(iii) This question continues from the setting of the previous questions. Recall that 3DVAR estimates the state of a partially observed dynamical system from the following sequential updates:

$$m_{j+1} = (I - KH)\Psi(m_j) + Ky_{j+1}.$$

Here, the $\{y_j\}$ denote the observations and the $\{m_j\}$ the state estimates; the map encapsulates a tradeoff between fitting to data and respecting the dynamics. Note that here $H = \begin{pmatrix} 1 & 0 \end{pmatrix}$ and recall that for 3DVAR the matrix $K$ satisfies the relations:

$$S = H\widehat{C}H^\top + \gamma^2, \qquad K = \widehat{C}H^\top S^{-1},$$

with $\widehat{C} \in \mathbb{R}^{2\times2}$ to be specified. Consider initializing 3DVAR from $m_0 = (0,0)^\top$ and suppose that $\widehat{C}$ is chosen to be a diagonal matrix. In this problem, show that there is only one degree of freedom. Play around with this parameter to find one that gives you a small $\sum_{j=1}^{20} |v_j - m_j|$. (This is an open-ended problem; you are encouraged to experiment.)

(iv) Repeat items (ii) and (iii) with the observations being on the state $w$ instead of $u$, e.g. $y_{j+1} = w_{j+1} + \eta_{j+1}$. What do you notice?

(v) Starting with $N \in \{5, 20, 50, 100\}$ random particles, sampled from a Gaussian $\mathcal{N}(0, I_2)$, apply particle filtering and report the effective sample size after each iteration of the dynamics. What do you observe?

(vi) What is the advantage of particle filtering for this problem over 3DVAR? Are there any disadvantages?

**Exercise 4** (Estimation of Model Parameters: the EM Algorithm)    Consider stochastic dynamics and data models given by

$$v_{j+1} = \Psi_\theta(v_j) + \xi_j, \qquad\qquad \xi_j \sim \mathcal{N}(0, \Sigma) \text{ i.i.d.}, \qquad (12.6)$$
$$y_{j+1} = Hv_{j+1} + \eta_{j+1}, \qquad\qquad \eta_j \sim \mathcal{N}(0, \Gamma) \text{ i.i.d.} \qquad (12.7)$$

with $v_0 \sim \mathcal{N}(m_0, C_0) \perp \{\xi_j\} \perp \{\eta_j\}$. Here, the vector $\theta \in \mathbb{R}^p$ parameterizes the dynamics. For a given and fixed integer $J$, set $V := \{v_0, \ldots, v_J\}$ and $Y := \{y_1, \ldots, y_J\}$. We seek to find $\theta$ that maximizes the likelihood function of $\theta$ given the observed data $Y$:

$$\mathbb{P}(Y \mid \theta) = \int \mathbb{P}(V, Y \mid \theta) \, dV. \qquad (12.8)$$

Here and below $\mathbb{P}(Y \mid \theta)$ denotes the pdf of $Y$ given that the dynamics map $\Psi_\theta$ in (12.6) is parameterized by $\theta$; $\mathbb{P}(V, Y \mid \theta)$ is defined similarly.

(i) Show that the joint distribution of $V$ and $Y$ admits the characterization

$$\begin{aligned}
\log \mathbb{P}(V, Y \mid \theta) = &-\frac{1}{2} \sum_{j=0}^{J-1} |y_{j+1} - H v_{j+1}|_\Gamma^2 - \frac{1}{2} |v_0 - m_0|_{C_0}^2 \\
&- \frac{1}{2} \sum_{j=0}^{J-1} |v_{j+1} - \Psi_\theta(v_j)|_\Sigma^2 + c,
\end{aligned} \tag{12.9}$$

where $c$ is a constant independent of $V$, $Y$, and $\theta$.

(ii) Show that, for any pdf $q$ with compatible support, it holds that

$$\log \mathbb{P}(Y \mid \theta) = \mathcal{L}(q, \theta) + d_{\mathrm{KL}}\big(q \| \mathbb{P}(V \mid Y, \theta)\big),$$

where

$$\mathcal{L}(q, \theta) := \int \log\left(\frac{\mathbb{P}(V, Y \mid \theta)}{q(V)}\right) q(V) \, dV$$

is a lower bound for the log-likelihood $\log \mathbb{P}(Y \mid \theta)$ since the Kullback–Leibler divergence is non-negative.

(iii) You will now derive an iterative algorithm to maximize the likelihood given the current iterate $\theta_\ell$. In particular, we define the new iterate $\theta_{\ell+1}$ in two steps, maximizing in turn the two components of the lower bound $\mathcal{L}(q, \theta)$:

    (a) First, show that $q_\ell(V) = \mathbb{P}(V \mid Y, \theta_\ell)$ maximizes the lower bound $\mathcal{L}(q, \theta_\ell)$ over pdf $q$.

    (b) Second, you will obtain $\theta_{\ell+1}$ by maximizing the lower bound $\mathcal{L}(q_\ell, \theta)$ over $\theta$. Show that the quantity to maximize is the expected value of the joint log-density $\log \mathbb{P}(V, Y \mid \theta)$ with respect to $q_\ell(V) = \mathbb{P}(V \mid Y, \theta_\ell)$.

Combining these two steps, you have derived the Expectation Maximization (EM) algorithm summarized below.

---

**Algorithm  Expectation Maximization**

---

1: **Input**: Initialization $\theta_0$.

2: For $\ell = 0, 1, \dots, L - 1$ do the following expectation and maximization steps:

3: **E-Step**: Compute

$$\mathbb{E}^{V \sim \mathbb{P}(V \mid Y, \theta_\ell)}\Big[\log \mathbb{P}(V, Y \mid \theta)\Big] = \int \log \mathbb{P}(V, Y \mid \theta) \, \mathbb{P}(V \mid Y, \theta_\ell) \, dV.$$

4: **M-Step**: Compute

$$\theta_{\ell+1} = \arg\max_\theta \mathbb{E}^{V \sim \mathbb{P}(V \mid Y, \theta_\ell)}\Big[\log \mathbb{P}(V, Y \mid \theta)\Big].$$

5: **Output**: Parameter $\theta^L$.

---

(iv) Let $\{\theta_\ell\}_{\ell=0}^{L-1}$ be the iterates of the EM algorithm. Show that, for $0 \le \ell \le L-1$, it holds that

$$\log \mathbb{P}(Y \mid \theta_\ell) \le \log \mathbb{P}(Y \mid \theta_{\ell+1}). \tag{12.10}$$

*Observation*   As a consequence of (12.10) the above inequality it is possible to deduce, under mild assumptions, that the iterates $\theta_\ell$ of the EM algorithm converge, as $\ell \to \infty$, to a local maximizer of the likelihood function. It is important to note, however, that the expectation in the E-step and the optimization in the M-step are often intractable. Monte Carlo, filtering, or smoothing algorithms may be employed to approximate the E-step, and optimization algorithms to approximate the M-step. Such approximations can cause loss of monotonicity and convergence guarantees.

**Exercise 5** (EM Algorithm with Ensemble Kalman Filter)   Consider the scalar stochastic dynamics and observation models given by

$$v_{j+1} = \theta v_j + \xi_j, \qquad \xi_j \sim \mathcal{N}(0, \sigma^2), \qquad v_0 \sim \mathcal{N}(m_0, c_0^2),$$
$$y_{j+1} = v_{j+1} + \eta_{j+1}, \qquad \eta_{j+1} \sim \mathcal{N}(0, \gamma^2),$$

where $\{\xi_j\}$ and $\{\eta_j\}$ are i.i.d. sequences and $v_0 \perp \{\xi_j\} \perp \{\eta_j\}$. Generate synthetic data $\{y_j\}_{j=1}^{10}$ from this model as in Exercise 2 using parameter $\theta^\star = 1.25$. You will derive an EM algorithm to find $\theta^\star$. Notice that the methodology you will derive is also applicable in nonlinear settings.

 (i) Implement an ensemble Kalman filtering algorithm with $N = 100$ particles, so that given parameter $\theta_\ell$ it outputs an ensemble $\{v_j^{(n)}\}_{n=1}^{100}$ for discrete time $j = 0, 1, \ldots, 10$.
 (ii) Using this ensemble Kalman filtering algorithm with parameter $\theta_\ell$, derive an (approximate) EM algorithm by setting

$$\theta_{\ell+1} = \arg\max_\theta \frac{1}{N} \sum_{n=1}^{N} \log \mathbb{P}(V^{(n)}, Y \mid \theta),$$

where we define, as in (12.9),

$$\log \mathbb{P}(V^{(n)}, Y \mid \theta) = -\frac{1}{2\gamma^2} \sum_{j=0}^{9} |y_{j+1} - v_{j+1}^{(n)}|^2 - \frac{1}{2c_0^2} |v_0^{(n)}$$
$$- m_0|^2 - \frac{1}{2\sigma^2} \sum_{j=0}^{9} |v_{j+1}^{(n)} - \theta v_j^{(n)}|^2.$$

Implement this EM algorithm with an initialization $\theta_0 = 1.5$ to recover $\theta^\star$.

**Exercise 6** (Likelihood: Linear-Gaussian Setting)   Suppose that, for each $0 \le j \le J-1$, the predictive distribution $\mathbb{P}(v_{j+1} \mid Y_j, \theta)$ of the stochastic dynamics and data models (12.6) and (12.7) is Gaussian with mean $\widehat{m}_{j+1}(\theta)$ and covariance $\widehat{C}_{j+1}(\theta)$. Show that then the log-likelihood function admits the following characterization

$$\log \mathbb{P}(Y \mid \theta) = -\frac{1}{2}\sum_{j=0}^{J-1} |y_{j+1} - H\widehat{m}_{j+1}(\theta)|^2_{S_{j+1}(\theta)} - \frac{1}{2}\sum_{j=0}^{J-1} \log \det\big(S_{j+1}(\theta)\big) + c,$$

where $S_{j+1}(\theta) = H\widehat{C}_{j+1}(\theta)H^\top + \Gamma$ and $c$ is a constant independent of $\theta$.

**Exercise 7** ($\chi^2$ Divergence in the Exponential Family)   The pdf $\pi_\theta(u)$ is in the exponential family $\mathcal{E}_F$ if it can be written in the form $\pi_\theta(u) = e^{\langle t(u), \theta\rangle - F(\theta) + \kappa(u)}$. We denote this distribution as $\mathcal{E}_F(\theta)$. Suppose the natural parameter space $\Theta = \{\theta \mid \int_{\mathbb{R}^d} \pi_\theta(u)du = 1\}$ is affine, meaning that $\sum_i w_i \theta_i \in \Theta$ if $\theta_i \in \Theta$ and $\sum_i w_i = 1$. Show that the $\chi^2$ divergence within the same exponential family $\mathcal{E}_F$ is characterized by

$$d_{\chi^2}\big(\mathcal{E}_F(\theta_1)\|\mathcal{E}_F(\theta_2)\big) = e^{F(2\theta_1 - \theta_2) - 2F(\theta_1) + F(\theta_2)} - 1.$$

**Exercise 8** ($\chi^2$ Divergence Between Gaussians)   Recall the exponential family introduced in Exercise 7.

(i) Let $p = \mathcal{N}(\mu, \Sigma)$ be a Gaussian on $\mathbb{R}^d$ with positive definite covariance matrix $\Sigma$. Show that it belongs to the exponential family, with parameter $\theta = [\Sigma^{-1}\mu; -\frac{1}{2}\Sigma^{-1}]$ where the natural parameter space $\mathbb{R}^d \oplus \mathbb{R}^{d\times d}$ inherits the inner products from the Euclidean space and the matrix space[4], $t(u) = [u; uu^\top]$, $F(\theta) = \frac{1}{2}\mu^\top\Sigma^{-1}\mu + \frac{1}{2}\log\det\Sigma$, and $\kappa(u) = -\frac{d}{2}\log(2\pi)$.

(ii) Let $p_1 = \mathcal{N}(\mu_1, \Sigma_1)$ and $p_2 = \mathcal{N}(\mu_2, \Sigma_2)$ be Gaussians on $\mathbb{R}^d$ with positive definite covariance matrices. Show that

$$d_{\chi^2}(p_1\|p_2) = \frac{\det W}{\sqrt{\det(2W - I)}} e^{w^\top \Sigma_1^{-1}(2W - I)^{-1}w} - 1,$$

where $W = \Sigma_2\Sigma_1^{-1}$ and $w = \mu_1 - \mu_2$.

---

[4]  The canonical inner product in the space of square matrices is defined to be the trace of the matrix product. We can also view this as an extension of the Euclidean inner product where the scalar in each coordinate is replaced by vectors.

# PART III

## KALMAN INVERSION

# 13

# Blending Inverse Problems and Data Assimilation

This chapter brings together the material in the first two parts of these notes, demonstrating how the principles and ideas underpinning the derivation of extended and ensemble Kalman filters for data assimilation can be used to design ensemble Kalman methods for inverse problems. We adopt an optimization perspective to the inverse problem and study gradient-based and ensemble algorithms for the minimization of two objective functions: a *data-misfit* objective defined by a loss function; and a *Tikhonov–Phillips* objective defined by appending the loss term with a regularization term. These objective functions will be introduced in Section 13.1, where we also show that they are particular instances of a general family of nonlinear least-squares objectives. Section 13.2 contains a short overview of Gauss–Newton and Levenberg–Marquardt optimization algorithms for nonlinear least-squares. In Section 13.3 we consider gradient-based extended Kalman methods for both objectives, highlighting their interpretation as standard Gauss–Newton and Levenberg–Marquardt optimization algorithms. Finally, in Section 13.4 we consider ensemble Kalman methods that avoid the calculation of gradients by invoking a statistical linearization defined with an ensemble of particles. The chapter closes in Section 13.5 with extensions and bibliographical remarks.

## 13.1 The Setting

Recall the inverse problem of finding an unknown $u \in \mathbb{R}^d$ from data $y \in \mathbb{R}^k$, where

$$y = G(u) + \eta, \quad \eta \sim \mathcal{N}(0, \Gamma), \tag{13.1}$$

and $G$ represents a given forward model. We consider an optimization approach to the inverse problem, seeking to recover the unknown $u$ by minimizing a data-misfit or a Tikhonov–Phillips objective function defined, respectively, by

$$J_{DM}(u) := \frac{1}{2}|y - G(u)|^2_\Gamma, \qquad J_{TP}(u) := \frac{1}{2}|y - G(u)|^2_\Gamma + \frac{1}{2}|u - \widehat{m}|^2_{\widehat{C}}. \quad (13.2)$$

As discussed in Section 3.1 and the examples therein, the data-misfit objective function $J_{DM}$ can be interpreted as a loss function and minimizing it promotes fitting the given data $y$; and the Tikhonov–Phillips objective $J_{TP}$ comprises a loss function appended with a regularization term that helps prevent overfitting the data. While in this chapter we focus on the optimization perspective, we recall that in the Bayesian perspective the regularization term can be interpreted as the negative log-density of a Gaussian prior $\rho(u) = \mathcal{N}(\widehat{m}, \widehat{C})$, in which case minimizing the Tikhonov–Phillips objective is equivalent to finding the MAP estimator.

The data-misfit and Tikhonov–Phillips objectives are examples of nonlinear least-squares objectives of the general form

$$J(u) = \frac{1}{2}|r(u)|^2. \quad (13.3)$$

To see this, note first that the data-misfit objective can be written in the form

$$J_{DM}(u) = \frac{1}{2}|r_{DM}(u)|^2, \qquad r_{DM}(u) := \Gamma^{-1/2}(y - G(u)). \quad (13.4)$$

Secondly, note that the Tikhonov–Phillips objective may be written in the form

$$J_{TP}(u) = \frac{1}{2}|y - G(u)|^2_\Gamma + \frac{1}{2}|u - \widehat{m}|^2_{\widehat{C}}$$
$$= \frac{1}{2}|z - h(u)|^2_Q,$$

where

$$z := \begin{bmatrix} y \\ \widehat{m} \end{bmatrix}, \qquad h(u) := \begin{bmatrix} G(u) \\ u \end{bmatrix}, \qquad Q := \begin{bmatrix} \Gamma & 0 \\ 0 & \widehat{C} \end{bmatrix}.$$

Therefore,

$$J_{TP}(u) = \frac{1}{2}|r_{TP}(u)|^2, \qquad r_{TP}(u) := Q^{-1/2}(z - h(u)). \quad (13.5)$$

Equations (13.4) and (13.5) show that both the data-misfit and the Tikhonov–Phillips objectives can be written in the general form (13.3).

## 13.2 Nonlinear Least-Squares Optimization

Gradient-based optimization algorithms for the nonlinear least-squares problem of minimizing (13.3) can be broadly classified into line-search and trust region methods, exemplified by the classical Gauss–Newton and Levenberg–Marquardt algorithms, respectively. We overview each of these in turn.

### 13.2.1 Gauss–Newton Method

The Gauss–Newton method applied to the general least-squares objective (13.3) is a line-search method which, starting from an initialization $u_0$, sets

$$u_{\ell+1} = u_\ell + \alpha_\ell v_\ell, \qquad \ell = 0, 1, \ldots, L-1,$$

where $v_\ell$ is a search direction defined by

$$v_\ell = \arg\min_v \mathsf{J}_\ell^{\mathrm{lin}}(v), \qquad \mathsf{J}_\ell^{\mathrm{lin}}(v) := \frac{1}{2}|Dr(u_\ell)v + r(u_\ell)|^2, \tag{13.6}$$

and $\alpha_\ell > 0$ is a user-chosen step-size parameter. Here and throughout this chapter, $Dr$ will denote the Jacobian of $r$, which here is assumed to exist. However, a significant outcome of the presentation in this chapter is the derivation of ensemble Kalman formulae for the search direction update, avoiding the need for the calculation of the Jacobian; these ensemble methods can be used when the Jacobian does not exist, or is too expensive to compute.

Our presentation in Sections 13.3 and 13.4 will focus on the derivation of extended and ensemble Kalman formulae, respectively, for the search direction update. Although the choice of step-size is crucial to the efficiency of all Gauss–Newton methods, it is not the focus of these notes. Consequently, we introduce algorithms viewing the number $L$ of iterations, and the mechanism for determining the step-size schedule $\{\alpha_\ell\}_{\ell=0}^{L-1}$, as given inputs.

***Remark 13.1*** In practice each step-size $\alpha_\ell$ is chosen adaptively based on the current state $u_\ell$ and search direction $v_\ell$. A unifying idea shared by many sophisticated line search strategies is to find an interval of desirable step-sizes and then try out a sequence of candidates within that interval, stopping when certain conditions are satisfied. For instance, a simple condition is to require reduction of J in which case $\alpha_\ell$ is required to satisfy

$$\mathsf{J}(u_\ell + \alpha_\ell v_\ell) < \mathsf{J}(u_\ell).$$

However, this condition is not sufficient to guarantee convergence and motivates the stronger Armijo condition: for some constant $c_1 \in (0, 1)$,

$$\mathsf{J}(u_\ell + \alpha_\ell v_\ell) \leq \mathsf{J}(u_\ell) + c_1 \alpha_\ell \langle D\mathsf{J}(u_\ell), v_\ell \rangle.$$

The choice of stopping criteria and adaptive step-sizes will be further discussed in Section 13.5. ◇

## 13.2.2 Levenberg–Marquardt Method

The Levenberg–Marquardt method applied to the general least-squares objective (13.3) is a trust region method which, starting from an initialization $u_0$, sets

$$u_{\ell+1} = u_\ell + v_\ell, \qquad \ell = 0, 1, \ldots, L - 1,$$

where

$$v_\ell = \arg\min_v J_\ell^{\mathrm{lin}}(v), \quad \text{such that } |v|_{\widehat{C}}^2 \leq \delta_\ell, \qquad J_\ell^{\mathrm{lin}}(v) := \frac{1}{2}|Dr(u_\ell)v + r(u_\ell)|^2.$$

Similar to Gauss–Newton methods, the increment $v_\ell$ is defined as the minimizer of a linearized objective, but now the minimization is constrained to a ball $\{|v|_{\widehat{C}}^2 \leq \delta_\ell\}$ in which we *trust* that the objective can be replaced by its linearization. For any $\delta_\ell$ there is an $\alpha_\ell \in (0, \infty]$ such that

$$v_\ell = \arg\min_v J_\ell^{\mathrm{UC}}(v),$$

where

$$J_\ell^{\mathrm{UC}}(v) = J_\ell^{\mathrm{lin}}(v) + \frac{1}{2\alpha_\ell}|v|_{\widehat{C}}^2. \tag{13.7}$$

The parameter $\alpha_\ell \in (0, \infty]$ acts as a Lagrange multiplier and plays an analogous role to the step-size in Gauss–Newton methods. We study Levenberg–Marquardt methods from the perspective of the unconstrained minimization problem for $J_\ell^{\mathrm{UC}}$ given by (13.7). Our presentation in Sections 13.3 and 13.4 will focus on the derivation of Kalman formulae for the increments $v_\ell$. As for Gauss–Newton methods, we view the number $L$ of iterations and the mechanism for determining the step-size schedule $\{\alpha_\ell\}_{\ell=0}^{L-1}$ as inputs to the algorithms we state here.

***Remark* 13.2**   In practice the parameter $\delta_\ell$ is chosen adaptively, for instance by monitoring the ratio

$$s_\ell = \frac{\mathsf{J}(u_\ell) - \mathsf{J}(u_\ell + v_\ell)}{\mathsf{Q}(0) - \mathsf{Q}(v_\ell)},$$

where $\mathsf{Q}(v)$ is a quadratic approximation to $\mathsf{J}(u_\ell + v)$. If $s_\ell$ is close to 1, this indicates that the objective (13.3) can be well approximated by a quadratic in a neighborhood of size $\delta_\ell$ around $u_\ell$, and thus that the next trust region can be enlarged. On the other hand, if $s_\ell$ is small, we may shrink the trust region in the next iteration. The choice of stopping criteria and adaptive step-sizes will be further discussed in Section 13.5.                                                     $\diamond$

Note that the Levenberg–Marquardt increment is the unconstrained minimizer of a *regularized* objective. It is for this reason that we say that Levenberg–Marquardt provides an implicit regularization. This regularization helps avoid

| Objective | Optimization | Gradient Method | Ensemble Method |
|-----------|--------------|-----------------|-----------------|
| $J_{TP}$ | Gauss–Newton | IExKF | IEnKF-SL |
| $J_{DM}$ | Levenberg–Marquardt | ExKI | EnKI-SL |
| $J_{TP}$ | Levenberg–Marquardt | TExKI | TEnKI-SL |

Table 13.1 *Summary of the algorithms considered in this chapter.*

overfitting when applied to the data-misfit objective which, unlike the Tikhonov–Phillips objective, is not regularized. On the other hand, Gauss–Newton methods do not provide implicit regularization and therefore should not be applied to the data-misfit objective when solving ill-posed inverse problems. We will therefore focus on gradient and ensemble methods that arise from the following three choices of objective function and optimization algorithm (see Table 13.1):

1 Tikhonov–Phillips and Gauss–Newton, leading to Iterative Extended and Iterative Ensemble Kalman Filters (IExKF and IEnKF-SL);
2 Data-misfit and Levenberg–Marquardt, leading to Extended and Ensemble Kalman Inversion (ExKI and EnKI-SL); and
3 Tikhonov–Phillips and Levenberg–Marquardt, leading to Tikhonov Extended and Tikhonov Ensemble Kalman Inversion (TExKI and TEnKI-SL).

Gradient methods will be introduced in Section 13.3 while their ensemble counterparts will be introduced in Section 13.4.

## 13.3 Extended Kalman Methods

In this section we derive closed formulae for the Gauss–Newton method applied to the Tikhonov–Phillips objective $J_{TP}$, as well as for the Levenberg–Marquardt method applied to the data-misfit objective $J_{DM}$ and the Tikhonov–Phillips objective $J_{TP}$. These formulae are the basis for the ensemble methods considered in the next section.

Since the search directions of Gauss–Newton and Levenberg–Marquardt methods are found by minimizing a linearization of the objective, it is instructive to consider first linear least-squares optimization before delving into the nonlinear setting. The following result characterizes the minimizer $m$ of the Tikhonov–Phillips objective $J_{TP}$ in the case of linear $G(u) = Au$. Note that it is a consequence of completing the square and is derived in the linear-Gaussian setting for inverse problems studied in Chapter 2; we record it here, as it will be used extensively in this chapter.

**Lemma 13.3**   *It holds that*

$$\frac{1}{2}|y - Au|_\Gamma^2 + \frac{1}{2}|u - \widehat{m}|_{\widehat{C}}^2 = \frac{1}{2}|u - m|_C^2 + \beta, \qquad (13.8)$$

*where $\beta$ does not depend on $u$, and*

$$C^{-1} = A^\top \Gamma^{-1} A + \widehat{C}^{-1}, \qquad (13.9)$$

$$C^{-1} m = A^\top \Gamma^{-1} y + \widehat{C}^{-1} \widehat{m}. \qquad (13.10)$$

*Equivalently,*

$$m = \widehat{m} + K(y - A\widehat{m}), \qquad (13.11)$$

$$C = (I - KA)\widehat{C}, \qquad (13.12)$$

*where $K$ is the Kalman gain matrix given by*

$$K = \widehat{C}A^\top (A\widehat{C}A^\top + \Gamma)^{-1} = CA^\top \Gamma^{-1}. \qquad (13.13)$$

*Proof*   The formulae (13.9) and (13.10) follow by matching linear and quadratic coefficients in $u$ between

$$\frac{1}{2}|u - m|_C^2 \quad \text{and} \quad \frac{1}{2}|u - \widehat{m}|_{\widehat{C}}^2 + \frac{1}{2}|y - Au|_\Gamma^2. \qquad (13.14)$$

The formulae (13.11) and (13.12) as well as the equivalent expressions for the Kalman gain $K$ in equation (13.13) can be obtained using the Woodbury matrix identity, Lemma 8.5.                                                   □

### 13.3.1  Iterative Extended Kalman Filter (IExKF)

In this subsection we introduce two ways of writing the Gauss–Newton update applied to the Tikhonov–Phillips objective $\mathsf{J}_{\mathrm{TP}}$. In order to apply the Gauss–Newton method to the Tikhonov–Phillips objective, we use (13.5). The following result is a direct consequence of Lemma 13.3.

**Lemma 13.4**   *The Gauss–Newton method applied to the Tikhonov–Phillips objective $\mathsf{J}_{\mathrm{TP}}$ admits the characterizations:*

$$u_{\ell+1} = u_\ell + \alpha_\ell C_\ell \left( G_\ell^\top \Gamma^{-1}(y - G(u_\ell)) + \widehat{C}^{-1}(\widehat{m} - u_\ell) \right), \qquad (13.15)$$

*and*

$$u_{\ell+1} = u_\ell + \alpha_\ell \left( K_\ell(y - G(u_\ell)) + (I - K_\ell G_\ell)(\widehat{m} - u_\ell) \right), \qquad (13.16)$$

*where $G_\ell = DG(u_\ell)$ and*

$$K_\ell = \widehat{C}G_\ell^\top (G_\ell \widehat{C} G_\ell^\top + \Gamma)^{-1},$$
$$C_\ell = (I - K_\ell G_\ell)\widehat{C}.$$

*Proof* The search direction $v_\ell$ of Gauss–Newton for the objective $\mathsf{J}_{\text{TP}}$ is given by

$$v_\ell = \arg\min_v \frac{1}{2}\left|Dr_{\text{TP}}(u_\ell)v + r_{\text{TP}}(u_\ell)\right|^2 \tag{13.17}$$

$$= \arg\min_v \frac{1}{2}\left|z - h(u_\ell) - Dh(u_\ell)v\right|_Q^2 \tag{13.18}$$

$$= \arg\min_v \left\{\frac{1}{2}\left|y - G(u_\ell) - DG(u_\ell)v\right|_\Gamma^2 + \frac{1}{2}\left|v - (\widehat{m} - u_\ell)\right|_{\widehat{C}}^2\right\}. \tag{13.19}$$

Applying Lemma 13.3, using formulae (13.10) and (13.12), we deduce that

$$v_\ell = C_\ell \left(G_\ell^\top \Gamma^{-1}(y - G(u_\ell)) + \widehat{C}^{-1}(\widehat{m} - u_\ell)\right),$$

which establishes the characterization (13.15). The equivalence between (13.15) and (13.16) follows from the identity (13.13), which implies that $C_\ell G_\ell^\top \Gamma^{-1} = K_\ell$ and $C_\ell \widehat{C}^{-1} = I - K_\ell G_\ell$. □

We refer to the Gauss–Newton method applied to $\mathsf{J}_{\text{TP}}$ as the Iterative Extended Kalman Filter (IExKF) algorithm. Discussion of how to choose the step-sizes adaptively can be found in Section 13.5.

---

**Algorithm 13.1** Iterative Extended Kalman Filter (IExKF)

---

1: **Input**: Initialization $u_0 = \widehat{m}$, rule for choosing the step-sizes $\{\alpha_\ell\}_{\ell=0}^{L-1}$.
2: For $\ell = 0, 1, \ldots, L - 1$ do:

    1 Set $K_\ell = \widehat{C}G_\ell^\top (G_\ell \widehat{C} G_\ell^\top + \Gamma)^{-1}, \qquad G_\ell = DG(u_\ell).$
    2 Set

$$u_{\ell+1} = u_\ell + \alpha_\ell \left(K_\ell (y - G(u_\ell)) + (I - K_\ell G_\ell)(\widehat{m} - u_\ell)\right). \tag{13.20}$$

3: **Output**: $u_1, u_2, \ldots, u_L$.

---

The next proposition shows that in the linear case, if $\alpha_\ell = 1$ for all $\ell \geq 0$, IExKF finds the minimizer of the objective (13.2) in one iteration, and further iterations still stay at the minimizer.

**Proposition 13.5** *Suppose that $G(u) = Au$ is linear and that $\alpha_\ell = 1$ for all $\ell \geq 0$. Then the output of Algorithm 13.1 satisfies*

$$u_\ell = m, \qquad \ell = 1, 2, \ldots,$$

*where m is the minimizer of the Tikhonov–Phillips objective* (13.2).

*Proof*   In the linear case we have

$$G_\ell = A, \qquad K_\ell = K = \widehat{C}A^\top(A\widehat{C}A^\top + \Gamma)^{-1}, \qquad \ell = 0, 1, \ldots$$

Therefore, update (13.20) simplifies as

$$u_{\ell+1} = \widehat{m} + K(y - A\widehat{m}), \quad \ell = 0, 1, \ldots$$

This implies that, for all $\ell \geq 1$, it holds that $u_\ell = m$ with $m$ defined in (13.11).   □

### 13.3.2  Extended Kalman Inversion (ExKI)

In this subsection we study the application of the Levenberg–Marquardt algorithm to the data-misfit objective $\mathsf{J}_{\mathrm{DM}}$. In order to apply the Levenberg–Marquardt method to the data-misfit objective $\mathsf{J}_{\mathrm{DM}}$, recall that this objective can be written in standard nonlinear least-squares form:

$$\mathsf{J}_{\mathrm{DM}}(u) = \frac{1}{2}|r_{\mathrm{DM}}(u)|^2, \qquad r_{\mathrm{DM}}(u) := \Gamma^{-1/2}(y - G(u)). \tag{13.21}$$

**Lemma 13.6**   *The Levenberg–Marquardt method applied to the data-misfit objective $\mathsf{J}_{\mathrm{DM}}$ admits the following characterization:*

$$u_{\ell+1} = u_\ell + K_\ell\left(y - G(u_\ell)\right), \tag{13.22}$$

*where*

$$K_\ell = \alpha_\ell \widehat{C} G_\ell^\top (\alpha_\ell G_\ell \widehat{C} G_\ell^\top + \Gamma)^{-1}, \qquad G_\ell = DG(u_\ell).$$

*Proof*   Note that the increment $v_\ell$ is defined as the unconstrained minimizer of

$$
\begin{aligned}
\mathsf{J}_{\mathrm{DM},\ell}^{\mathrm{UC}}(v) &= \frac{1}{2}|Dr_{\mathrm{DM}}(u_\ell)v + r_{\mathrm{DM}}(u_\ell)|^2 + \frac{1}{2\alpha_\ell}|v|_{\widehat{C}}^2 \\
&= \frac{1}{2}|y - G(u_\ell) - DG(u_\ell)v|_\Gamma^2 + \frac{1}{2\alpha_\ell}|v|_{\widehat{C}}^2.
\end{aligned}
\tag{13.23}
$$

The result follows from Lemma 13.3.   □

The previous lemma motivates the following Extended Kalman Inversion (ExKI) algorithm. Discussion of how to choose the step-sizes adaptively can be found in Section 13.5.

---

**Algorithm 13.2** Extended Kalman Inversion (ExKI)

---

1: **Input**: Initialization $u_0 = \widehat{m}$, rule for choosing the step-sizes $\{\alpha_\ell\}_{\ell=0}^{L-1}$.
2: For $\ell = 0, 1, \ldots, L-1$ do:

  1 Set $K_\ell = \alpha_\ell \widehat{C} G_\ell^\top (\alpha_\ell G_\ell \widehat{C} G_\ell^\top + \Gamma)^{-1}$,      $G_\ell = DG(u_\ell)$.
  2 Set

$$u_{\ell+1} = u_\ell + K_\ell\Big(y - G(u_\ell)\Big). \tag{13.24}$$

3: **Output**: $u_1, u_2, \ldots, u_L$.

---

When $\alpha_0 = 1$, the following linear-case result shows that ExKI reaches the minimizer of $\mathsf{J}_{\mathrm{TP}}$ in one iteration. However, in contrast to IExKF, further iterations of ExKI will typically no longer agree with the minimizer of $\mathsf{J}_{\mathrm{TP}}$.

**Proposition 13.7** *Suppose that $G(u) = Au$ is linear and $\alpha_0 = 1$. Then the output of Algorithm 13.2 satisfies*

$$u_1 = \arg\min_u \mathsf{J}_{\mathrm{TP}}(u),$$

*where $\mathsf{J}_{\mathrm{TP}}$ is the Tikhonov–Phillips objective* (13.2).

*Proof* The proof is identical to that of Proposition 13.5, noting that in the linear case $u_{\ell+1} = u_\ell + K(y - Au_\ell)$.       □

### 13.3.3 Tikhonov Extended Kalman Inversion (TExKI)

In this subsection we describe the application of the Levenberg–Marquardt algorithm to the Tikhonov–Phillips objective $\mathsf{J}_{\mathrm{TP}}$.

**Lemma 13.8** *The Levenberg–Marquardt method applied to the Tikhonov–Phillips objective $\mathsf{J}_{\mathrm{TP}}$ admits the following characterization:*

$$u_{\ell+1} = u_\ell + K_\ell\Big(z - h(u_\ell)\Big),$$

*where*

$$K_\ell = \alpha_\ell \widehat{C} H_\ell^\top (\alpha_\ell H_\ell \widehat{C} H_\ell^\top + Q)^{-1}, \qquad H_\ell = Dh(u_\ell).$$

*Proof* Note that the increment $v_\ell$ is defined as the unconstrained minimizer of

$$\mathsf{J}_{\mathrm{TP},\ell}^{\mathrm{UC}}(v) = \mathsf{J}_{\mathrm{TP},\ell}^\ell(v) + \frac{1}{2\alpha_\ell}|v|_{\widehat{C}}^2 \tag{13.25}$$

$$= \frac{1}{2}|z - h(u_\ell) - Dh(u_\ell)v|_Q^2 + \frac{1}{2\alpha_\ell}|v|_{\widehat{C}}^2. \tag{13.26}$$

This has the form of equation (13.23), replacing $y$ with $z$, $G$ with $h$, and $\Gamma$ with $Q$. □

The previous lemma motivates the following Tikhonov Extended Kalman Inversion (TExKI) algorithm. Discussion of how to choose the step-sizes adaptively can be found in Section 13.5.

---

**Algorithm 13.3** Tikhonov Extended Kalman Inversion (TExKI)

---

**Input**: Initialization $u_0 = \widehat{m}$, rule for choosing the step-sizes $\{\alpha_\ell\}_{\ell=0}^{L-1}$.
For $\ell = 0, 1, \dots, L - 1$ do:

1 Set $K_\ell = \alpha_\ell \widehat{C} H_\ell^\top (\alpha_\ell H_\ell \widehat{C} H_\ell^\top + Q)^{-1}$,     $H_\ell = Dh(u_\ell)$.
2 Set

$$u_{\ell+1} = u_\ell + K_\ell \big(z - h(u_\ell)\big). \tag{13.27}$$

**Output**: $u_1, u_2, \dots, u_L$.

---

When $\alpha_0 = 1$, the following linear-case result shows that TExKI reaches in one iteration the minimizer of a $\mathsf{J}_{\text{TP}}$ objective appended with an additional regularization term.

**Proposition 13.9**   *Suppose that $G(u) = Au$ is linear and $\alpha_0 = 1$. Then the output of Algorithm 13.2 satisfies*

$$u_1 = \arg\min_u \Big(\mathsf{J}_{\text{TP}}(u) + \frac{1}{2}|u - \widehat{m}|_{\widehat{C}}^2\Big),$$

*where $\mathsf{J}_{\text{TP}}$ is the Tikhonov–Phillips objective (13.2).*

*Proof*   Notice that setting $H = \begin{bmatrix} A \\ I \end{bmatrix}$ we have

$$u_1 = \widehat{m} + \widehat{C} H^\top (H\widehat{C} H^\top + Q)^{-1}(z - H\widehat{m}).$$

Lemma 13.3 then implies that $u_1$ minimizes

$$\frac{1}{2}|z - Hu|_Q^2 + \frac{1}{2}|u - \widehat{m}|_{\widehat{C}}^2,$$

which implies the result. □

**Remark 13.10**   It is illustrative to compare Propositions 13.5, 13.7, and 13.9. These results show that in a linear setting: (i) IExKF reaches in one iteration the minimizer of $\mathsf{J}_{\text{TP}}$, and that further iterates remain at the minimizer; (ii) ExKI reaches in one iteration the minimizer of $\mathsf{J}_{\text{TP}}$; and (iii) TExKI reaches in one iteration the minimizer of a $\mathsf{J}_{\text{TP}}$ objective appended with an additional regularization term. ◇

## 13.4 Ensemble Kalman Methods

In this section we review three subfamilies of iterative methods that update an ensemble $\{u_\ell^{(n)}\}_{n=1}^N$ employing Kalman-based formulae, where $\ell = 0, 1, \ldots$ denotes the iteration index and $N$ is a fixed ensemble size. Each ensemble member $u_\ell^{(n)}$ is updated by optimizing an objective defined using the current ensemble $\{u_\ell^{(n)}\}_{n=1}^N$. The optimization is performed without evaluating derivatives by invoking a *statistical linearization* of a Gauss–Newton or Levenberg–Marquardt algorithm. In analogy with the previous section, the three subfamilies of ensemble methods we consider differ in the choice of the objective and in the choice of the optimization algorithm.

Given an ensemble $\{u_\ell^{(n)}\}_{n=1}^N$ we use the following notation for ensemble empirical means

$$m_\ell := \frac{1}{N} \sum_{n=1}^N u_\ell^{(n)}, \qquad \overline{G}_\ell := \frac{1}{N} \sum_{n=1}^N G(u_\ell^{(n)}),$$

and empirical covariances and cross-covariances

$$\widehat{C}_\ell^{uu} := \frac{1}{N} \sum_{n=1}^N (u_\ell^{(n)} - m_\ell)(u_\ell^{(n)} - m_\ell)^\top,$$

$$\widehat{C}_\ell^{uy} := \frac{1}{N} \sum_{n=1}^N (u_\ell^{(n)} - m_\ell)(G(u_\ell^{(n)}) - \overline{G}_\ell)^\top,$$

$$\widehat{C}_\ell^{yy} := \frac{1}{N} \sum_{n=1}^N (G(u_\ell^{(n)}) - \overline{G}_\ell)(G(u_\ell^{(n)}) - \overline{G}_\ell)^\top.$$

Here and in what follows $(\widehat{C}_\ell^{uu})^{-1}$ denotes the pseudoinverse of $\widehat{C}_\ell^{uu}$.

The overarching theme that underlies the derivation of the ensemble methods studied in this section is the use of statistical linearization to avoid evaluation of derivatives. The idea behind statistical linearization is this: if $G(u) = Au$ is linear, we have

$$\widehat{C}_\ell^{uy} = \widehat{C}_\ell^{uu} A^\top.$$

Thus, if $\widehat{C}_\ell^{uu}$ is invertible, $A = (\widehat{C}_\ell^{uy})^\top (\widehat{C}_\ell^{uu})^{-1}$. Here and in what follows $(\widehat{C}_\ell^{uu})^{-1}$ denotes the inverse of $\widehat{C}_\ell^{uu}$ if this inverse exists, and the pseudoinverse otherwise. Noting that $A$ is the derivative of $G(\cdot)$ in the linear case, this calculation motivates the following *approximation* in the general nonlinear case:

$$DG(u_\ell^{(n)}) \approx G_\ell := (\widehat{C}_\ell^{uy})^\top (\widehat{C}_\ell^{uu})^{-1}, \qquad n = 1, \ldots, N, \tag{13.28}$$

Note that (13.28) gives the same approximation of the derivative for every particle $n$, and indeed that it leads to an approximation that may be used at any point.

Other useful approximations follow from this. For example, note that the exact gradient of $J_{DM}(u)$ from (13.2) is given by

$$DJ_{DM}(u) = DG(u)^\top \Gamma^{-1}(y - G(u)).$$

This suggests the approximation, for $G_\ell$ given by (13.28),

$$DJ_{DM}(u_\ell^{(n)}) \approx G_\ell^\top \Gamma^{-1}(y - G(u_\ell^{(n)})), \tag{13.29a}$$

$$= (\widehat{C}_\ell^{uu})^{-1} \widehat{C}_\ell^{uy} \Gamma^{-1}(y - G(u_\ell^{(n)})). \tag{13.29b}$$

### 13.4.1 Iterative Ensemble Kalman Filter with Statistical Linearization (IEnKF-SL)

Given an ensemble $\{u_\ell^{(n)}\}_{n=1}^N$, consider the following Gauss–Newton update for each $n$:

$$u_{\ell+1}^{(n)} = u_\ell^{(n)} + \alpha_\ell v_\ell^{(n)}, \tag{13.30}$$

where $\alpha_\ell > 0$ is the step-size, and $v_\ell^{(n)}$ is the minimizer of the following (linearized) Tikhonov–Phillips objective (see (13.19))

$$J_{TP,\ell}^{(n)}(v) = \frac{1}{2}|y - G(u_\ell^{(n)}) - G_\ell v|_\Gamma^2 + \frac{1}{2}|\widehat{m} - u_\ell^{(n)} - v|_{\widehat{C}}^2. \tag{13.31}$$

It is important to appreciate that we adopt the statistical linearization (13.28) in the above formulation. This couples the different objective functions $J_{TP,\ell}^{(n)}$ indexed by $\ell$. Applying Lemma 13.3, the minimizer $v_\ell^{(n)}$ of $J_{TP,\ell}^{(n)}$ can be calculated as

$$v_\ell^{(n)} = C_\ell\left(G_\ell^\top \Gamma^{-1}(y - G(u_\ell^{(n)})) + \widehat{C}^{-1}(\widehat{m} - u_\ell^{(n)})\right), \tag{13.32}$$

or, in an equivalent form,

$$v_\ell^{(n)} = K_\ell(y - G(u_\ell^{(n)})) + (I - K_\ell G_\ell)(\widehat{m} - u_\ell^{(n)}), \tag{13.33}$$

where

$$C_\ell = \left(G_\ell^\top \Gamma^{-1} G_\ell + \widehat{C}^{-1}\right)^{-1},$$

$$K_\ell = \widehat{C} G_\ell^\top (G_\ell \widehat{C} G_\ell^\top + \Gamma)^{-1}.$$

Crucially each $v_\ell^{(n)}$ depends on all the $\{u_\ell^{(m)}\}_{m=1}^N$.

Combining (13.30) and (13.33) leads to the Iterative Ensemble Kalman Filter with Statistical Linearization (IEnKF-SL) algorithm. Discussion on how to choose the step-sizes adaptively can be found in Section 13.5.

---

**Algorithm 13.4** Iterative Ensemble Kalman Filter with Statistical Linearization

**Input**: Initial ensemble $\{u_0^{(n)}\}_{n=1}^N$ sampled from $\mathcal{N}(\widehat{m}, \widehat{C})$, rule for choosing the step-sizes $\{\alpha_\ell\}_{\ell=0}^{L-1}$.
For $\ell = 0, 1, \ldots, L-1$ do:

1 Set $K_\ell = \widehat{C} G_\ell^\top (G_\ell \widehat{C} G_\ell^\top + \Gamma)^{-1}$,    $G_\ell = (\widehat{C}_\ell^{uy})^\top (\widehat{C}_\ell^{uu})^{-1}$.
2 Set

$$u_{\ell+1}^{(n)} = u_\ell^{(n)} + \alpha_\ell \left( K_\ell \big( y - G(u_\ell^{(n)}) \big) + (I - K_\ell G_\ell)\big(\widehat{m} - u_\ell^{(n)}\big) \right), \qquad 1 \le n \le N. \tag{13.34}$$

**Output**: Ensemble means $m_1, m_2, \ldots, m_L$.

---

Notice that IEnKF-SL is a natural ensemble-based version of the derivative-based IExKF Algorithm 13.1 with update (13.20). Other statistical linearizations and approximations of the Gauss–Newton scheme are possible.

## 13.4.2 Ensemble Kalman Inversion with Statistical Linearization (EnKI-SL)

Given an ensemble $\{u_\ell^{(n)}\}_{n=1}^N$, consider the following Levenberg–Marquardt update for each $n$:

$$u_{\ell+1}^{(n)} = u_\ell^{(n)} + v_\ell^{(n)}, \tag{13.35}$$

where $v_\ell^{(n)}$ is the minimizer of the following regularized (linearized) data-misfit objective (see (13.23))

$$\mathsf{J}_{\mathrm{DM},\ell}^{(n),\mathrm{UC}}(v) = \frac{1}{2}\big|y - G(u_\ell^{(n)}) - G_\ell v\big|_\Gamma^2 + \frac{1}{2\alpha_\ell}|v|_{\widehat{C}}^2, \tag{13.36}$$

and $\alpha_\ell > 0$ will be regarded as a step-size. Notice that we adopt the statistical linearization (13.28) in the above formulation. Applying Lemma 13.3, we can calculate the minimizer $v_\ell^{(n)}$ explicitly:

$$v_\ell^{(n)} = (G_\ell^\top \Gamma^{-1} G_\ell + \alpha_\ell^{-1} \widehat{C}^{-1})^{-1} G_\ell^\top \Gamma^{-1}\big(y - G(u_\ell^{(n)})\big), \tag{13.37}$$

or, in an equivalent form,

$$v_\ell^{(n)} = \widehat{C} G_\ell^\top (G_\ell \widehat{C} G_\ell^\top + \alpha_\ell^{-1}\Gamma)^{-1}\big(y - G(u_\ell^{(n)})\big). \tag{13.38}$$

As in the preceding subsection, each $v_\ell^{(n)}$ depends on all the $\{u_\ell^{(m)}\}_{m=1}^N$. This leads to the Ensemble Kalman Inversion (EnKI-SL) with Statistical Linearization method. Discussion of how to choose the step-sizes adaptively can be found in Section 13.5.

---

**Algorithm 13.5** Ensemble Kalman Inversion with Statistical Linearization

---

**Input**: Initial ensemble $\{u_0^{(n)}\}_{n=1}^N$ sampled from $\mathcal{N}(\widehat{m}, \widehat{C})$, rule for choosing the step-sizes $\{\alpha_\ell\}_{\ell=0}^{L-1}$.

For $\ell = 0, 1, \ldots, L - 1$ do:

1 Set $K_\ell = \widehat{C} G_\ell^\top (G_\ell \widehat{C} G_\ell^\top + \alpha_\ell^{-1} \Gamma)^{-1}$, $\quad G_\ell = (\widehat{C}_\ell^{uy})^\top (\widehat{C}_\ell^{uu})^{-1}$.

2 Set

$$u_{\ell+1}^{(n)} = u_\ell^{(n)} + K_\ell \left( y - G(u_\ell^{(n)}) \right), \qquad 1 \le n \le N. \tag{13.39}$$

**Output**: Ensemble means $m_1, m_2, \ldots, m_L$.

---

Notice that EnKI-SL is a natural ensemble-based version of the derivative-based ExKI Algorithm 13.2.

### 13.4.3 Tikhonov Ensemble Kalman Inversion with Statistical Linearization (TEnKI-SL)

Recall that we define

$$z := \begin{bmatrix} y \\ \widehat{m} \end{bmatrix}, \qquad h(u) := \begin{bmatrix} G(u) \\ u \end{bmatrix}, \qquad Q := \begin{bmatrix} \Gamma & 0 \\ 0 & \widehat{C} \end{bmatrix}.$$

Then, given an ensemble $\{u_\ell^{(n)}\}_{n=1}^N$, we can define

$$\overline{h}_\ell := \frac{1}{N} \sum_{n=1}^N h(u_\ell^{(n)}),$$

and empirical covariances

$$\widehat{C}_\ell^{zz} := \frac{1}{N} \sum_{n=1}^N \left( h(u_\ell^{(n)}) - \overline{h}_\ell \right) \left( h(u_\ell^{(n)}) - \overline{h}_\ell \right)^\top,$$

$$\widehat{C}_\ell^{uz} := \frac{1}{N} \sum_{n=1}^N \left( u_\ell^{(n)} - m_\ell \right) \left( h(u_\ell^{(n)}) - \overline{h}_\ell \right)^\top.$$

Furthermore, we define the statistical linearization $H_\ell$:

$$Dh(u_\ell^{(n)}) \approx (\widehat{C}_\ell^{uz})^\top (\widehat{C}_\ell^{uu})^{-1} =: H_\ell. \tag{13.40}$$

Notice that

$$H_\ell = \begin{bmatrix} G_\ell \\ I \end{bmatrix},$$

with $G_\ell$ defined in (13.28).

Given an ensemble $\{u_\ell^{(n)}\}_{n=1}^N$, consider the following Levenberg–Marquardt update for each $n$:

$$u_{\ell+1}^{(n)} = u_\ell^{(n)} + v_\ell^{(n)},$$

where $v_\ell^{(n)}$ is the minimizer of the following regularized (linearized) Tikhonov–Phillips objective (see (13.26))

$$\mathsf{J}_{\mathrm{TP},\ell}^{(n),\mathrm{uc}}(v) = \frac{1}{2}|z - h(u_\ell^{(n)}) - H_\ell v|_Q^2 + \frac{1}{2\alpha_\ell}|v|_{\widehat{C}}^2, \qquad (13.41)$$

and $\alpha_\ell > 0$ will be regarded as a step-size. We can calculate the minimizer $v_\ell^{(n)}$ explicitly, applying Lemma 13.3:

$$v_\ell^{(n)} = (H_\ell^\top Q^{-1} H_\ell + \alpha_\ell^{-1} \widehat{C}^{-1})^{-1} H_\ell^\top Q^{-1}(z - h(u_\ell^{(n)})), \qquad (13.42)$$

or, in an equivalent form,

$$v_\ell^{(n)} = \widehat{C} H_\ell^\top (G_\ell \widehat{C} H_\ell^\top + \alpha_\ell^{-1} Q)^{-1}(z - h(u_\ell^{(n)})). \qquad (13.43)$$

Once again each $v_\ell^{(n)}$ depends on all the $\{u_\ell^{(m)}\}_{m=1}^N$.

This leads to Tikhonov Ensemble Kalman Inversion with Statistical Linearization (TEnKI-SL), described in Algorithm 13.6. Discussion on how to choose the step-sizes adaptively can be found in Section 13.5.

---

**Algorithm 13.6** Tikhonov Ensemble Kalman Inversion with Statistical Linearization

---

**Input**: Initial ensemble $\{u_0^{(n)}\}_{n=1}^N$ sampled from $\mathcal{N}(m, P)$, rule for choosing the step-sizes $\{\alpha_\ell\}_{\ell=0}^{L-1}$.

For $\ell = 0, 1, \ldots, L - 1$ do:

1 Set $K_\ell = \widehat{C} H_\ell^\top (G_\ell \widehat{C} H_\ell^\top + \alpha_\ell^{-1} Q)^{-1}$, $\qquad H_\ell = (\widehat{C}_\ell^{uz})^\top (\widehat{C}_\ell^{uu})^{-1}$.

2 Set

$$u_{\ell+1}^{(n)} = u_\ell^{(n)} + K_\ell\left(z - h(u_\ell^{(n)})\right), \qquad 1 \le n \le N. \qquad (13.44)$$

**Output**: Ensemble means $m_1, m_2, \ldots, m_L$.

---

Notice that TEnKI-SL is a natural ensemble-based version of the derivative-based TExKI Algorithm 13.3.

## 13.5  Discussion and Bibliography

The presentation in this chapter follows the conceptual approach to this subject overviewed and systematized in Chada et al. (2021): Kalman methods for inverse problems are studied from the optimization perspective, and classified in terms of the objective function they seek to minimize and the nonlinear least-squares optimization algorithm they are based on. For background on nonlinear least-squares optimization we refer to Nocedal and Wright (2006) and Dennis Jr. and Schnabel (1996) where, in particular, a detailed discussion on the adaptive choice of the step-size parameters can be found; note that the algorithms stated in this chapter have been agnostic regarding the step-size choice strategy as we have concentrated on the use of ideas from Kalman filtering within optimization. Furthermore, following the presentation in Chada et al. (2021), we have considered only nonlinear least-squares objectives and quadratic regularizers. However, ensemble Kalman methods for inverse problems that use other objective functions (or loss functions) and other regularizers are starting to emerge; in particular cross-entropy loss (Kovachki and Stuart, 2019), logistic loss (Pidstrigach and Reich, 2023) and regularizers that promote sparsity (Lee, 2021; Schneider et al., 2022; Kim et al., 2023) have all been considered.

There are a number of other ways in which Kalman filtering methods may be used to study inverse problems. The review by Calvello et al. (2022) emphasizes the Bayesian approach to inversion and, in particular, shows how ideas from the sequential Monte Carlo (SMC) (Del Moral et al., 2006) approach to Bayesian inversion can be adapted to the use of ensemble Kalman methods. This possibility is highlighted in Reich (2017), which is focused on sequential data assimilation; note, however, that the analysis step (7.1) in sequential data assimilation requires solution of a Bayesian inverse problem and thus the ideas in that paper are relevant for inverse problems in general, beyond data assimilation. The reader interested in the use of SMC for inverse problems is directed to Kantas et al. (2014) and Beskos et al. (1994) and the references therein; the former paper demonstrates use of the methodology for an inverse problem arising from the Navier–Stokes equation, and the latter paper contains a simple proof of convergence of the particle filter in the context of SMC for inverse problems, following the analysis in Rebeschini and Handel (2015) for particle filters in sequential data assimilation.

Another class of methods for inverse problems, which may be applied in both the optimization and Bayesian approaches, revolves around the idea of preconditioned gradient descent in ensemble Kalman methods for inversion; in particular, use of the pre-conditioned gradient

$$\widehat{C}_\ell^{uu} D\mathsf{J}_{\mathrm{DM}}(u_\ell^{(n)}) \approx \widehat{C}_\ell^{uy}\Gamma^{-1}\big(y - G(u_\ell^{(n)})\big),$$

which follows from (13.29). This leads to iterative optimization methods (Iglesias et al., 2014a; Schillings and Stuart, 2017, 2018), based on gradient descent, and to Bayesian sampling methods (Garbuno-Inigo et al., 2020b,a). A key feature of the preconditioned gradient is that it leads to algorithms which are affine invariant (Goodman and Weare, 2010), and hence to convergence rates which are uniform across wide classes of problems; see Calvello et al. (2022) for further discussion.

Finally, we note that Kalman methods are based on a Gaussian approximation, and hence on matching first and second order moments when studying Bayesian inversion. Therefore, it is natural to study Kalman methods for inverse problems which are applied to (possibly stochastic) dynamical systems whose long-term properties exactly solve the optimization or Bayesian approach to inversion in the linear-Gaussian setting; this idea is developed in Huang et al. (2022b, 2022a).

The gradient-based IExKF algorithm was developed in the control theory literature (Jazwinski, 2007) without reference to the Gauss–Newton optimization method; the correspondence between both methods was established in Bell and Cathey (1993). Ensemble Kalman methods were also first introduced as filtering schemes for sequential data assimilation, as described in Chapter 10. Their use for state and parameter estimation and inverse problems was further developed in Anderson (2001), Lorentzen et al. (2001), and Skjervheim et al. (2011). The idea of *iterating* these methods was considered in Chen and Oliver (2002), Emerick and Reynolds (2013), and Reich (2017). Ensemble Kalman methods are now popular in both inverse problems and data assimilation; they have also shown some potential in machine learning applications (Haber et al., 2018; Guth et al., 2020; Kovachki and Stuart, 2019). There are two main computational benefits in updating an ensemble of candidate reconstructions rather than a single estimate. First, the ensemble update can be performed without evaluating derivatives of $G$, effectively approximating them using statistical linearization. This is important in applications where computing derivatives of $G$ is expensive, or where the map $G$ needs to be treated as a black-box. Second, the use of empirical rather than model covariances can significantly reduce the computational cost whenever the ensemble size $N$ is smaller than the dimension $d$ of the unknown $u$. Another advantage of the ensemble approach is that, for problems that are not strongly nonlinear, the spread of the ensemble may contain meaningful information on the uncertainty in the reconstruction. Statistical linearization has also been used within unscented Kalman methods, see Ungarala (2012), Huang et al. (2022b, 2021).

In this chapter we have considered three families of ensemble algorithms characterized by a choice of objective function and optimization algorithm: (i) Tikhonov–Phillips and Gauss–Newton; (ii) data-misfit and Levenberg–Marquardt; and (iii) Tikhonov–Phillips and Levenberg–Marquardt. Each family of ensemble Kalman methods stems from a choice of objective and a derivative-based optimization scheme that is approximated with the ensemble. There is substantial freedom as to how to use the ensemble to approximate a derivative-based method. We have focused on randomized-maximum likelihood implementations (Gu and Oliver, 2007; Kelly et al., 2014), but square-root approaches (Anderson, 2001; Tippett et al., 2003) can also be considered.

Algorithms in the first family were originally introduced in petroleum engineering and the geophysical sciences (Aanonsen et al., 2009; Chen and Oliver, 2002; Emerick and Reynolds, 2013; Gu and Oliver, 2007; Li and Reynolds, 2007; Reynolds et al., 2006) and were inspired by iterative, gradient-based, extended Kalman filters (Bell, 1994; Bell and Cathey, 1993; Jazwinski, 2007). More challenging problems with strongly nonlinear dynamics are considered in Sakov et al. (2012). In this chapter we have presented the iterative IEnKF-SL as a prototypical example of an algorithm that belongs to this family. IEnKF-SL was introduced in Chada et al. (2021) as a slight modification of the iterative ensemble Kalman algorithm proposed in Ungarala (2012). One of the earliest applications of iterative ensemble Kalman methods for inversion in the petroleum engineering literature was proposed in Reynolds et al. (2006), which considered the alternative characterization of the Gauss–Newton update (13.32). Moreover, instead of using a different preconditioner $C_\ell$ for each step, Reynolds et al. (2006) used a fixed preconditioner.

Algorithms in the second family were introduced in the applied mathematics literature (Iglesias, 2016; Iglesias et al., 2014a) building on ideas from classical inverse problems (Hanke, 1997). Recent theoretical work has focused on developing continuous-time and mean-field limits, as well as various convergence results (Blömker et al., 2019; Blömker et al., 2018; Chada and Tong, 2022; Herty and Visconti, 2019; Ding and Li, 2021; Kovachki and Stuart, 2019; Schillings and Stuart, 2017). Methodological extensions based on Bayesian hierarchical techniques were introduced in Chada (2018); Chada et al. (2018) and the incorporation of constraints has also been investigated (Albers et al., 2019; Chada et al., 2019). In this chapter we use EnKI-SL as a prototypical example of an algorithm that belongs to this subfamily. Its connection with the Ensemble Kalman Inversion algorithm from Iglesias et al. (2014a) is discussed in Chada et al. (2021).

The third family, which has emerged more recently, combines explicit regularization through the Tikhonov–Phillips objective and an implicitly regularizing optimization scheme (Chada et al., 2020; Chada and Tong, 2022). In this chapter we use TEnKI-SL as a prototypical example of an algorithm that belongs to this subfamily.

Our presentation has focused on the derivation of Kalman formulae for the search direction update of Gauss–Newton and Levenberg–Marquardt algorithms and their ensemble approximations. All the algorithms studied in this chapter require specifying appropriate step-size parameters that determine the size of the updates along the search direction. For gradient-based methods, there is abundant literature on the adaptive choice of step-sizes (Nocedal and Wright, 2006). Gauss–Newton methods can be shown to converge when the step-sizes are chosen according to Armijo or Wolfe conditions; the line search is often performed with a backtracking strategy (Nocedal and Wright, 2006; Dennis Jr. and Schnabel, 1996). When using Levenberg–Marquardt schemes for inverse problems, it is important to ensure that the step-sizes, as well as the stopping criteria, provide sufficient implicit regularization to alleviate the ill-posedness of inverse problems (Hanke, 1997). For ensemble Kalman methods, the use and analysis of adaptive step-sizes is a topic of current research (Chada and Tong, 2022; Iglesias and Yang, 2021). In practice, ensemble methods are often run with short step-sizes, in which case the algorithms may be interpreted as being defined by discretization of (stochastic) differential equations, see e.g. Reich (2017), Chada et al. (2021), and Schillings and Stuart (2017). Finally, we point out that the original descriptions of some of the algorithms studied in this chapter, e.g. EnKI and TEnKI in Iglesias et al. (2014a) and Chada et al. (2020), do not discuss the inclusion of step-size parameters. This would correspond to setting $\alpha_\ell = 1$ for all $\ell \geq 0$ in our terminology.

# References

Aanonsen, S. I., Nævdal, G., Oliver, D. S., Reynolds, A. C., and Vallès, B. 2009. The ensemble Kalman filter in reservoir engineering–a review. *SPE Journal*, **14**(03), 393–412.

Abarbanel, H. 2013. *Predicting the Future: Completing Models of Observed Complex Systems*. Springer.

Agapiou, S., Larsson, S., and Stuart, A. M. 2013. Posterior contraction rates for the Bayesian approach to linear ill-posed inverse problems. *Stochastic Processes and their Applications*, **123**(10), 3828–3860.

Agapiou, S., Papaspiliopoulos, O., Sanz-Alonso, D., and Stuart, A. M. 2017a. Importance sampling: Intrinsic dimension and computational cost. *Statistical Science*, **32**(3), 405–431.

Agapiou, S., Burger, M., Dashti, M., and Helin, T. 2017b. Sparsity-promoting and edge-preserving maximum a posteriori estimators in non-parametric Bayesian inverse problems. *Inverse Problems*, **34**(4), 045002.

Agrawal, S., Kim, H., Sanz-Alonso, D., and Strang, A. 2022. A variational inference approach to inverse problems with gamma hyperpriors. *SIAM/ASA Journal on Uncertainty Quantification*, **10**(4), 1533–1559.

Akyildiz, Ö. D., and Míguez, J. 2021. Convergence rates for optimised adaptive importance samplers. *Statistics and Computing*, **31**(2), 1–17.

Al Ghattas, O., and Sanz-Alonso, D. 2022. Non-asymptotic analysis of ensemble Kalman updates: effective dimension and localization. *arXiv preprint arXiv:2208.03246*.

Albers, D. J., Blancquart, P.-A., Levine, M. E., Seylabi, E. E., and Stuart, A. M. 2019. Ensemble Kalman methods with constraints. *Inverse Problems*, **35**(9), 095007.

Anderson, B., and Moore, J. B. 1979. *Optimal Filtering*. Prentice-Hall Information and System Sciences Series. Prentice Hall.

Anderson, E. C. 2014. Monte Carlo methods and importance sampling. Lecture Notes for Statistical Genetics. Unpublished lecture notes, available at https://ib.berkeley.edu/labs/slatkin/eriq/classes/guest_lect/mc_lecture_notes.pdf

Anderson, J. L. 2001. An ensemble adjustment Kalman filter for data assimilation. *Monthly Weather Review*, **129**(12), 2884–2903.

Asch, M., Bocquet, M., and Nodet, M. 2016. *Data Assimilation: Methods, Algorithms, and Applications*. Vol. 11 of Fundamentals of Algorithms. Society for Industrial and Applied Mathematics.

Ayanbayev, B., Klebanov, I., Lie, H. C., and Sullivan, T. J. 2021. Γ-convergence of Onsager–Machlup functionals: I. With applications to maximum a posteriori estimation in Bayesian inverse problems. *Inverse Problems*, **38**(2), 025005.

Bain, A., and Crisan, D. 2008. *Fundamentals of Stochastic Filtering*. Vol. 60 of Stochastic Modelling and Applied Probability. Springer Science & Business Media.

Bal, G. 2012. Introduction to Inverse Problems. *Lecture Notes-Department of Applied Physics and Applied Mathematics, Columbia University, New York*. Available at www.stat.uchicago.edu/~guillaumebal/PAPERS/IntroductionInverse Problems.pdf

Bassiri, P., Holmes, C., and Walker, S. 2016. A general framework for updating belief distributions. *Journal of the Royal Statistical Society: Series B (Statistical Methodology)*, **78**(5), 1103–1130.

Bayes, T. 1763. An essay towards solving a problem in the doctrine of chances. *Philosophical Transactions of the Royal Society of London*, **53**, 370–418.

Bell, B. M. 1994. The iterated Kalman smoother as a Gauss–Newton method. *SIAM Journal on Optimization*, **4**(3), 626–636.

Bell, B. M., and Cathey, F. W. 1993. The iterated Kalman filter update as a Gauss-Newton method. *IEEE Transactions on Automatic Control*, **38**(2), 294–297.

Beskos, A., Jasra, A., Law, K. J. H., Tempone, R., and Zhou, Y. 1994. Multilevel sequential Monte Carlo samplers. *Stochastic Processes and their Applications*, **127**(5), 1417–1440.

Bickel, P., Li, B., and Bengtsson, T. 2008. Sharp failure rates for the bootstrap particle filter in high dimensions. Pages 318–329 of: *Pushing the Limits of Contemporary Statistics: Contributions in Honor of Jayanta K. Ghosh*. Institute of Mathematical Statistics.

Bishop, C. M. 2006. *Pattern Recognition and Machine Learning*. Vol. 128 of Information Science and Statistics. Springer.

Bishop, C. H., Etherton, B. J., and Majumdar, S. J. 2001. Adaptive sampling with the ensemble transform Kalman filter. Part I: Theoretical aspects. *Monthly Weather Review*, **129**(3), 420–436.

Blei, D. M., Kucukelbir, A., and McAuliffe, J. D. 2017. Variational inference: A review for statisticians. *Journal of the American Statistical Association*, **112**(518), 859–877.

Blömker, D., Schillings, C., and Wacker, P. 2018. A strongly convergent numerical scheme from ensemble Kalman inversion. *SIAM Journal on Numerical Analysis*, **56**(4), 2537–2562.

Blömker, D., Schillings, C., Wacker, P., and Weissmann, S. 2019. Well posedness and convergence analysis of the ensemble Kalman inversion. *Inverse Problems*, **35**(8), 085007.

Bocquet, M., Brajard, J., Carrassi, A., and Bertino, Laurent. L. 2020. Bayesian inference of chaotic dynamics by merging data assimilation, machine learning and expectation-maximization. *Foundations of Data Science*, **2**(1), 55–80.

Bottou, L., Curtis, F. E., and Nocedal, J. 2018. Optimization methods for large-scale machine learning. *SIAM Review*, **60**(2), 223–311.

Boyd, S., Boyd, S. P., and Vandenberghe, L. 2004. *Convex Optimization*. Cambridge University Press.

Brajard, J., Carrassi, A., Bocquet, M., and Bertino, L. 2020. Combining data assimilation and machine learning to emulate a dynamical model from sparse and noisy observations: a case study with the Lorenz 96 model. *Journal of Computational Science*, **44**, 101171.

Branicki, M., Majda, A. J., and Law, K. J. H. 2018. Accuracy of some approximate Gaussian filters for the Navier–Stokes equation in the presence of model error. *Multiscale Modeling & Simulation*, **16**(4), 1756–1794.

Brett, C., Lam, K., Law, K. J. H., McCormick, D., Scott, M., and Stuart, A. M. 2013. Accuracy and stability of filters for dissipative PDEs. *Physica D: Nonlinear Phenomena*, **245**(1), 34–45.

Bröcker, J. 2013. Existence and uniqueness for four-dimensional variational data assimilation in discrete time. *SIAM Journal on Applied Dynamical Systems*, **16**(1), 361–374.

Brooks, S., Gelman, A., Jones, G., and Meng, X. 2011. *Handbook of Markov Chain Monte Carlo*. CRC Press.

Bugallo, M. F., Elvira, V., Martino, L., Luengo, D., Miguez, J., and Djuric, P. M. 2017. Adaptive importance sampling: The past, the present, and the future. *IEEE Signal Processing Magazine*, **34**(4), 60–79.

Bui-Thanh, T., Ghattas, O., Martin, J., and Stadler, G. 2013. A computational framework for infinite-dimensional Bayesian inverse problems Part I: The linearized case, with application to global seismic inversion. *SIAM Journal on Scientific Computing*, **35**(6), A2494–A2523.

Caflisch, R. E. 1998. Monte Carlo and quasi-Monte Carlo methods. *Acta Numerica*, **7**, 1–49.

Calvello, E., Reich, S., and Stuart, A. M. 2022. Ensemble Kalman methods: A mean field perspective. *arXiv preprint arXiv:2209.11371*.

Calvetti, D., and Somersalo, E. 2007. *An Introduction to Bayesian Scientific Computing: Ten Lectures on Subjective Computing*. Vol. 2 of Surveys and Tutorials in the Applied Mathematical Sciences. Springer Science & Business Media.

Carrassi, A., Bocquet, M., Bertino, L., and Evensen, G. 2018. Data assimilation in the geosciences: An overview of methods, issues, and perspectives. *Wiley Interdisciplinary Reviews: Climate Change*, **9**(5).

Carrillo, J.A., Hoffmann, F., Stuart, A. M., and Vaes, U. 2022. The Ensemble Kalman filter in the near-Gaussian setting. *arXiv preprint arXiv:2212.13239*.

Chada, N. K. 2018. Analysis of hierarchical ensemble Kalman inversion. *arXiv preprint arXiv:1801.00847*.

Chada, N., and Tong, X. 2022. Convergence acceleration of ensemble Kalman inversion in nonlinear settings. *Mathematics of Computation*, **91**(335), 1247–1280.

Chada, N. K., Iglesias, M. A., Roininen, L., and Stuart, A. M. 2018. Parameterizations for ensemble Kalman inversion. *Inverse Problems*, **34**(5), 055009.

Chada, N. K., Schillings, C., and Weissmann, S. 2019. On the incorporation of box-constraints for ensemble Kalman inversion. *Foundations of Data Science*, **1**(4), 433.

Chada, N. K., Stuart, A. M., and Tong, X. T. 2020. Tikhonov regularization within ensemble Kalman inversion. *SIAM Journal on Numerical Analysis*, **58**(2), 1263–1294.

Chada, N. K., Chen, Y., and Sanz-Alonso, D. 2021. Iterative ensemble Kalman methods: A unified perspective with some new variants. *Foundations of Data Science*, **3**(3), 331–369.

Chatterjee, S., and Diaconis, P. 2018. The sample size required in importance sampling. *The Annals of Applied Probability*, **28**(2), 1099–1135.

Chen, Y., and Oliver, D. 2002. Ensemble randomized maximum likelihood method as an iterative ensemble smoother. *Mathematical Geosciences*, **44**(1), 1–26.

Chen, Y., Sanz-Alonso, D., and Willett, R. 2022. Auto-differentiable ensemble Kalman filters. *SIAM Journal on Mathematics of Data Science*, **4**(2), 801–833.

Chopin, N., and Papaspiliopoulos, O. 2020. *An Introduction to Sequential Monte Carlo*. Springer.

Cotter, S., Dashti, M., and Stuart, A. M. 2010. Approximation of Bayesian inverse problems for PDE's. *SIAM Journal on Numerical Analysis*, **48**(1), 322–345.

Cotter, S. L., Roberts, G. O., Stuart, A. M., and White, D. 2013. MCMC methods for functions: modifying old algorithms to make them faster. *Statistical Science*, 424–446.

Crisan, D., and Doucet, A. 2002. A survey of convergence results on particle filtering methods for practitioners. *Signal Processing, IEEE Transactions on*, **50**(3), 736–746.

Crisan, D., and Rozovskii, B. 2011. *The Oxford Handbook of Nonlinear Filtering*. Oxford University Press.

Crisan, D., Moral, P., and Lyons, T. 1998. Discrete filtering using branching and interacting particle systems. *Université de Toulouse. Laboratoire de Statistique et Probabilités [LSP]*.

Dashti, M., and Stuart, A. M. 2017. Bayesian approach to inverse problems. Pages 311–428 of: *Handbook of Uncertainty Quantification*. Springer.

Dashti, M., Law, K. J. H., Stuart, A. M., and Voss, J. 2013. MAP estimators and their consistency in Bayesian nonparametric inverse problems. *Inverse Problems*, **29**(9), 095017.

De Finetti, B. 2017. *Theory of Probability: A Critical Introductory Treatment*. Vol. 6 of Wiley Series in Probability and Statistics. John Wiley & Sons.

Del Moral, P. 2004. *Feynman-Kac Formulae: Genealogical and Interacting Particle Systems with Applications*. Springer Science & Business Media.

Del Moral, P., Doucet, A., and Jasra, A. 2006. Sequential Monte Carlo samplers. *Journal of the Royal Statistical Society: Series B (Statistical Methodology)*, **68**(3), 411–436.

Deniz Akyildiz, Ö. 2022. Global convergence of optimized adaptive importance samplers. *arXiv preprint arXiv:2201.00409*.

Dennis Jr., J. E., and Schnabel, R. B. 1996. *Numerical Methods for Unconstrained Optimization and Nonlinear Equations*. Society for Industrial and Applied Mathematics.

Dick, J., Kuo, F. Y., and Sloan, I. H. 2013. High-dimensional integration: the quasi-Monte Carlo way. *Acta Numerica*, **22**, 133.

Ding, Z., and Li, Q. 2021. Ensemble Kalman sampler: mean-field limit and convergence analysis. *SIAM Journal on Mathematical Analysis*, **53**(2), 10.1137.

Doob, J. L. 1949. Application of the theory of martingales. Pages 23–27 of: *Le calcul des probabilités et ses applications*, Éditions du Centre National de la Recherche Scientifique (C. N. R. S.).

Doucet, A., Godsill, S., and Andrieu, C. 2000. On sequential Monte Carlo sampling methods for Bayesian filtering. *Statistics and Computing*, **10**(3), 197–208.

Doucet, A., Freitas, N. de, and Gordon, N. 2001. An introduction to sequential Monte Carlo methods. Pages 3–14 of: *Sequential Monte Carlo Methods in Practice*. Springer.

Dunlop, M. M. 2019. Multiplicative noise in Bayesian inverse problems: Well-posedness and consistency of MAP estimators. *arXiv preprint arXiv:1910.14632*.

Emerick, A., and Reynolds, A. 2013. Investigation of the sampling performance of ensemble-based methods with a simple reservoir model. *Computational Geosciences*, **17**(2), 325–350.

Engl, H., Hanke, M., and Neubauer, A. 1996. *Regularization of Inverse Problems*. Springer Science and Business Media.

Ernst, O., Sprungk, B., and Starkloff, H. 2015. Analysis of the ensemble and polynomial chaos Kalman filters in Bayesian inverse problems. *SIAM/ASA Journal on Uncertainty Quantification*, **3**(1), 823–851.

Evensen, G. 1995. Sequential data assimilation with a nonlinear quasi-geostrophic model using Monte Carlo methods to forecast error statistics. *Journal of Geophysical Research: Oceans*, **99**(c5), 10143–10162.

Evensen, G. 2009. *Data Assimilation: the Ensemble Kalman Filter*. Springer Science and Business Media.

Evensen, G., and Leeuwen, P. Van. 1996. Assimilation of Geosat altimeter data for the Agulhas current using the ensemble Kalman filter with a quasigeostrophic model. *Monthly Weather Review*, **124**(1), 85–96.

Evensen, G., and Van Leeuwen, P. J. 2000. An ensemble Kalman smoother for nonlinear dynamics. *Monthly Weather Review*, **128**(6), 1852–1867.

Evensen, G., Vossepoel, F. C., and van Leeuwen, P. J. 2022. *Data Assimilation Fundamentals: A Unified Formulation of the State and Parameter Estimation Problem*. Springer.

Farchi, A., and Bocquet, M. 2018. Comparison of local particle filters and new implementations. *Nonlinear Processes in Geophysics*, **25**(4), 765–807.

Fienberg, S. E. 2006. When did Bayesian inference become "Bayesian"? *Bayesian Analysis*, **1**(1), 1–40.

Fisher, M., Nocedal, J., Trémolet, Y., and Wright, S. 2009. Data assimilation in weather forecasting: a case study in PDE-constrained optimization. *Optimization and Engineering*, **10**(3), 409–426.

Franklin, J. 1970. Well-posed stochastic extensions of ill-posed linear problems. *Journal of Mathematical Analysis and Applications*, **31**(3), 682–716.

Frei, M., and Künsch, H. R. 2013. Bridging the ensemble Kalman and particle filters. *Biometrika*, **100**(4), 781–800.

Gamerman, D., and Lopes, H. 2006. *Markov Chain Monte Carlo: Stochastic Simulation for Bayesian Inference*. CRC Press.

Garbuno-Inigo, A., Nüsken, N., and Reich, S. 2020a. Affine invariant interacting Langevin dynamics for Bayesian inference. *SIAM Journal on Applied Dynamical Systems*, **19**(3), 1633–1658.

Garbuno-Inigo, A., Hoffmann, F., Li, W., and Stuart, A. M. 2020b. Interacting Langevin diffusions: Gradient structure and ensemble Kalman sampler. *SIAM Journal on Applied Dynamical Systems*, **19**(1), 412–441.

Garcia Trillos, N., and Sanz-Alonso, D. 2018. Continuum limits of posteriors in graph Bayesian inverse problems. *SIAM Journal on Mathematical Analysis*, **50**(4), 4020–4040.

Garcia Trillos, N., and Sanz-Alonso, D. 2020. The Bayesian update: variational formulations and gradient flows. *Bayesian Analysis*, **15**(1), 29–56.

Garcia Trillos, N., Kaplan, Z., and Sanz-Alonso, D. 2019. Variational characterizations of local entropy and heat regularization in deep learning. *Entropy*, **21**(5), 511.

Garcia Trillos, N., Kaplan, Z., Samakhoana, T., and Sanz-Alonso, D. 2020. On the consistency of graph-based Bayesian semi-supervised learning and the scalability of sampling algorithms. *Journal of Machine Learning Research*, **21**(28), 1–47.

Gelb, A., Kasper, J. F., Nash, R. A., Price, C. F., and Sutherland, A. A. 1974. *Applied Optimal Estimation*. MIT Press.

Gelman, A., Carlin, J. B, Stern, H. S., Dunson, D. B., Vehtari, A., and Rubin, D. B. 2013. *Bayesian Data Analysis*. Chapman and Hall/CRC.

Ghil, M., Cohn, S., Tavantzis, J., Bube, K., and Isaacson, E. 1981. Applications of estimation theory to numerical weather prediction. Pages 139–224 of: *Dynamic Meteorology: Data Assimilation Methods*. Springer.

Gibbs, A., and Su, F. 2002. On choosing and bounding probability metrics. *International Statistical Review*, **70**(3), 419–435.

Giles, M. 2015. Multilevel Monte Carlo methods. *Acta Numerica*, **24**, 259–328.

Gine, E., and Nickl, R. 2015. *Mathematical Foundations of Infinite-dimensional Statistical Models*. Cambridge University Press.

Giordano, M., and Nickl, R. 2020. Consistency of Bayesian inference with Gaussian process priors in an elliptic inverse problem. *Inverse Problems*, **36**(8), 085001.

Gland, F., Monbet, V., and Tran, V. 2009. Large sample asymptotics for the ensemble Kalman filter. *PhD Thesis*.

Goodfellow, I., Bengio, Y., and Courville, A. 2016. *Deep Learning*. MIT Press.

Goodman, J., and Weare, J. 2010. Ensemble samplers with affine invariance. *Communications in Applied Mathematics and Computational Science*, **5**(1), 65–80.

Gottwald, G. A., and Majda, A. J. 2013. A mechanism for catastrophic filter divergence in data assimilation for sparse observation networks. *Nonlinear Processes in Geophysics*, **20**(5), 705–712.

Gottwald, G. A., and Reich, S. 2021. Supervised learning from noisy observations: Combining machine-learning techniques with data assimilation. *Physica D: Nonlinear Phenomena*, **423**, 132911.

Gu, Y., and Oliver, D. S. 2007. An iterative ensemble Kalman filter for multiphase fluid flow data assimilation. *SPE Journal*, **12**(04), 438–446.

Guth, P. A., Schillings, C., and Weissmann, S. 2020. Ensemble Kalman filter for neural network based one-shot inversion. *arXiv preprint arXiv:2005.02039*.

Haber, E., Lucka, F., and Ruthotto, L. 2018. Never look back – A modified EnKF method and its application to the training of neural networks without back propagation. *arXiv preprint arXiv:1805.08034*.

Hairer, M., Stuart, A. M., and Voss, J. 2011. Signal processing problems on function space: Bayesian formulation, stochastic PDEs and effective MCMC methods. Pages 833–873 of: *The Oxford Handbook of Nonlinear Filtering*. Oxford University Press.

Hairer, M., Stuart, A. M., Voss, J., and Wiberg, P. 2013. Analysis of SPDEs arising in path sampling. Part I: The Gaussian case. *Communications in Mathematical Sciences*, **3**(4), 587–603.

Hairer, M., Stuart, A. M., and Vollmer, S. J. 2014. Spectral gaps for a Metropolis–Hastings algorithm in infinite dimensions. *The Annals of Applied Probability*, **24**(6), 2455–2490.

Hammersley, J., and Handscomb, D. 1964. Percolation processes. Pages 134–141 of: *Monte Carlo Methods*, Springer.

Hanke, M. 1997. A regularizing Levenberg-Marquardt scheme, with applications to inverse groundwater filtration problems. *Inverse Problems*, **13**(1), 79–95.

Harlim, J., Sanz-Alonso, D., and Yang, R. 2020. Kernel methods for Bayesian elliptic inverse problems on manifolds. *SIAM/ASA Journal on Uncertainty Quantification*, **8**(4), 1414–1445.

Harvey, A. 1964. *Forecasting, Structural Time Series Models and the Kalman Filter*. Cambridge University Press.

Hastings, W. K. 1970. Monte Carlo sampling methods using Markov chains and their applications. *Biometrika*, **57**(1), 97–109.

Hayden, K., Olson, E., and Titi, E. 2011. Discrete data assimilation in the Lorenz and 2D Navier–Stokes equations. *Physica D: Nonlinear Phenomena*, **240**(18), 1416–1425.

Helin, T., and Burger, M. 2015. Maximum a posteriori probability estimates in infinite-dimensional Bayesian inverse problems. *Inverse Problems*, **31**(8), 085009.

Herty, M., and Visconti, G. 2019. Kinetic methods for inverse problems. *Kinetic & Related Models*, **12**(5), 1109.

Hosseini, B. 2017. Well-posed Bayesian inverse problems with infinitely divisible and heavy-tailed prior measures. *SIAM/ASA Journal on Uncertainty Quantification*, **5**(1), 1024–1060.

Hosseini, B., and Nigam, N. 2017. Well-posed Bayesian inverse problems: priors with exponential tails. *SIAM/ASA Journal on Uncertainty Quantification*, **5**(1), 436–465.

Houtekamer, P. L., and Derome, J. 1995. Methods for ensemble prediction. *Monthly Weather Review*, **123**(7), 2181–2196.

Houtekamer, P. L., and Mitchell, H. 1998. Data assimilation using an ensemble Kalman filter technique. *Monthly Weather Review*, **126**(3), 796–811.

Huang, D. Z., and Huang, J. 2021. Unscented Kalman inversion: efficient Gaussian approximation to the posterior distribution. *arXiv preprint arXiv:2103.00277*.

Huang, D. Z., Schneider, T., and Stuart, A. M. 2021. Unscented Kalman inversion. *arXiv preprint arXiv:2102.01580*.

Huang, D. Z., Huang, J., Reich, S., and Stuart, A. M. 2022a. Efficient derivative-free Bayesian inference for large-scale inverse problems. *arXiv preprint arXiv:2204.04386*.

Huang, D. Z., Schneider, T., and Stuart, A. M. 2022b. Iterated Kalman methodology for inverse problems. *Journal of Computational Physics*, **463**, 111262.

Iglesias, M. A. 2016. A regularizing iterative ensemble Kalman method for PDE-constrained inverse problems. *Inverse Problems*, **32**(2), 025002.

Iglesias, M. A., and Yang, Y. 2021. Adaptive regularisation for ensemble Kalman inversion. *Inverse Problems*, **37**(2), 025008.

Iglesias, M. A., Law, K. J. H., and Stuart, A. M. 2014a. Ensemble Kalman methods for inverse problems. *Inverse Problems*, **29**(4), 045001.

Iglesias, M. A., Lin, K., and Stuart, A. M. 2014b. Well-posed Bayesian geometric inverse problems arising in subsurface flow. *Inverse Problems*, **30**(11), 114001.

Jazwinski, A. 2007. *Stochastic Processes and Filtering Theory*. Courier Corporation.

Johansen, A., and Doucet, A. 2008. A note on auxiliary particle filters. *Statistics and Probability Letters*, **78**(12), 1498–1504.

Jordan, M. I., Ghahramani, Z., Jaakkola, T. S., and Saul, L. K. 1999. An introduction to variational methods for graphical models. *Machine Learning*, **37**(2), 183–233.

Kahn, H. 1955. *Use of Different Monte Carlo Sampling Techniques*. Rand Corporation.

Kahn, H., and Marshall, A. W. 1953. Methods of reducing sample size in Monte Carlo computations. *Journal of the Operations Research Society of America*, **1**(5), 263–278.

Kaipio, J., and Somersalo, E. 2006. Statistical and Computational Inverse Problems. *Springer Science & Business Media*, **160**.

Kalman, R. 1960. A new approach to linear filtering and prediction problems. *Journal of Basic Engineering*, **82**(1), 35–45.

Kalman, R., and Bucy, R. 1961. New results in linear filtering and prediction theory. *Journal of Basic Engineering*, **83**(1), 95–108.

Kalnay, E. 2003. *Atmospheric Modeling, Data Assimilation and Predictability*. Cambridge University Press.

Kantas, N., Beskos, A., and Jasra, A. 2014. Sequential Monte Carlo methods for high-dimensional inverse problems: a case study for the Navier Stokes equations. *SIAM Journal on Uncertainty Quantification*, **2**(1), 464–489.

Kawai, R. 2017. Adaptive importance sampling Monte Carlo simulation for general multivariate probability laws. *Journal of Computational and Applied Mathematics*, **319**, 440–459.

Kelly, D., and Stuart, A. M. 2019. Ergodicity and accuracy of optimal particle filters for Bayesian data assimilation. *Chinese Annals of Mathematics, Series B*, **40**(5), 811–842.

Kelly, D., Law, K. J. H., and Stuart, A. M. 2014. Well-posedness and accuracy of the ensemble Kalman filter in discrete and continuous time. *Nonlinearity*, **27**(10), 2579.

Kiefer, J., and Wolfowitz, J. 1952. Stochastic estimation of the maximum of a regression function. *The Annals of Mathematical Statistics*, **23**(3), 462–466.

Kim, H., Sanz-Alonso, D., and Strang, A. 2023. Hierarchical ensemble Kalman methods with sparsity-promoting generalized gamma hyperpriors. *Foundations of Data Science*, **5**(3), 366–388.

Knapik, B., van der Vaart, A., and van Zanten, J. 2011. Bayesian inverse problems with Gaussian priors. *Annals of Statistics*, **39**(5), 2626–2657.

Kovachki, N. B., and Stuart, A. M. 2019. Ensemble Kalman inversion: A derivative-free technique for machine learning tasks. *Inverse Problems*, **35**(9), 095005.

Krishnan, R., Shalit, U., and Sontag, D. 2017. Structured inference networks for nonlinear state space models. In: *Proceedings of the AAAI Conference on Artificial Intelligence*, **31**(1), 2101–2109.

Kwiatkowski, E., and Mandel, J. 2015. Convergence of the square root ensemble Kalman filter in the large ensemble limit. *SIAM/ASA Journal on Uncertainty Quantification*, **3**(1), 1–17.

Lalley, S. P. 1999. Beneath the noise, chaos. *The Annals of Statistics*, **27**(2), 461–479.

Lasanen, S. 2012a. Non-Gaussian statistical inverse problems. Part I: Posterior distributions. *Inverse Problems & Imaging*, **6**(2), 215–266.

Lasanen, S. 2012b. Non-Gaussian statistical inverse problems. Part II: Posterior convergence for approximated unknowns. *Inverse Problems & Imaging*, **6**(2), 267.

Latz, J. 2020. On the well-posedness of Bayesian inverse problems. *SIAM/ASA Journal on Uncertainty Quantification*, **8**(1), 451–482.

Law, K. J. H, and Zankin, V. 2022. Sparse online variational Bayesian regression. *SIAM/ASA Journal on Uncertainty Quantification*, **10**(3), 1070–1100.

Law, K. J. H., Shukla, A., and Stuart, A. M. 2014. Analysis of the 3DVAR filter for the partially observed Lorenz'63 model. *Discrete and Continuous Dynamical Systems*, **34**(3), 1061–1078.

Law, K. J. H., Stuart, A. M., and Zygalakis, K. 2015. *Data Assimilation*. Springer.

Law, K. J. H., Sanz-Alonso, D., Shukla, A., and Stuart, A. M. 2016. Filter accuracy for the Lorenz 96 model: Fixed versus adaptive observation operators. *Physica D: Nonlinear Phenomena*, **325**, 1–13.

Lee, Y. 2021. $l_p$ regularization for ensemble Kalman inversion. *SIAM Journal on Scientific Computing*, **43**(5), A3417–A3437.

Leeuwen, P. Van, Cheng, Y., and Reich, S. 2015. *Nonlinear Data Assimilation*. Springer.

Lehtinen, M. S., Paivarinta, L., and Somersalo, E. 1989. Linear inverse problems for generalised random variables. *Inverse Problems*, **5**(4), 599.

Levine, M., and Stuart, A. 2022. A framework for machine learning of model error in dynamical systems. *Communications of the American Mathematical Society*, **2**(7), 283–344.

Li, G., and Reynolds, A. C. 2007. An iterative ensemble Kalman filter for data assimilation. In: *SPE Annual Technical Conference and Exhibition*. Society of Petroleum Engineers.

Lieberman, C., Willcox, K., and Ghattas, O. 2010. Parameter and state model reduction for large-scale statistical inverse problems. *SIAM Journal on Scientific Computing*, **32**(5), 2535–2542.

Lindvall, T. 2002. *Lectures on the Coupling Method*. Springer.

Liu, J. S. 2008. *Monte Carlo Strategies in Scientific Computing*. Springer Science & Business Media.

Lorenc, A. 1986. Analysis methods for numerical weather prediction. *Quarterly Journal of the Royal Meteorological Society*, **112**(474), 1177–1194.

Lorenc, A. C., Ballard, S. P., Bell, R. S., Ingleby, N. B., Andrews, P. L. F., Barker, D. M., Bray, J. R., Clayton, A. M., Dalby, T., Li, D., et al. 2000. The Met. Office global three-dimensional variational data assimilation scheme. *Quarterly Journal of the Royal Meteorological Society*, **126**(570), 2991–3012.

Lorentzen, R., Fjelde, R., FrØyen, J., Lage, A., Naevdal, G., and Vefring, E. 2001. Underbalanced and low-head drilling operations: Real time interpretation of measured data and operational support. *SPE Annual Technical Conference and Exhibition*.

Lu, Y., Stuart, A. M., and Weber, H. 2017. Gaussian approximations for probability measures on $\mathbb{R}^d$. *SIAM/ASA Journal on Uncertainty Quantification*, **5**(1), 1136–1165.

MacKay, D. 2003. *Information Theory, Inference and Learning Algorithms*. Cambridge University Press.

Majda, A. J., and Harlim, J. 2012. *Filtering Complex Turbulent Systems*. Cambridge University Press.

Mandel, J., Cobb, L., and Beezley, J. D. 2011. On the convergence of the ensemble Kalman filter. *Applications of Mathematics*, **56**(6), 533–541.

Martin, J., Wilcox, L., Burstedde, C., and Omar, G. 2012. A stochastic Newton MCMC method for large-scale statistical inverse problems with application to seismic inversion. *SIAM Journal on Scientific Computing*, **34**(3), A1460–A1487.

Martino, L., Elvira, V., and Louzada, F. 2017. Effective sample size for importance sampling based on discrepancy measures. *Signal Processing*, **131**, 386–401.

Marzouk, Y., and Xiu, D. 2009. A stochastic collocation approach to Bayesian inference in inverse problems. *Communications in Computational Physics*, **6**(4), 826–847.

Mattingly, J., Stuart, A.M., and Higham, D. 2002. Ergodicity for PDE's and approximations: locally Lipschitz vector fields and degenerate noise. *Stochastic Processes and Their Applications*, **101**(2), 185–232.

Metropolis, N., Rosenbluth, A. W., Rosenbluth, M. N., Teller, A. H., and Teller, E. 1953. Equation of state calculations by fast computing machines. *The Journal of Chemical Physics*, **21**(6), 1087–1092.

Meyn, S., and Tweedie, R. 2012. *Markov Chains and Stochastic Stability*. Springer Science and Business Media.

Miller, E. L., and Karl, W. C. 2003. Fundamentals of Inverse Problems. Unpublished lecture notes, available at https://ece.northeastern.edu/fac-ece/elmiller/eceg398 f03/notes.pdf.

Minka, T. P. 2013. Expectation propagation for approximate Bayesian inference. *arXiv preprint arXiv:1301.2294*.

Moodey, A., Lawless, A., Potthast, R., and Leeuwen, P. Van. 2013. Nonlinear error dynamics for cycled data assimilation methods. *Inverse Problems*, **29**(2), 025002.

Morzfeld, M., Hodyss, D., and Snyder, C. 2017. What the collapse of the ensemble Kalman filter tells us about particle filters. *Tellus A: Dynamic Meteorology and Oceanography*, **69**(1), 1283809.

Nickl, R. 2020. Bernstein–von Mises theorems for statistical inverse problems I: Schrödinger equation. *Journal of the European Mathematical Society*, **22**(8), 2697–2750.

Nickl, R. 2022. Bayesian Non-linear Statistical Inverse Problems. *Lecture Notes, Department of Mathematics, ETH Zürich*.

Nickl, R., and Paternain, G. 2021. On some information-theoretic aspects of non-linear statistical inverse problems. *arXiv preprint arXiv:2107.09488*.

Nickl, R., and Söhl, J. 2019. Bernstein–von Mises theorems for statistical inverse problems II: compound Poisson processes. *Electronic Journal of Statistics*, **13**(2), 3513–3571.

Nickl, R., van de Geer, S., and Wang, S. 2020. Convergence rates for penalised least squares estimators in PDE-constrained regression problems. *SIAM/ASA Journal on Uncertainty Quantification*, **8**(1), 374–413.

Nielsen, F., and Garcia, V. 2009. Statistical exponential families: A digest with flash cards. *arXiv preprint arXiv:0911.4863*.

Nocedal, J., and Wright, S. 2006. *Numerical Optimization*. Springer Science & Business Media.

Oliver, D., Reynolds, A., and Liu, N. 2008. *Inverse Theory for Petroleum Reservoir Characterization and History Matching*. Cambridge University Press.

Oljaca, L., Brocker, J., and Kuna, T. 2018. Almost sure error bounds for data assimilation in dissipative systems with unbounded observation noise. *SIAM Journal on Applied Dynamical Systems*, **17**(4), 2882–2914.

Owhadi, H., Scovel, C., Sullivan, T. J., McKerns, M., and Ortiz, M. 2013. Optimal uncertainty quantification. *SIAM Review*, **55**(2), 271–345.

Owhadi, H., Scovel, C., and Sullivan, T. J. 2015a. Brittleness of Bayesian inference under finite information in a continuous world. *Electronic Journal of Statistics*, **9**(1), 1–79.

Owhadi, H., Scovel, C., and Sullivan, T. J. 2015b. On the brittleness of Bayesian inference. *SIAM Review*, **57**(4), 566–582.

Paulin, D., Jasra, A., Crisan, D., and Beskos, A. 2018. On concentration properties of partially observed chaotic systems. *Advances in Applied Probability*, **50**(2), 440–479.

Paulin, D., Jasra, A., Crisan, D., and Beskos, A. 2019. Optimization based methods for partially observed chaotic systems. *Foundations of Computational Mathematics*, **19**(3), 485–559.

Pavliotis, G. A. 2014. *Stochastic Processes and Applications: Diffusion Processes, the Fokker-Planck and Langevin Equations*. Vol. 60 of Texts in Applied Mathematics. Springer.

Pecora, L. M., and Carroll, T. L. 1990. Synchronization in chaotic systems. *Physical Review Letters*, **64**(8), 821.

Petersen, K., and Pedersen, M. 2008. *The Matrix Cookbook*. Technical University of Denmark.

Petra, N., Martin, J., Stadler, G., and Ghattas, O. 2014. A computational framework for infinite-dimensional Bayesian inverse problems, Part II: Stochastic Newton MCMC with application to ice sheet flow inverse problems. *SIAM Journal on Scientific Computing*, **36**(4), A1525–A1555.

Pidstrigach, J., and Reich, S. 2023. Affine-invariant ensemble transform methods for logistic regression. *Foundations of Computational Mathematics*, **23**(2), 675–708.

Pinski, F., Simpson, F., Stuart, A. M., and Weber, H. 2015a. Algorithms for Kullback–Leibler approximation of probability measures in infinite dimensions. *SIAM Journal on Scientific Computing*, **37**(6), A2733–A2757.

Pinski, F., Simpson, F., Stuart, A. M., and Weber, H. 2015b. Kullback–Leibler approximation for probability measures on infinite dimensional spaces. *SIAM Journal on Mathematical Analysis*, **47**(6), 4091–4122.

Pitt, M., and Shephard, N. 1999. Filtering via simulation: Auxiliary particle filters. *Journal of the American Statistical Association*, **94**(446), 590–599.

Rauch, H., Striebel, C., and Tung, F. 1965. Maximum likelihood estimates of linear dynamic systems. *AIAA Journal*, **3**(8), 1445–1450.

Rawlins, F., Ballard, S. P., Bovis, K. J., Clayton, A. M., Li, D., Inverarity, G. W., Lorenc, A. C., and Payne, T. J. 2007. The Met Office global four-dimensional variational data assimilation scheme. *Quarterly Journal of the Royal Meteorological Society: A Journal of the Atmospheric Sciences, Applied Meteorology and Physical Oceanography*, **133**(623), 347–362.

Rebeschini, P., and Handel, R. Van. 2015. Can local particle filters beat the curse of dimensionality? *Annals of Applied Probability*, **25**(5), 2809–2866.

Reich, S. 2017. A dynamical systems framework for intermittent data assimilation. *BIT Numerical Mathematics*, **51**(1), 235–249.

Reich, S. 2019. Data assimilation: the Schrödinger perspective. *Acta Numerica*, **28**, 635–711.

Reich, S., and Cotter, C. 2015. *Probabilistic Forecasting and Bayesian Data Assimilation*. Cambridge University Press.

Reynolds, A. C., Zafari, M., and Li, G. 2006. Iterative forms of the ensemble Kalman filter. Pages cp–23 of: *ECMOR X-10th European conference on the mathematics of oil recovery*. European Association of Geoscientists & Engineers.

Robbins, H., and Monro, S. 1951. A stochastic approximation method. *The Annals of Mathematical Statistics*, **22**(3), 400–407.

Robert, C., and Casella, G. 2013. *Monte Carlo Statistical Methods*. Springer Science & Business Media.

Roberts, G. O., Rosenthal, J. S., et al. 2001. Optimal scaling for various Metropolis-Hastings algorithms. *Statistical Science*, **16**(4), 351–367.

Ryu, E. K., and Boyd, S. P. 2014. Adaptive importance sampling via stochastic convex programming. *arXiv preprint arXiv:1412.4845*.

Sakov, P., Oliver, D. S., and Bertino, L. 2012. An iterative EnKF for strongly nonlinear systems. *Monthly Weather Review*, **140**(6), 1988–2004.

Sanz-Alonso, D. 2018. Importance sampling and necessary sample size: An information theory approach. *SIAM/ASA Journal on Uncertainty Quantification*, **6**(2), 867–879.

Sanz-Alonso, D., and Stuart, A. M. 2015. Long-time asymptotics of the filtering distribution for partially observed chaotic dynamical systems. *SIAM/ASA Journal on Uncertainty Quantification*, **3**(1), 1200–1220.

Sanz-Alonso, D., and Stuart, A. M. 2017. Gaussian approximations of small noise diffusions in Kullback-Leibler divergence. *Communications in Mathematical Sciences*, **15**(7), 2087–2097.

Sanz-Alonso, D., and Wang, Z. 2021. Bayesian update with importance sampling: Required sample size. *Entropy*, **23**(1), 22.

Särkkä, S. 2013. *Bayesian Filtering and Smoothing*. Vol. 3 of Institute of Mathematical Statistics Textbooks. Cambridge University Press.

Savage, L. J. 1972. *The Foundations of Statistics*. Courier Corporation.

Schillings, C., and Stuart, A. M. 2017. Analysis of the ensemble Kalman filter for inverse problems. *SIAM Journal on Numerical Analysis*, **55**(3), 1264–1290.

Schillings, C., and Stuart, A. M. 2018. Convergence analysis of ensemble Kalman inversion: the linear, noisy case. *Applicable Analysis*, **97**(1), 107–123.

Schneider, T., Stuart, A. M., and Wu, J.-L. 2022. Ensemble Kalman inversion for sparse learning of dynamical systems from time-averaged data. *Journal of Computational Physics*, **470**, 111559.

Skjervheim, J.-A., Evensen, G., Hove, J., and Vabø, J. G. 2011. An ensemble smoother for assisted history matching. In: *SPE Reservoir Simulation Symposium*. OnePetro.

Sloan, I. H., and Woźniakowski, H. 1998. When are quasi-Monte Carlo algorithms efficient for high dimensional integrals? *Journal of Complexity*, **14**(1), 1–33.

Smith, R. C. 2013. *Uncertainty Quantification: Theory, Implementation, and Applications*. Vol. 12 of Computational Science and Engineering. Society for Industrial and Applied Mathematics.

Snyder, C. 2011. Particle filters, the "optimal" proposal and high-dimensional systems. Pages 161–170 of: *Proceedings of the ECMWF Seminar on Data Assimilation for Atmosphere and Ocean*, European Centre for Medium-Range Weather Forecasts.

Snyder, C., Bengtsson, T., and Morzfeld, M. 2015. Performance bounds for particle filters using the optimal proposal. *Monthly Weather Review*, **143**(11), 4750–4761.

Snyder, C., Bengtsson, T., Bickel, P., and Anderson, J. L. 2016. Obstacles to high-dimensional particle filtering. *Monthly Weather Review*, **136**(12), 4629–4640.

Stordal, A. S., Karlsen, H. A., Nævdal, G., Skaug, H. J, and Vallès, B. 2011. Bridging the ensemble Kalman filter and particle filters: the adaptive Gaussian mixture filter. *Computational Geosciences*, **15**(2), 293–305.

Stuart, A. M. 2010. Inverse problems: a Bayesian perspective. *Acta Numerica*, **19**, 451–559.

Stuart, A. M., and Humphries, A. R. 1998. *Dynamical Systems and Numerical Analysis*. Vol. 2 of Cambridge Monographs on Applied and Computational Mathematics. Cambridge University Press.

Sullivan, T. J. 2015. *Introduction to Uncertainty Quantification*. Vol. 63 of Texts in Applied Mathematics. Springer.

Tarantola, A. 2015a. *Inverse Problem Theory and Methods for Model Parameter Estimation*. Society for Industrial and Applied Mathematics.

Tarantola, A. 2015b. Towards adjoint-based inversion for rheological parameters in nonlinear viscous mantle flow. *Physics of the Earth and Planetary Interiors*, **234**, 23–34.

Tikhonov, A. N., and Arsenin, V. Y. 1977. *Solutions of Ill-Posed Problems*. Washington, Winston & Sons.

Tippett, M. K., Anderson, J. L., Bishop, C. H., Hamill, T. M., and Whitaker, J. S. 2003. Ensemble square root filters. *Monthly Weather Review*, **131**(7), 1485–1490.

Tokdar, S., Kass, S., and Kass, R. 2010. Importance sampling: a review. *Wiley Interdisciplinary Reviews: Computational Statistics*, **2**(1), 54–60.

Tong, X. T., Majda, A. J., and Kelly, D. 2015. Nonlinear stability of the ensemble Kalman filter with adaptive covariance inflation. *Nonlinearity*, **29**(2), 54–60.

Tong, X. T., Majda, A. J, and Kelly, D. 2016. Nonlinear stability and ergodicity of ensemble based Kalman filters. *Nonlinearity*, **29**(2), 657.

Ungarala, S. 2012. On the iterated forms of Kalman filters using statistical linearization. *Journal of Process Control*, **22**(5), 935–943.

Van der Vaart, A. 1998. *Asymptotic Statistics*. Cambridge University Press.

Vogel, C. R. 2002. *Computational Methods for Inverse Problems*. Society for Industrial and Applied Mathematics.

Wainwright, M. J., and Jordan, M. I. 2008. Graphical Models, Exponential Families, and Variational Inference. *Foundations and Trends in Machine Learning*, **1**(1–2), 1–305.

# Index

205